FAE Elective

Business Decisions Transaction Taxes (NI)

2016–2017

Published in 2016 by
Chartered Accountants Ireland
Chartered Accountants House
47–49 Pearse Street
Dublin 2
www.charteredaccountants.ie

ISBN: 978-1-910374-61-0

Typeset by Deanta Global Publishing Services
Printed by eprint, Dublin

Contents

Chapter 7 Capital Taxes Planning for Individuals

General Framework: European Union Law and State Aid

Learning Objectives

After studying this chapter you will understand:

■ The four fundamental freedoms contained in the Treaty on the Functioning of the European Union (TFEU) and the implications of same.

■ The primacy of EU law, with specific reference to the principal cases:

● *Commission v. French Republic* (Case C–270/83);

● *Marks & Spencer v. Halsey* (Case C–446/03); and

● *Cadbury Schweppes and Cadbury Schweppes Overseas* (Case C–196/04).

■ The provenance of the state aid rules and their impact on domestic tax law.

■ The procedures applicable to an investigation of state aid by the European Commission and the possible implications for businesses availing of tax reliefs that contravene the state aid rules.

■ The practical aspects of claiming EU Treaty benefits.

1.1 The Treaty on the Functioning of the European Union

The UK's membership of the European Union (EU) has an impact on direct and indirect tax law. The relevant treaty is the Treaty on the Functioning of the European Union (TFEU). This was originally the 1957 Treaty of Rome, then became the EC Treaty and has since been renamed as a result of the Lisbon Treaty that came into effect on 1 December 2009.

The numbering of the Articles of the EC Treaty was changed by the Treaty of Amsterdam in 1999 and has subsequently been amended by the Lisbon Treaty. Cases decided by the European Court of Justice (ECJ) on issues arising before 1 December 1999 will refer to the old numbering. Therefore, an awareness of the previous numbering of the Articles is useful. The ECJ is officially known as the Court of Justice of the European Union (CJEU), but is still generally referred to as the ECJ. Students should be aware of this other abbreviation as you may come across it in your studies.

The main goal of the EU is the progressive integration of its Member States' economic and political systems and the establishment of a single market based on the free movement of goods, people, money and services. To this end, Member States cede part of their sovereignty under the TFEU, which empowers EU institutions to enact laws. These laws (regulations, directives and decisions) take precedence over national law and are binding on national authorities. The EU also issues non-binding instruments, such as recommendations and opinions, as well as rules governing how EU institutions and programmes work, etc.

The European Commission is responsible for ensuring compliance by Member States with these rules. The Commission acts on its own initiative (where it detects a failure to comply with EU law) or in response to complaints. It first attempts to bring about compliance by contacting the Member State in question. If needs be, it takes the matter to the ECJ, which delivers a judgment providing a definitive interpretation of the EU law. Most differences of opinion are settled during the first stage; in most cases, Member States bring their legislation into line with Community law early in the procedure, before the matter goes to the ECJ. The Commission also contributes to the interpretation of Community law by submitting its observations on questions referred by national courts to the ECJ for a preliminary ruling (Article 267 TFEU).

Before considering the four fundamental freedoms of the Treaty, it is worthwhile looking at the other provisions of the Treaty that have an impact on tax. This will aid your understanding of the jurisprudence of the ECJ. The full text of the Treaty can be viewed at http://eur-lex.europa.eu/legal-content/EN/TXT/?uri=OJ:C:2016:202:TOC. Decisions of the ECJ can be obtained from the Court's website at http://curia.europa.eu/.

Title I of the Treaty sets out the areas of competency of the European Union. Article 3 gives the EU exclusive competence over certain areas, including the customs union, the establishing of competition rules necessary for the functioning of the internal market and the common commercial policy. Article 2(1) states that, where the EU has exclusive competence, only the Union may legislate and enact legally binding Acts. This means that the Member States of the EU have given up their rights to freely legislate in these areas.

In a referendum held on 23 June 2016, the UK voted to leave the EU. At the time of writing, the Government has signalled the intention to wait until the end of 2016 before triggering the exit process, which will take up to two years to complete. The EU Treaty will continue to apply to the UK in the meantime.

1.2 The Four Fundamental Freedoms

1.2.1 The Four Fundamental Freedoms

The **four fundamental freedoms** is a common term for a set of Treaty provisions, secondary legislation and court decisions protecting the ability of goods, services, capital and labour to move freely within the internal market of the EU. These four freedoms form part of the substantive law of the EU and are fundamental to the common market.

The four freedoms are:

1. **Freedom of Movement of Workers**
2. **Freedom of Establishment**
3. **Freedom to Provide Services**
4. **Free Movement of Capital**

These freedoms flow from the original economic purpose of the EU Treaty, and it is intended that they should be used as an aid to the development and promotion of a common market across Member States.

1.2.2 Freedom of Movement of Workers

The first freedom is the freedom of movement of workers, contained in Article 45 (previously Article 39 EC), which guarantees free movement for workers within the EU. Article 45(2) states that this should entail the abolition of any discrimination based on nationality. Article 45(3) makes the right subject to limitations justified on the grounds of public policy, public security or public health.

For direct tax purposes, the key determinant for taxation in a Member State is generally residence rather than nationality. The connection between residence and nationality was discussed in the first tax case to come before the ECJ regarding the freedom of movement of workers: *Biehl* (1990) (Case C–175/88).

Biehl

Mr Biehl was a German national who had been resident and employed in Luxembourg for a number of years. He returned to Germany partway through a tax year and applied for over-deductions of income tax from his salary in Luxembourg to be repaid by the Luxembourg Tax Authority.

Luxembourg tax law included a provision which stated that over-deductions of income tax belonging to individuals who became resident outside Luxembourg during a tax year became the property of the Treasury. Mr Biehl claimed that such a provision was precluded by Article 45.

The ECJ stated that equality of treatment forbade not only overt discrimination but also all forms of covert discrimination. It held that, although the Luxembourg tax provision on repaying an over-deduction of tax used the criterion of residence and applied irrespective of the nationality of the taxpayer, there was a risk that it would work in particular against taxpayers who were nationals of other Member States. Therefore, the provision of Luxembourg tax law was incompatible with the freedom of movement of workers.

The Court also considered tax provisions in other workers' cases that applied on the grounds of residence, rather than nationality, to be indirect discrimination prohibited by Article 45, including *Bachmann* (1992) (Case C–204/90) and *Schumacker* (1995) (Case C–279/93).

1.2.3   Freedom of Establishment

The second fundamental freedom is contained in Article 49 (previously Article 43 EC) and prohibits restrictions on the freedom of establishment. The freedom of establishment includes the right to take up and pursue activities as self-employed persons and to set up and manage undertakings. The prohibition also applies to restrictions on the setting-up of agencies, branches or subsidiaries in any Member State.

Article 52 allows measures providing for special treatment of foreign nationals on the grounds of public policy, public security or public health. These exclusions have been narrowly interpreted by the ECJ.

Article 54 states that companies or firms formed in accordance with the law of a Member State, and having their registered office, central administration or principal place of business within the EU, shall be treated in the same way as natural persons for the purposes of the freedom of establishment.

Daily Mail

An important case on the freedom of establishment is *Daily Mail* (1988) (Case C–81/87).

Daily Mail & General Trust PLC, a company both incorporated and resident in the UK, wished to move its tax residence to the Netherlands in order to minimise tax on the sale of certain investments. Under the legislation in place in the UK at that time, consent for this move was required from the UK Treasury. Daily Mail was unable to obtain this consent from the Treasury and initiated proceedings in the UK courts, claiming that Articles 49 and 54 gave it the right to transfer its tax residence to another Member State without prior consent. The UK courts referred the matter to the ECJ.

Daily Mail argued that Article 54 gave companies the same right of primary establishment as natural persons and that it was planning to establish itself in the Netherlands by locating its centre of decision making there.

The ECJ stated that companies can exercise their right of establishment by setting up agencies, branches or subsidiaries. It held that the freedom of establishment cannot be interpreted as conferring on companies incorporated under the law of a Member State a right to transfer their central management and control to another Member State while retaining their status as companies incorporated under the legislation of the first Member State.

The *Daily Mail* decision is interpreted as meaning that Articles 49 and 54 grant companies only the right of secondary establishment (e.g. setting up a branch or incorporating a subsidiary) and not the right of primary establishment. This was reiterated by the ECJ in *Cartesio* (2008) (Case C–210/06), where the Court held that the freedom of establishment did not entitle a limited partnership established under Hungarian law to move its place of management to Italy while retaining its legal personality under Hungarian law.

This can be contrasted with the decision in *National Grid Indus* (2011) (Case C–371/10). In this case, it was held that where the migration of a company from one EU Member State to another (by virtue of the company transferring its place of central management and control) triggered a tax charge, then the company incorporated in the first Member State could use freedom of establishment to challenge the lawfulness of the tax so levied.

The ECJ's judgment in *Daily Mail* was favourable for the taxpayer in one regard. The Court pointed out that, although the Articles on the freedom of establishment are mainly directed at ensuring that foreign nationals and companies are not subject to discrimination in the host Member State (i.e. the state in which they wish to establish themselves), they also prohibit the Member State of origin (i.e. the state where the national or company is currently established) from hindering the establishment in another Member State. Many of the subsequent tax cases on freedom of establishment for taxpayers have been based on this principle, e.g. *Marks & Spencer* and *Cadbury Schweppes* (see **Sections 1.4** and **1.5** below).

One of the issues that has come before the ECJ in tax cases is which of the freedoms applies to the situation in question. In *Asscher* (1996) (Case C–107/94), the Court held that Mr Asscher, the director of a company of which he was the sole shareholder, was pursuing an activity as a self-employed person. Therefore, the freedom of establishment applied to his situation and not the freedom of movement of workers.

1.2.4   Freedom to Provide Services

The freedom to provide services is set out in Article 56 (previously Article 49 EC), which prohibits restrictions on the freedom to provide services between nationals of Member States. This freedom has been the subject of a number of tax cases, including *Eurowings* (1999) (Case C–294/97) and *Vestergaard* (1999) (Case C–55/98).

Eurowings

Eurowings, a German company, leased an aircraft from an Irish company. Under German tax law, it was required to add back half of the lease payments for trade tax purposes, as the Irish company was not subject to trade tax. As a recipient of leasing services, Eurowings could rely on Article 56, and the ECJ held that this provision of German tax law was incompatible with Article 56. The incompatible provision was not justified by the lessor being subject to lower taxation in Ireland.

Vestergaard

Mr Vestergaard was a Danish auditor who went to a tax training course on the island of Crete in Greece. Under Danish tax law, he was denied a deduction for the costs, as the course was held in an ordinary tourist resort in another Member State. The ECJ held that the Danish tax rules subjected the provision of services to different tax treatment depending on the place of provision, which was prohibited by Article 56.

1.2.5 Free Movement of Capital

The fourth and final freedom is the free movement of capital and payments. Article 63 (previously Article 56 EC) prohibits all restrictions on the movement of capital between Member States, and between Member States and third countries (non-EU members). The extending of the freedom of movement of capital to third countries is unique to this freedom and does not apply to the previous three freedoms.

Article 64 introduces a 'grandfathering' provision to protect measures of national law existing on 31 December 1993, which are restrictions on the movement of capital to or from third countries.

Article 65 permits Member States to apply relevant provisions of their tax law that distinguish between taxpayers who are not in the same situation with regard to their place of residence or with regard to the place where their capital is invested. It also allows them to take all necessary measures to prevent infringements of national law, in particular in the field of taxation. However, Article 65(3) states that these must not constitute a means of arbitrary discrimination or a disguised restriction on the free movement of capital.

The application of this freedom can be demonstrated by looking at the ECJ's decisions in *Lasertec* (2007) (Case C–492/04) and *Holböck* (2007) (Case C–157/05).

Lasertec

German tax law reclassified interest paid by Lasertec, a German company, to its Swiss shareholder as a covert distribution of profits. The ECJ had to determine if the German rules classifying loan interest paid by a German resident company to a shareholder established in a non-member country, who had a substantial holding in the capital of that company, as a covert distribution of profit (in certain circumstances) were incompatible with the free movement of capital.

In order to answer the questions put to it, the ECJ considered whether the freedom of establishment or the freedom of movement of capital was in point. The ECJ referred to its earlier decisions, including *Cadbury Schweppes*, where it had been held that, in ascertaining whether national legislation falls within one or other of the freedoms, the purpose of the legislation must be taken into consideration. The ECJ had also previously held that national laws relating to holdings giving the holder a definite influence on the decisions of the company concerned and allowing him to determine its activities fall within the freedom of establishment, rather than the freedom of movement of capital.

The German law at issue applied where the non-resident lending company had a holding of over 25% in the resident borrowing company. The Swiss lending company in this case held two-thirds of the nominal capital in the German borrowing company, giving it a determinative influence on the German company's decisions and activities.

The ECJ therefore held that the case fell within the freedom of establishment, which does not apply to third countries. Any restrictive effects on the free movement of capital were an unavoidable consequence of the restriction on the freedom of establishment and did not justify examination under Articles 56–58 EC.

Holböck

Mr Holböck was an Austrian resident who owned two-thirds of a Swiss company and received dividends from that company. The dividends from the Swiss company were subject to higher income tax in Austria than dividends from domestic companies. Mr Holböck claimed that this higher taxation constituted a restriction on the free movement of capital.

As in *Lasertec*, the company looked at the purpose of the legislation in question. It distinguished the legislation in question from the legislation at issue in *Cadbury Schweppes*, as the Austrian legislation was not intended to apply only to those shareholdings that enable the holder to have a definite influence on a company's decisions and activities. The national legislation could fall within the scope of the freedom of establishment and the freedom of movement of capital.

The freedom of establishment did not apply to Switzerland as a non-EU Member State.

The ECJ had already held in *Lenz* (2004) (Case C–315/02) that the Austrian legislation at issue constituted a restriction on the free movement of capital between Member States. However, as Switzerland is a third country, the Court had to consider the exception in Article 64 for national laws existing on 31 December 1993.

The ECJ held that it was for the national court to determine the content of legislation existing on that date, but it did provide guidance. A national measure adopted after that date was not automatically excluded from the derogation. A provision substantially identical to the previous legislation, or limited to reducing or eliminating an obstacle to the exercise of Community rights and freedoms in the earlier legislation, will be covered by the derogation.

1.2.6   Discrimination, Restrictions and Justifications

A provision of domestic law can be held to be incompatible with one of the four fundamental freedoms where it operates in a discriminatory manner or places a restriction on the exercise of the freedom in question.

Discrimination occurs when there is different treatment of the same situation or the same treatment of different situations. This was the case in *Biehl* (see above), where the discrimination was indirect (covert) as opposed to direct (overt).

There have been a number of tax cases focusing on restrictions on the exercise of one of the freedoms. For instance, in *Cadbury Schweppes*, where the taxpayer argued that the UK's controlled foreign company (CFC) legislation restricted its freedom to establish subsidiaries in other Member States (see **Section 1.5**).

Justifications

Over the years, the ECJ has accepted a number of justifications for national measures that restrict the exercise of the freedoms. To be valid, the justification for a restriction on a fundamental freedom must meet all four conditions of the imperative requirements doctrine. This doctrine requires that the restriction must be:

1.   applied in a non-discriminatory manner;
2.   justified by imperative requirement in the public interest;
3.   suitable for securing the attainment of the objective which those measures pursue; and
4.   no more than what is necessary to obtain that objective (i.e. proportionality).

Some of the justifications accepted by the ECJ in tax cases include:

- symmetry/balanced allocation of taxing powers;
- cohesion of the tax system;
- preventing losses from being used twice;
- the need for fiscal supervision;
- territoriality; and
- prevention of tax avoidance.

1.3 Commission v. French Republic (Avoir Fiscal) (Case C–270/83)

1.3.1 Background

The supremacy of EU law over conflicting national laws of Member States was established in the early 1960s in *Van Gend en Loos* (1963) (Case–26/62). However, it was not until 1986 that the consequences for national tax systems were highlighted when *Avoir Fiscal* came before the ECJ. This case was brought by the European Commission against France and concerned the differing treatment of subsidiaries and branches of insurance companies.

1.3.2 Facts

Under French tax law at that time, a tax credit (*avoir fiscal*) was granted to the recipient of dividends distributed by French companies. An insurance company whose registered offices were in France, including subsidiaries set up in France by foreign insurance companies, benefitted from the tax credit in respect of its shares in French companies. However, insurance companies based in other Member States and who established branches in France did not benefit from the tax credit.

The Commission argued that the rules on the tax credit discriminated against branches of insurance companies whose registered office was situated in another Member State and that they constituted an indirect restriction on the freedom to set up a secondary establishment under Article 49 (then Article 52).

1.3.3 Judgment

At paragraphs 13, 14 and 18 of its judgment, the ECJ reiterated the importance of the freedom of establishment in Community law and related it to the facts in question.

In order for a provision of national law to be discriminatory on the grounds of nationality, the situation of nationals and non-nationals must be comparable. The ECJ dealt with this issue at paragraph 20, holding that the situations of an insurance company established in France and a French branch of an insurance company established in another Member State were comparable as both were subject to corporation tax on profits arising in France, but not on profits arising outside France.

The ECJ stated:

"Since the rules at issue place companies whose registered office is in France, and branches and agencies situated in France of companies whose registered office is abroad, on the same footing for the purposes of taxing their profits, those rules cannot, without giving rise to discrimination, treat them differently in regard to the grant of an advantage related to taxation, such as shareholders' tax credit."

Justifications

The ECJ did not accept the French Government's argument that the difference in treatment could be justified by other advantages enjoyed by branches over companies. At paragraph 22, the ECJ stated that what is now Article 49:

"... expressly leaves traders free to choose the appropriate legal form in which to pursue their activities in another Member State and that freedom of choice must not be limited by discriminatory tax provisions."

The French Government also argued that the difference in treatment could be justified as direct tax laws had not been harmonised within the Community and the interaction of tax laws between different Member States was governed by double tax treaties, as expressly recognised by Article 293 EC. The ECJ did not accept this argument, stating at paragraph 24:

"It must first be noted that the fact that the laws of the Member States on corporation tax have not been harmonized cannot justify the difference of treatment in this case. Although it is true that in the absence of such harmonization a company's tax position depends on the national law applied to it, [Article 49] prohibits the Member States from laying down in their laws conditions for the pursuit of activities by persons exercising their right of establishment which differ from those laid down for its own nationals."

The ECJ rejected France's argument that the rules were necessary to prevent tax evasion. The ECJ held that Article 49 did not prevent any derogation from the fundamental principle of freedom of establishment on the grounds of preventing the risk of tax avoidance. This can be contrasted with the ECJ's later findings on the justification of tax avoidance in the cases of *Marks & Spencer* and *Cadbury Schweppes* (see **Sections 1.4** and **1.5**).

The ECJ further held that the French Government was wrong to contend that the difference of treatment was due to double tax agreements. At paragraph 26 it stated:

"the rights conferred by [Article 49] are unconditional and a Member State cannot make respect for them subject to the contents of an agreement concluded with another Member State."

1.3.4   Outcome

The ECJ's decision was that refusing to grant the tax credit to branches was discrimination constituting a restriction of the right of establishment of insurance companies, which was contrary to Article 43.

1.3.5   Summary of Avoir Fiscal

- *Avoir fiscal* is a tax credit granted to the recipient of a French dividend.
- *Avoir fiscal* is not granted to French branches.
- Since branches and subsidiaries are on the same tax footing, they cannot be treated differently without giving rise to discrimination.
- Article 49 gives the right to choose an appropriate legal form to undertake business.
- Article 49 does not permit any derogation in respect of the risk of tax avoidance (contrast with *Marks & Spencer* and *Cadbury Schweppes* cases).
- The rights conferred by Article 49 are unconditional and cannot be made subject to a double tax convention.

1.4   Marks & Spencer plc v. David Halsey (HMIT) (Case C–446/03)

1.4.1   Facts

The *Marks & Spencer* (2005) case concerned the UK's group relief rules for corporation tax. The group relief rules in place at the time permitted losses of UK companies to be surrendered to other UK companies where there was a common parent. Marks & Spencer had loss-making subsidiaries in France, Belgium and Germany, and it sought to set the losses generated by these companies against the profits of its UK subsidiaries. The subsidiaries in Belgium and Germany had ceased to trade and the French subsidiary had been sold to a third party by the time the case came before the ECJ.

The Inland Revenue refused to allow Marks & Spencer's group relief claim for its non-UK subsidiaries. Marks & Spencer took the case to the Special Commissioners, where it lost, and subsequently appealed to the High Court. The High Court referred a number of questions to the ECJ for a preliminary ruling.

The ECJ was asked whether Articles 49 and 54 precluded provisions of a Member State that prevent a resident parent company from deducting from its taxable profits losses incurred in another Member State by a subsidiary established in that Member State, although they allow it to deduct losses incurred by a resident subsidiary. In other words, did the UK group relief provisions, which allow only UK losses to be utilised, constitute a restriction on the freedom of establishment? (Paragraphs 27 and 28)

1.4.2   Judgment

As usual, the ECJ's judgment started with a re-cap of the principles previously established, as follows:

1. Although direct tax falls within the competence of Member States, that competence must be exercised consistently with Community law (paragraph 29).
2. The freedom of establishment includes the right for companies to exercise their activity in another Member State through a subsidiary, branch or agency (paragraph 30).
3. Although the wording of the freedom of establishment is aimed at preventing discrimination in the host state, it also prohibits the state of origin from hindering one of its nationals from establishing in another Member State (paragraph 31).

At paragraphs 32–34, the ECJ held that **the UK group relief rules were a restriction on the freedom of establishment.**

The ability to surrender losses within the group allowed immediate use of the losses and, therefore, represented a cash flow advantage for the group. The fact that this advantage did not exist when the subsidiaries were established in other Member States hindered the exercise by the parent company of its freedom of establishment by deterring it from setting up subsidiaries in other Member States. There was a restriction due to the difference in treatment for tax purposes between losses of a resident subsidiary and losses of a non-resident subsidiary.

Imperative Requirements Doctrine

At paragraph 35, the ECJ set out the conditions to be met for such a restriction to be permissible. The ECJ first had to determine if the UK legislation pursued a legitimate objective that was compatible with the EC Treaty and justified by imperative reasons in the public interest.

The UK and other Member States argued that resident subsidiaries and non-resident subsidiaries were not in comparable tax situations, as the principle of territoriality gave the UK no tax jurisdiction over the non-resident subsidiaries.

The ECJ held that the fact that the UK did not tax the profits of non-resident subsidiaries of a UK parent did not, in itself, justify restricting group relief to losses incurred by UK companies (paragraph 40).

Justifications

The ECJ decided that, in order to determine whether the restriction was justified, it was necessary to consider the consequences of extending the group relief to non-UK subsidiaries (paragraph 41). The UK and other Member States put forward three factors to justify the restriction (paragraph 43), as follows:

1. Symmetry/balanced allocation of the power to impose taxes.
2. Losses could be taken into account twice.
3. The risk of tax avoidance.

In considering the first justification, the ECJ restated the position established in earlier cases that the reduction in tax revenue of a Member State is not an overriding reason in the public interest capable of justifying a restriction on a freedom (paragraph 44).

However, the ECJ agreed with the UK Government on the importance of preserving the allocation of the power to impose taxes between Member States (paragraph 45). It held, at paragraph 46, that:

> "to give companies the option to have their losses taken into account in the Member State in which they are established, or in another Member State, would **significantly jeopardise a balanced allocation of the power to impose taxes between Member States**, as the taxable basis would be increased in the first state and reduced in the second to the extent of the losses transferred." [Emphasis added.]

The ECJ also accepted that Member States must be able to prevent losses being used twice. At paragraph 48, it held that:

> "Such a danger does in fact exist if group relief is extended to the losses of non-resident subsidiaries. It is avoided by a rule which precludes relief in respect of those losses."

The risk of tax avoidance was dealt with at paragraphs 49 and 50:

> "49. As regards, last, the third justification, relating to the risk of tax avoidance, it must be accepted that the possibility of transferring the losses incurred by a non-resident company to a resident company entails a risk that within a group of companies losses will be transferred to companies established in the Member States which apply the highest rates of taxation and in which the tax value of the losses is therefore the highest.
>
> 50. To exclude group relief for losses incurred by non-resident subsidiaries prevents such practices, which may be inspired by the realisation that the rates of taxation applied in the various Member States vary significantly."

At paragraph 51, the ECJ held that the "**three justifications, taken together**" meant that the restrictive provisions of the UK group relief rules did pursue legitimate objectives compatible with the EC Treaty and constituted overriding reasons in the public interest and that they were apt to ensure the attainment of those objectives.

Taking three justifications together to justify a restriction was a new approach for the ECJ and sparked academic debate. The issue has been subsequently addressed by the ECJ in other cross-border loss relief cases: *Oy AA* (2005) (Case C–254/04) and *Lidl Belgium* (2008) (Case C–414/06).

Next, the ECJ had to determine if the restrictive provisions went beyond what was necessary to attain the objectives pursued (paragraph 53). The ECJ partially accepted the arguments put forward by Marks & Spencer and the European Commission that less restrictive measures could be used to attain the objectives. At paragraph 55, the ECJ held that the restrictive measures went beyond what was necessary where:

"– the non-resident subsidiary has exhausted the possibilities available in its State of residence of having the losses taken into account for the accounting period concerned ... and also for previous accounting periods ... and

– there is no possibility for the foreign subsidiary's losses to be taken into account in its State of residence for future periods."

In other words, the ECJ ruled that not making intra-EU group relief available for terminal losses was incompatible with the Treaty.

1.4.3 Outcome

As the ECJ only rules on points of EU law, the case made its way through the UK Courts, which applied the principles set out in the ECJ judgment to the factual situation at hand.

As a result of the ECJ decision, the UK amended its group relief legislation to permit limited use of cross-border losses.

For accounting periods beginning on or after 1 April 2006, a non-resident company that is resident or carrying on a trade in an EEA Member State (other than through a UK permanent establishment) may surrender losses to a UK resident company where the non-resident company is either a 75% subsidiary of the UK resident claimant company or a fellow 75% subsidiary of a UK resident company.

The companies also need to meet the following four conditions:

1. The equivalence condition (section 114 CTA 2010) – the amount surrendered must be in relation to a loss that would have qualified for group relief if it had arisen in the UK.
2. The EEA tax loss condition (sections 115–116 CTA 2010) – the loss must be calculated in accordance with the rules of the state in which it has arisen.
3. The qualifying loss condition (sections 117–120 CTA 2010) – the loss must not be available for any other type of relief. This condition is so restrictive that it is generally held to mean that only subsidiaries that have ceased trading or are prohibited from carrying forward losses in their home territory are able to satisfy it.
4. The precedence condition (section 121 CTA 2010) – where there is an intermediate company between the UK parent and the 75% EEA subsidiary, then, if relief is possible in the territory where the intermediate company is resident, no UK group relief will be available.

The ability for a group to surrender losses of a non-UK resident company is only available where the foreign loss remains a loss after having been recalculated under UK tax rules.

In October 2011 the Court of Appeal published its judgment in the case, now known as *Commissioners for HMRC v. Marks and Spencer plc* ([2011] EWCA Civ 1156). Both sides appealed to the Supreme Court. Some particular points regarding the conditions to be met for loss relief to be claimed (as outlined above) have been clarified as the case has proceeded through the courts. For example, the issues considered by the Court of Appeal were as follows:

1. "Is the test that the ECJ established to identify those circumstances in which it would be unlawful to preclude cross-border relief for losses, the 'no possibilities' test, to be applied (as the Revenue contend) at the end of accounting period in which the losses crystallised rather than (as M&S contends) the date

of claim? This question involves deciding whether the Court of Appeal (in the First Appeal), reached a binding decision on that issue and whether it remains binding on this court in light of subsequent decisions of the ECJ."

Appeal by HMRC refused – "no possibilities" test to be applied at the date of claim.

2. "Can sequential/cumulative claims be made (as M&S contends) by the same company for the same losses of the same surrendering company in respect of the same accounting period? The Revenue asserts that that is not a question decided by the Court of Appeal and is precluded both by UK fiscal rules and by the underlying jurisprudence of the ECJ."

Appeal by HMRC refused – "M&S is permitted to make successive claims to the same loss and rely on the claim which satisfies the … criteria, and then withdraw any earlier claims to the same surrendered losses."

3. "If a surrendering company has some losses which it has or can utilise and others which it cannot, does the no possibilities test (as the Revenue contend) preclude transfer of that proportion of the losses which it has no possibility of using?"

Appeal by HMRC refused – "The 'no possibilities' test is to be applied on a euro by euro basis so that at the time the claim is made the … criteria may be fulfilled even if a proportion of the losses do not satisfy them."

4. "Does the principle of effectiveness require M&S to be allowed to make fresh 'pay and file' claims now that the ECJ has identified the circumstances in which losses may be transferred cross-border, when at the time M&S made those claims there was no means of foreseeing the test established by the court?"

Appeal by M&S refused – "There is no principle that a reasonable time must be afforded to a claimant in which to bring about the circumstances which would generate the community law right."

5. "What is the correct method of calculating the losses available to be transferred?"

Appeal by HMRC refused – "Once you move from identifying the local losses (computed under local rules) to identifying their equivalent under UK rules, you also have to move from local time of recognition to UK timing of recognition."

In September 2008 the European Commission issued a formal request to the UK to properly implement the judgment. The Commission considers that the legislation meant to implement the *Marks & Spencer* ruling imposes conditions on cross-border group relief that make it virtually impossible for taxpayers to benefit from the relief, and referred the UK to the ECJ for improper implementation of the original ECJ ruling. In February 2015, the CJEU dismissed the complaint (*European Commission v. United Kingdom* (C-172/13)).

1.4.4   *Summary of* Marks & Spencer

- Marks & Spencer claimed group relief for the losses of subsidiaries in Belgium, Germany and France.
- The ECJ held that group relief confers a cash advantage on a group.
- There was a restriction on the freedom of establishment as different treatment applied for tax purposes to the losses of resident and non-resident subsidiaries.
- The fact that the UK did not tax the profits of non-resident subsidiaries did not justify restricting group relief.
- The restriction could be justified by **three justifications, taken together**:

- preservation of the allocation of the power to impose taxes;
- danger that losses could be used twice; and
- a risk of tax avoidance.
- Did the restriction go beyond what was necessary to achieve the objectives?
  - Yes – but only where the non-resident subsidiary had exhausted the possibilities of having the losses taken into account in its state of residence and there was no possibility of the losses being taken into account in the future.

1.5 *Cadbury Schweppes plc & Cadbury Schweppes Overseas Ltd v. Commissioners of Inland Revenue* (Case C–196/04)

1.5.1 Background

Cadbury Schweppes (2006) concerns the operation of the UK controlled foreign company (CFC) provisions. This legislation is covered in detail in **Chapter 10**. The CFC provisions are anti-avoidance legislation aimed at cancelling tax advantages that UK companies can obtain by establishing subsidiaries in lower tax jurisdictions. Where none of the exemptions set out in the legislation are met, the profits of the overseas subsidiary are attributed to its UK parent and taxed at the full rate of UK corporation tax.

1.5.2 Facts

Cadbury Schweppes, a UK company, had established two subsidiaries in the International Financial Services Centre (IFSC) in Dublin to take advantage of the favourable tax regime, under which the subsidiaries paid tax at 10%. The business of both subsidiaries was to raise finance and provide that finance to other subsidiaries in the group.

HMRC assessed the profits of the Irish subsidiaries to UK tax under the CFC legislation. Cadbury Schweppes appealed to the Special Commissioners, maintaining that the UK legislation was contrary to Article 49 (freedom of establishment), Article 56 (freedom to provide services) and Article 63 (freedom of movement of capital).

The Special Commissioners referred the issue to the ECJ for a preliminary ruling.

1.5.3 Judgment

Which Freedom Applied?

The ECJ first considered which of the freedoms were at issue. It reiterated its previous case law that national provisions applying to holdings giving the shareholder definite influence on the company's decisions and allowing the shareholder to determine the company's activities fall within the definition of freedom of establishment.

As the UK CFC legislation applied where the UK company had a controlling holding in subsidiaries established outside the UK, the legislation had to be examined under freedom of establishment (paragraph 32). If there were any restrictive effects on the free movement of services and the free movement of capital, these were an unavoidable consequence of any restrictions on the freedom of establishment and did not justify an independent examination of the legislation under Articles 56 and 63 (paragraph 33).

The decision that the CFC legislation was to be examined solely under freedom of establishment had important consequences. As discussed above, freedom of establishment applies only between Member States, whereas free movement of capital can apply between Member States and non-EU members.

Was there an Abuse of the Freedom of Establishment?

Before examining the UK legislation under Articles 49 and 54, the ECJ had to consider whether Cadbury Schweppes had abused the freedom of establishment by establishing and capitalising subsidiaries in the

Republic of Ireland solely because of the more favourable tax regime there (paragraph 34). This issue was discussed at paragraphs 35–38 and the ECJ made reference to its earlier decisions in *Centros* (1999) (Case C–212/97) and *Inspire Art* (2003) (Case C–167/01).

At paragraph 38, the ECJ concluded that the fact that Cadbury Schweppes decided to establish subsidiaries:

> "… in the IFSC for the avowed purpose of benefiting from the favourable tax regime which that establishment enjoys does not **in itself** constitute abuse." [Emphasis added.]

Was there a Restriction on the Freedom?

As there was no abuse of the freedom of establishment, the ECJ then examined whether Articles 49 and 54 precluded the application of the CFC legislation. The ECJ set out the basic principles of the freedom of establishment, as determined in cases like *Marks & Spencer*.

It was common ground that the CFC legislation involved a difference in treatment of UK resident companies on the basis of the level of taxation imposed on their subsidiaries (paragraph 43). The difference in treatment created a tax disadvantage for UK companies subject to the CFC legislation, as they are subjected to tax on the profits of another legal person (paragraph 45).

At paragraph 46, the ECJ held that the different tax treatment and the resulting tax disadvantage hindered the exercise of the freedom of establishment by UK companies, dissuading them from establishing, acquiring or maintaining a subsidiary in a Member State where it would be subject to a lower level of taxation. **The CFC legislation therefore constituted a restriction on the freedom of establishment.**

Justifications

The ECJ then considered whether the restriction could be justified by overriding reasons of public interest (paragraph 47). At paragraph 48, the UK Government argued that the CFC legislation was intended to:

> "counter a specific type of tax avoidance involving the artificial transfer by a resident company of profits from the Member State in which they were made to a low-tax State."

At paragraph 49, the ECJ referred to its *Avoir Fiscal* judgment and stated that:

> "it is settled case-law that any advantage resulting from the low taxation to which a subsidiary established in a Member State, other than the one in which the parent company was incorporated, is subject cannot, by itself, authorise that Member State to offset that advantage by less favourable tax treatment of the parent company."

There was no general presumption of tax evasion just because a resident company established a secondary establishment in another Member State (paragraph 50). However, at paragraph 51, the ECJ stated, with reference to paragraph 57 of *Marks & Spencer*, that:

> "a national measure restricting freedom of establishment may be justified where it specifically relates to **wholly artificial arrangements aimed at circumventing the application of the legislation** of the Member State concerned." [Emphasis added.]

In assessing whether a taxpayer had entered into a wholly artificial arrangement aimed at circumventing national tax legislation, it was necessary to look at the objective pursued by the freedom of establishment (paragraph 52). At paragraph 53, the ECJ stated that:

> "freedom of establishment is intended to allow a Community national **to participate, on a stable and continuing basis, in the economic life of a Member State** other than his State of origin and to profit therefrom." [Emphasis added.]

Paragraph 54 is one of the most important paragraphs of the *Cadbury Schweppes* judgment, as it addressed the issue of the substance required in a Member State:

"Having regard to that objective of integration in the host Member State, the concept of establishment within the meaning of the Treaty provisions on freedom of establishment involves the **actual pursuit of an economic activity through a fixed establishment in that State for an indefinite period**. Consequently, it presupposes **actual establishment** of the company concerned in the host Member State and the **pursuit of genuine economic activity** there." [Emphasis added.]

Paragraph 55 of the judgment is the key statement of the ECJ's position on the justification of preventing tax avoidance.

"It follows that, in order for a restriction on the freedom of establishment to be justified on the ground of prevention of abusive practices, **the specific objective of such a restriction must be to prevent conduct involving the *creation of wholly artificial arrangements which do not reflect economic reality*, with a view to escaping the tax normally due on the profits generated by activities carried out on national territory**." [Emphasis added.]

At paragraph 56, the ECJ referred to paragraphs 46 and 49 of *Marks & Spencer* and linked the prevention of abusive tax practices to the exercise of tax jurisdiction by Member States and the need to ensure a balanced allocation between Member States of the power to impose taxes.

Having set out the principles, the ECJ moved on to determine if the restriction on freedom of establishment in the CFC legislation could be justified on the ground of preventing wholly artificial arrangements and, if so, whether it was proportionate (paragraph 57). The ECJ held that the legislation made it possible to thwart practices having no purpose other than to escape tax normally due on the profits generated by activities carried on in the national territory and was therefore suitable to achieve its objective (paragraph 59).

The ECJ then considered if the legislation was proportionate, i.e. whether it went beyond what was necessary to achieve the objective (paragraph 60). Where none of the specific exemptions in the CFC legislation were met (i.e. *de minimus* exemption, publicly quoted exemption, acceptable distribution policy, exempt activities or excluded country), an attribution of profits from the subsidiary to its UK parent could be avoided if the motive test in section 748(3) ICTA 1988 was met. As set out in paragraph 62, this required passing both the 'transactions' leg and the 'diversion of profits' leg.

At paragraph 64, the ECJ applied the test on abusive tax practices developed in the indirect tax case *Halifax plc* (2006) (Case C–255/02). In order to conclude that there is a wholly artificial arrangement intended solely to escape tax, there must be:

1. a subjective element consisting in the intention to obtain a tax advantage; and
2. objective circumstances showing that the objective pursued by the freedom of establishment has not been achieved.

The ECJ's conclusion, at paragraph 65, was that the taxation provided for by the CFC legislation must be excluded where, despite the existence of tax motives, the incorporation of a subsidiary reflected economic reality. Economic reality would exist where there was an actual establishment intended to carry on genuine economic activities in the host Member State (paragraph 66). This would be determined by looking at objective factors ascertainable by third parties, particularly at the extent to which the CFC physically existed in terms of premises, staff and equipment (paragraph 67).

If checking those factors led to the finding that the CFC was a fictitious establishment not carrying on any genuine economic activity, the creation of the CFC would be regarded as having the characteristics of a wholly artificial arrangement (paragraph 68).

1.5.4 Outcome

Cadbury Schweppes was to be given an opportunity to produce evidence that the CFCs were actually established and that their activities were genuine (paragraph 70). This did not occur, as Cadbury Schweppes reached a settlement with HM Revenue and Customs (HMRC).

The ECJ stated that it was for the national court to determine whether the motive test in section 748(3) ICTA 1988 lent itself to an interpretation that enabled the taxation provided for by the CFC legislation to be restricted to wholly artificial arrangements.

The UK courts have applied the ECJ's decision in *Cadbury Schweppes* in the *Vodafone 2* case (2008) (Case C-203/05). The Court of Appeal held that the motive test in section 747(3) ICTA 1988 could be interpreted in a manner that complied with the freedom of establishment.

Legislative Change

Following the *Cadbury Schweppes* case, the UK introduced section 751A into the CFC legislation in an attempt to make the motive defence compatible with EU law. Tax advisors have argued it does not sufficiently incorporate the principles in the *Cadbury Schweppes* judgment. The result of the *Cadbury Schweppes* and *Vodafone 2* judgments has been uncertainty for taxpayers in applying the UK CFC legislation to subsidiaries established in other EU Member States. This applies to both tax compliance and planning.

After some interim reform of the rules, the UK CFC legislation was the subject of wholesale reform in 2012. It is hoped that this will result in clarity and certainty in this area. Full details of the current legislation can be found in **Chapter 10**.

1.5.5 Summary of Cadbury Schweppes

- UK CFC rules applied to UK parent with two subsidiaries in the Republic of Ireland.
- The CFC rules apply where there is a controlling holding, therefore the freedom of establishment applies.
- The issue of abuse of the freedom of establishment was considered.
- A tax disadvantage was found, as a resident company is taxed on the profits of another legal person.
- Could the restriction on the freedom of establishment be justified on the ground of prevention of abusive practices?
  - Establishment involves the actual pursuit of economic activity through a fixed establishment in a state for an indefinite period.
  - The specific objective of the anti-avoidance legislation must be to prevent conduct involving the creation of wholly artificial arrangements not reflecting economic reality with a view to escaping the tax normally due.
  - Wholly artificial arrangements = subjective element consisting of an intention to obtain a tax advantage + objective circumstances showing the objective pursued by the freedom of establishment has not been achieved.
- The UK courts had to interpret the motive test.

1.6 EC Treaty Articles on State Aid

The state aid rules are designed to prevent the distortion of competition within the EU internal market. One Member State may not grant an aid to certain sectors or regions, as this causes a disadvantage for operators in other Member States. An aid can be positive (e.g. the grant of a subsidy) or negative (e.g. special tax rules).

Article 107(1) states that "any aid granted by a Member State or through State resources ... which distorts or threatens to distort competition by favouring certain undertakings or the production of certain goods shall ... be incompatible with the internal market." Articles 107(2) and 107(3) contain derogations from this principle. Article 107(3) considers aids with the following purposes, amongst others, to be compatible with the common market:

1. to promote the economic development of areas where the standard of living is abnormally low or there is serious underemployment;
2. to promote the execution of an important project of common European interest or to remedy a serious disturbance in the economy of a Member State;
3. to facilitate the development of certain economic activities or of certain economic areas; and
4. to promote culture and heritage conservation.

Article 108 deals with the European Commission's powers in respect of state aid. In accordance with Article 108(1), the Commission keeps existing aids under review and proposes appropriate measures to the states. Under Article 108(2), if the Commission finds that aid is not compatible with the internal market, it decides that the state shall abolish or alter the aid within a period of time set by the Commission. If the State does not comply, the Commission or an interested Member State may refer the matter to the ECJ. Article 108(3) requires Member States to inform the Commission of any plans to grant or alter aid. If the Commission considers that any such plan is not compatible with the internal market, the procedures in Article 108(2) are initiated and a Member State may not put its proposed measures into effect until the procedure has resulted in a final decision.

1.7   Impact of State Aid Rules on Domestic Tax Law

The European Commission considered that the question of whether a tax measure could be qualified as aid under Article 107(1) required clarification and it therefore issued the 'EC Commission Notice of 11 November 1998 on the Application of the State Aid Rules to Measures relating to Direct Business Taxation (98/C384/03)' ('the Notice').

The Notice followed from the *Code of Conduct for Business Taxation* issued by the European Council on 1 December 1997. The *Code of Conduct* was designed to curb harmful tax measures. The Council acknowledged the positive effects of fair competition, but noted that tax competition could lead to tax measures with harmful effects.

The *Code of Conduct* was a reaction to the OECD's work on harmful tax competition, which invited tax havens (e.g. the Channel Islands, British Virgin Islands) to become more transparent and identified a number of harmful tax practices in OECD member countries, including EU countries (e.g. the holding company regime in Luxembourg and coordination centres in Belgium). There is a link between these harmful tax practices and State aid, therefore the Commission undertook, at paragraph J of the *Code of Conduct*, to draw up guidance on state aid and direct business taxation, which led to the 1998 Notice.

1.7.1   European Commission Notice

The Notice was based on decisions of the judiciary on state aid. It was already settled case law that it is the effect of a measure, not its purpose or the form which it may take, that determines whether it is state aid. This was reiterated at paragraph 7 of the Notice.

At paragraphs 8–12, the Commission specified four cumulative criteria for identifying aid within the meaning of Article 107(1):

1. The measure must confer a financial advantage. The advantage may be provided through a reduction in a firm's tax burden in various ways, including:
    (a) a reduction in the tax base (e.g. accelerated depreciation arrangements);
    (b) a total or partial reduction in the amount of tax;
    (c) deferment or cancellation of a tax debt.
2. The advantage must be granted by the state or through state resources, including regional or local bodies.
3. The measure must directly or indirectly affect competition and trade between Member States. The mere fact that the aid strengthens the firm's position compared with competitors is enough to reach the conclusion that intra-Community trade is affected.
4. The measure must be specific or selective in that it favours "certain undertakings or the production of certain goods". However, the selective nature of a measure may be justified by the nature or general scheme of the system.

At paragraph 13, the Commission states that tax measures open to all economic agents operating within a Member State are, in principle, general measures. It further states that the following measures do not constitute state aid, provided that they apply without distinction to all firms and the production of all goods:

- tax measures of a purely technical nature (e.g. setting the tax rate, rules on loss carry forward, etc.); and
- measures pursuing general economic policy objectives (e.g. promoting research and development).

Paragraph 16 states that the main criterion in applying Article 107(1) to a tax measure is that the measure provides an exception to the application of the tax system in favour of certain undertakings. If the exception does not derive directly from the basic or guiding principles of the tax system in the Member State concerned, state aid will be involved.

1.7.2 Illustrations

These principles can be illustrated by looking at certain provisions of tax law in the Republic of Ireland (RoI).

Before the reduction of the corporation tax rate for trading activities to 12.5%, the RoI had a reduced tax rate for manufacturing companies. The Commission determined this to be state aid, as it favoured the manufacturing sector.

Similarly, one of the harmful tax practices identified by the OECD was the International Financial Services Centre (IFSC) regime in Dublin, which provided for special tax reductions for companies conducting financial activities there. This was a harmful tax practice, as it encouraged highly mobile activities (i.e. financing) to locate in the RoI for tax reasons. It constituted state aid as it provided reductions in the tax base not normally available. The IFSC regime had initially been covered by the derogation in Article 107(3).

In contrast, the reduction of the corporation tax rate to 12.5% for trading activities does not constitute state aid as it applies to all economic agents operating in the entire territory.

Similarly, the Commission examined the RoI participation exemption and concluded that the exemption of capital gains from the sale of substantive participations was not state aid, as it did not amount to favourable treatment of certain undertakings.

1.7.3   ECJ Case Law on State Aid

Examples of state aid cases that have come before the ECJ include:

▤ exemptions and waiving of levies granted to racecourse undertakings by the French government (*France v. Commission (Ladbroke Racing)* (2000) (Case C–83/98));

▤ a rebate on energy consumption taxes in Austria that benefitted only undertakings manufacturing goods (*Adria-Wien Pipeline GmbH* (2001) (Case C–143/99)); and

▤ tax measures introduced by Portugal for the reduction in the rate of income tax for natural and legal persons having their tax residence in the Azores (*Portugal v. Commission* (2006) (Case C–88/03)).

1.8   Procedures Applicable to a State Aid Investigation

A distinction must be made between new and existing aids when looking at the procedural rules. Generally, existing aids are those which were in force before the EC Treaty became applicable (i.e. when a Member State joined the EU) and those which have already been approved by the Commission. All others are new aids.

1.8.1   New Aids

In respect of new aids, Article 108(3) requires Member States to notify the Commission of all their plans to grant or alter aid, including tax aid, and provides that any proposed measures may not be put into effect without the Commission's prior approval.

This is routinely done where a Member State intends to introduce or amend an aid. For example, where the UK wishes to introduce or amend a tax measure that applies only to small or medium-sized enterprises (SMEs), e.g. an enhanced scheme for R&D tax credits, it will apply to the Commission for a ruling that the measure is not state aid prohibited by the Treaty.

1.8.2   Existing Aids

In respect of existing aids, the Commission keeps all systems of aid, including tax aids, under constant review, as set out in Article 108(1). To allow any such review to be undertaken, the Member States have to submit reports to the Commission every year on their fiscal State aid systems and provide an estimate of budgetary revenue lost.

If the Commission undertakes a review of an existing aid and decides that it is not, or is no longer, compatible with the common market, it will propose that the Member State amend or abolish it.

The Member State can refuse the Commission's recommendation. The Commission may then start the formal investigation procedure and conclude that the aid is incompatible with the internal market. In exceptional circumstances, a Member State may apply to the Council, which may act unanimously, to decide that the aid is compatible with the Treaty, by way of derogation.

1.9   Possible Implications for Businesses

State aid is a matter to be dealt with by the governments of Member States and the institutions of the EU (the Commission, the ECJ and the Council). However, there are potentially severe implications for businesses that have benefitted from illegal state aid where a government has not followed the procedures set out above. The Commission recently concluded a state-aid investigation where it concluded that the RoI granted illegal tax benefits to Apple (the US multinational technology company) that enabled it to pay substantially less tax than other businesses over many years. The Commission has ordered that RoI must recover the unpaid taxes, from 2003 to 2014, of up to €13 billion, plus interest. The RoI government is to appeal the ruling. Again, a distinction should be drawn between new and existing state aids.

1.9.1 New Aids

Where a Member State enacts an aid without the Commission's prior approval, the aid is considered illegal. If, after examination of the new aid, the Commission finds that the aid is incompatible with the internal market, it requires the Member State to recover the aid granted. The exception is where that would be contrary to a general principle of Community law, in particular legitimate expectations to which the Commission's behaviour can give rise.

In the case of state aid in the form of tax measures, the amount to be recovered is calculated on the basis of a comparison between the tax actually paid and the amount which should have been paid if the generally applicable rule had been applied. This is irrespective of the fact that a taxpayer may not have entered into a given transaction had the aid not been granted. Interest is then added to this amount.

Therefore, taxpayers need to take care if they are taking advantage of a tax aid that has not already been approved by the Commission, as they could be forced to repay the tax advantage plus interest.

1.9.2 Existing Aids

Where the Commission reviews an existing aid and deems it incompatible with the common market, it cannot demand recovery of the aid. This is because the aid is legal until declared incompatible by the Commission with a final decision. In addition, the Commission may recognise that the beneficiaries of the existing aid had legitimate expectations of relying on the aid for some time in the future and may grant a transitional period before suppressing the existing aid, during which the aid can be legally granted.

1.10 Practical Aspects of Claiming Treaty Reliefs

If a taxpayer believes that a transaction should be tax relieved under the terms of the EC Treaty, an initial claim should be made in the relevant tax return with full disclosure of the legal basis of the claim (i.e. UK law, relevant freedom(s) and why they apply). It is likely that HMRC will reject the claim if it can distinguish it from previously successful EU-style claims.

If HMRC chooses to reject the claim, then, as the EU Commission is responsible for ensuring that Community law is correctly applied, the next step is to challenge the Member State (in this case the UK) by lodging a complaint against the measure (legislative, regulatory or administrative) or widespread administrative practice considered incompatible with Community law. If the complaint appears to be well-founded, the Commission may initiate infringement proceedings. However, such proceedings can only result in a declaration that a provision or practice is indeed incompatible. It is therefore in the interests of complainants to use the remedies available at national level in order to uphold their rights and obtain redress in their individual cases; national courts are the only ones competent to, for example, award damages or grant an injunction against the administration.

This process can be very expensive, and therefore should only be considered if a large amount of tax is at stake, or a group litigation order (GLO) can be set up. A GLO is where companies/individuals with similar-style claims all come together to fund the costs of litigating the issue.

A test case to the EU courts commences with the EU Commission considering whether the decision of HMRC on a claim is compatible with Community law. As part of this process, HMRC will present its views regarding the facts stated in the complaint and the Commission will issue its initial legal assessment – through what is known as 'the letter of formal notice'. At this point, HMRC may decide the claim, or continue to debate the matter with the EU.

If HMRC does not accept the claim and the Commission decides that the case is reasonable, the next step is for the EU to issue a 'reasoned opinion'. This will express the Commission's view that an infringement of one of the four freedoms exists and why, and will ask HMRC to remove it.

If HMRC does not satisfactorily respond to the reasoned opinion (i.e. by allowing the claim), the issue will then be referred to the ECJ.

It is important to note that any finding by the ECJ has no impact on the specific rights of a taxpayer because the Court does not rule on individual cases. The ECJ makes decisions on the application of EU law to certain issues and merely obliges the Member State to comply with Community law.

Therefore, once the ECJ rules that the denial of the claim by HMRC is in breach of one of the four freedoms, it will be necessary to take this judgment and use it as a basis to seek redress through the UK national courts.

In general, however, once the ECJ has ruled in a taxpayer's favour, the national courts will only be deciding on how the mechanics of the claim should operate, as the principle of whether a claim is successful or not has already been decided.

This process can be very lengthy. As the UK time limits for making claims are in some cases only two years from the end of the relevant tax period, it is important that protective claims are filed with HMRC as soon as it is considered that they may be available. This is because, if the claim is delayed until there is a favourable ECJ judgment, it may be out of time and will fail on this procedural point even if the legal basis behind the claim is proven to be correct.

Questions

Review Questions

(See Suggested Solutions to Review Questions at the end of this textbook.)

Question 1.1

In the tax year 2008/09, Mrs Jones, a UK resident and domiciled taxpayer, received a dividend from London Ltd, a UK company. Mrs Jones was entitled to a notional tax credit on this dividend with the result that, as a higher rate taxpayer, the effective rate of income tax on the dividend was reduced from 32.5% to 25%.

In the same tax year, Mrs Jones also received dividends from Paris SA, a French company, and Toronto Inc, a Canadian company. UK tax law did not permit a notional tax credit to be applied to the foreign dividends, so the effective rate of income tax paid by Mrs Jones on these dividends was 32.5%.

Mrs Jones owned 10% of the share capital of each of the companies in question.

Your partner is revisiting Mrs Jones's tax return for 2008/09 and has asked you to consider whether the UK legislation that granted an individual a notional tax credit for dividends received from a UK company, but not dividends received from another EU Member State or third country, could be incompatible with the fundamental freedoms set out in the EC Treaty.

Requirement

(a) Explain which of the freedoms could apply to the French dividend with reference to Articles 45, 49, 56, 63 and to relevant ECJ case law, where appropriate.

(b) Discuss whether the UK legislation at issue, as it relates to the French dividend, could be discriminatory or constitute a restriction on one or more of the freedoms, with reference to ECJ case law.

(c) State how your answers to (a) and (b) would differ when considering the Canadian dividend, rather than the French dividend.

Challenging Question

(Suggested Solutions to Challenging Questions are available through your lecturer.)

Question 1.1

Your firm has a new client, Watermelon Ltd, a UK company engaged in the wholesale distribution of fruit. Watermelon Ltd has a number of subsidiaries in other EU countries. It has recently set up a subsidiary, Finco Ltd, in the Republic of Ireland to engage in financing activities and take advantage of a lower level of taxation.

Finco does not meet any of the exemptions in the CFC legislation. The only method of avoiding an attribution of profits from Finco to Watermelon is to claim the motive defence, as interpreted by the ECJ in *Cadbury Schweppes*.

At present, Finco has no employees other than two directors, only one of whom is resident in the Republic of Ireland. One director is Mr Edwards, managing director of Watermelon, who is based in Belfast. The Irish resident director is an employee of a corporate management company in Dublin. The only establishment of Finco in the Republic of Ireland is a letterbox at the corporate management company's offices, which is Finco's registered office.

Requirement

Your partner has asked you to draft a letter to Mr Edwards, advising Watermelon on the following:

1. The impact of the *Cadbury Schweppes* decision for Watermelon and its RoI subsidiary, Finco.
2. The factors required to improve Finco's establishment in the Republic of Ireland in order to avoid Finco being seen as a wholly artificial arrangement designed to avoid tax in the UK and its profits therefore being attributed to Watermelon under the UK CFC legislation.

Note: You are not required to discuss the UK CFC legislation in detail.

Appendix 1.1

Current EU Member States (year of entry)

Austria (1995)

Belgium (1952)

Bulgaria (2007)

Croatia (2013)

Cyprus (2004)

Czech Republic (2004)

Denmark (1973)

Estonia (2004)

Finland (1995)

France (1952)

Germany (1952)

Greece (1981)

Hungary (2004)

Ireland (1973)

Italy (1952)

Latvia (2004)

Lithuania (2004)

Luxembourg (1952)

Malta (2004)

Netherlands (1952)

Poland (2004)

Portugal (1986)

Romania (2007)

Slovakia (2004)

Slovenia (2004)

Spain (1986)

Sweden (1995)

United Kingdom (1973)

Candidate Countries

Former Yugoslav Republic of Macedonia

Albania

Montenegro

Serbia

Turkey

International Issues in Taxation

Learning Objectives

After studying chapter you will understand:

■ The provenance and principles of the OECD Model Treaty.
■ The main provisions of the UK/Ireland double tax treaties as they relate to a particular client's circumstances (complex calculations are not expected).
■ The granting of unilateral credit relief for tax on foreign activities.
■ The concept of the foreign profits regime, including the worldwide debt cap, dividend exemption and overseas branch exemption.
■ The issue of corporate residence and the options regarding corporate presence in another jurisdiction.

2.1 The OECD Model Treaty and Commentary

2.1.1 The Organisation for Economic Co-operation and Development (OECD)

The Organisation for Economic Co-operation and Development (OECD) was formed in 1961. It currently has 34 member countries, including the United Kingdom and the Republic of Ireland.

The OECD Committee on Fiscal Affairs (CFA) is "responsible for the method by which taxation can be used to promote improved allocation of and use of economic resources, both domestically and internationally, and for proposing ways of increasing the effectiveness of taxation as a policy instrument for achieving Government objectives."

The OECD CFA has a number of working parties, one of which is responsible for drafting the OECD Model Tax Convention and the Commentary on the Model Convention. The *Draft Double Tax Convention on Income and Capital* was published in 1963, and the *Model Double Tax Convention on Income and Capital* (the "OECD Model Treaty") was first published in 1977. There have been a number of revised versions of the OECD Model Treaty and Commentary since that date; the latest version is the *Model Tax Convention on Income and on Capital* which was issued in 2014 (see www.oecd.org).

2.1.2 Introduction to the OECD Model Treaty

OECD member countries use the OECD Model Treaty when negotiating double tax treaties with each other. The format of the Model Treaty is as follows:

Chapter I:	Scope of the Convention
	Article 1 – Persons covered
	Article 2 – Taxes covered
Chapter II:	Definitions
	Article 3 – General definitions
	Article 4 – Resident
	Article 5 – Permanent establishment
Chapter III:	Taxation of Income
	Articles 6–21 – Various, covering differing sources of income
Chapter IV:	Taxation of Capital
	Article 22 – Capital
Chapter V:	Methods for Elimination of Double Taxation
	Article 23A – Exemption method
	Article 23B – Credit method
Chapter VI:	Special Provisions
	Articles 24–29 – Various, including non-discrimination, mutual agreement procedure, territorial extension, etc.
Chapter VII:	Final Provisions
	Article 30 – Entry into force
	Article 31 – Termination

The OECD Commentary on the Model Treaty is used to interpret the provisions of a specific treaty. There has been some debate in academic circles, and in court cases in certain jurisdictions, about which version of the Commentary should be used as an interpretative guide to a treaty. The issue has been whether the version of the Commentary in use when the Treaty was negotiated or the most recent version of the Commentary should be used. All references below are to the 2014 Model Treaty and related Commentary.

In addition to the *Model Tax Convention on Income and on Capital*, the OECD has also published a *Draft Convention for the Avoidance of Double Taxation with Respect to Taxes on Estates and Inheritances*. The equivalent UK/Ireland Convention, known as the "Capital Taxes Treaty", is discussed at **Section 2.3**.

It is likely that the Model Treaty will need to be amended in future years to take account of changes resulting from the ongoing Base Erosion and Profit Shifting (BEPS) project. The OECD's *Action Plan on Base Erosion and Profit Shifting* was published in July 2013, with a view to addressing perceived flaws in international tax rules. The 40-page plan, which was negotiated and drafted with the active participation of its member states, contained 15 separate action points, some of which were further split into specific actions or outputs. BEPS is likely to result in changes being required to the Model Treaty article on permanent establishments, among other areas.

2.1.3 Taxes Covered by the Model Treaty

The 2014 OECD Model Treaty is specifically for taxes on income and capital. It therefore covers:

- income tax;
- corporation tax;
- capital gains tax (CGT);
- Pay As You Earn (PAYE); and
- withholding tax (WHT).

The taxes that are **not** covered by the 2014 Model Treaty include:

■ VAT;
■ inheritance tax (IHT);
■ stamp duty; and
■ stamp duty land tax (SDLT).

2.1.4   The Purpose of Double Tax Treaties

The purpose of double tax treaties (DTTs) is to deal with the interaction of tax rules of two different jurisdictions. In the absence of a DTT, double taxation may arise as two or more states may claim the right to tax. Tax treaties aim to allocate taxing rights between two jurisdictions as follows:

1. the state of residence (the country where the taxpayer resides); and
2. the state of source (the country where the income or gain arises).

2.1.5   Chapter I: Scope of the Convention

The main Articles of the 2014 Model Treaty will now be discussed, with reference to the Commentary as appropriate.

Article 1 states that the Treaty applies to "persons" who are "residents" of one or both of the "Contracting States" (i.e. the parties to the Treaty). "Person" is defined in Article 3(1)(a), and includes an individual and a company. Residence in a state is the key to being able to claim the benefit of a treaty. This is dealt with in Article 4.

Article 2 permits the Contracting States to specifically list the taxes covered by the Treaty. These will generally include the taxes outlined at **Section 2.1.3**, above.

2.1.6   Chapter II: Definitions

Article 3: General Definitions

Article 3 contains definitions of certain terms, including "persons", "company", "enterprise", "national" and "business".

Article 3(2) is important as it states that "any term not defined ... shall ... have the meaning that it has at that time under the law of [the Contracting] State for the purposes of the taxes to which the Convention applies." It would not be practical for a double tax treaty to contain all the relevant definitions for tax law. However, given the different meanings which could be applied to a term in different jurisdictions, this provision can lead to difficulties in the interpretation of a treaty.

Article 4: Resident

Article 4 defines the term "resident" for the purposes of the Model Treaty.

Article 4(1) defines the term "resident of a Contracting State" as "any person who, under the laws of that state, is liable to tax therein by reason of his domicile, residence, place of management or any other criterion of a similar nature ..." These are the individuals or companies who are entitled to rely on the Treaty. Therefore, a person who is considered by HMRC to be tax resident in the UK under domestic law would be entitled to rely on the UK's extensive network of DTTs in dealing with the tax authorities of states with which the UK has a treaty.

Article 4(2): Individuals

Article 4(2) is the 'tie-breaker' test for the residence of an individual. It is possible that both Contracting States, by applying their domestic tax law, consider that an individual is tax resident in their jurisdiction. In the absence of this test, both could claim primary taxing rights over the income of the individual to tax, resulting in double taxation.

Article 4(2) sets out a number of tests to be applied to determine in which of the states the individual is resident for the purposes of the Treaty:

1. They shall be deemed to be a resident only of the state in which they have a **permanent home** available to them; if they have a permanent home in both states, they shall be deemed to be a resident only of the state with which their personal and economic relations are closer (**centre of vital interests**).
2. If the state in which they have their centre of vital interests cannot be determined, or if they do not have a permanent home in either state, they shall be deemed to be a resident only of the state in which they have a **habitual abode**.
3. If they have a habitual abode in both or neither states, they shall be deemed to be a resident only of the state of which they are a **national**.
4. If they are a national of both or neither states, the competent authorities of the Contracting States (i.e. the tax authorities) shall settle the question by **mutual agreement**.

Article 4(2) is the key article to be considered when an individual wishes to move their tax residence from one jurisdiction to another. Ideally, where this is mainly motivated by tax reasons, the individual should ensure that they are considered non-resident under the domestic law of the state they are leaving.

Where this is not possible, Article 4(2) of the treaty between the state being left and the state in which they wish to become resident should be considered and advice given based on the tests set out, to ensure that they are considered resident under the "permanent home", "centre of vital interests" and "habitual abode" tests in the new state. This is referred to as being "treaty resident" in that state. Where none of the tests, 1.–4. above, is met, the individual's residence can only be determined by mutual agreement between the tax authorities of the two states. This is a situation to be avoided when undertaking tax planning based on the residence of a taxpayer.

The Commentary on Article 4 gives guidance on the terms in Article 4(2).

"Permanent home" – A permanent home can be rented or owned, but must be arranged and retained for the individual's permanent use, i.e. available to them at all times continuously.

"Centre of vital interests" – In ascertaining an individual's centre of vital interests, regard will be had to factors including: family and social relations; occupations; political, cultural or other activities; and place of business.

"Habitual abode" – Determining an individual's habitual abode requires examining the time spent in both states to conclude where they stay most frequently.

Example 2.1

Mr Benn is currently resident in, and is also a national of, Monrovia. He wishes to become tax resident in Utopia due to the lower rates of income tax and CGT. He is single and owns an apartment in Monrovia. He is a pilot on international routes for the Monrovian national airline. He is a keen showjumper and owns two horses, which are stabled near his home. He is reluctant to sell his Monrovian apartment due to the depressed condition of the housing market in Monrovia. The DTT between Monrovia and Utopia is based on the OECD Model Treaty.

What advice would you give Mr Benn to ensure that he is considered to be tax resident in Utopia under Article 4(2) of the Monrovia/Utopia DTT?

continued overleaf

Solution

As a national of Monrovia, Mr Benn will be considered to be tax resident there under test 3. if his residence cannot be determined by tests 1. and 2. Therefore, in order to be considered tax resident in Utopia and benefit from the lower rates of taxation, he should do as much as possible to ensure that he meets the permanent home, centre of vital interests or habitual abode tests set out at Article 4(2)(a) and (b).

Mr Benn should rent or buy a property in Utopia, which can become his permanent home in that state. As he is unwilling to sell his Monrovian apartment, he should consider letting it out so that it is no longer continuously available to him. If this is not feasible, as he may need to use it to be close to the airport for his employment duties, he would then have a permanent home in both states.

If Mr Benn has a permanent home in both states, he will need to ensure that his centre of vital interests is in Utopia, in order that he can be tax resident in that state under the DTT. The OECD Commentary requires regard to be had to his family and social relations, his occupations and his political, cultural or other activities. It can be difficult to demonstrate that a person's centre of vital interests has moved, so Mr Benn should do as much as possible to show that he has moved his centre of vital interests to Utopia, and not retained it in Monrovia.

Mr Benn's employment will continue to be based in Monrovia, as a pilot for the Monrovian national airline. He is single but, as a national of Monrovia, it is likely that he has family connections in that state. One way in which he could demonstrate that his centre of vital interests has moved to Utopia is to move his horses to stables near his new home in Utopia. He could then join a local showjumping team and take part in competitions in Utopia.

If Mr Benn has a permanent home in both states, and it is not possible to demonstrate in which one he has his centre of vital interests, he will be deemed to be resident in the state where he has his habitual abode. This is likely to be the state where he stays more frequently, and the OECD Commentary states that regard must be had not only to stays at his permanent home in the state in question but also at any other place in the same state.

Mr Benn should aim to spend as little time as possible in Monrovia. He will clearly be required to stay there, either in his apartment or a hotel, to undertake his pilot duties. He is also likely to wish to spend some time with family and friends. As a pilot on international routes, he will also be spending significant amounts of time staying in neither state. Mr Benn should keep a careful record of the amount of time spent in each state and ensure that a clear majority of his time is spent in Utopia.

Due to the nature of Mr Benn's occupation, as he may have difficulty with the centre of vital interests and habitual abode tests, the advice should be that he not retain a permanent home in Utopia and instead stay in hotels when access to the airport is required.

Article 4(3): Companies

Article 4(3) is the tie-breaker test for companies. Where a company is resident under domestic law in both states, it is deemed to be a resident only of the place in which its place of effective management is situated.

The 2008 Model Treaty introduced a new proposed Article 4(3) within its commentary, which states that it is for the competent authorities to reach agreement on the place of residence of a corporate entity. Treaties negotiated under previous versions of the Model Treaty (such as the UK/RoI DTT) use the "place of effective management test".

New treaties (such as the new UK/Netherlands DTT) use the new Article 4(3), which states that corporate residence is to be determined by the competent authorities. In the absence of agreement regarding corporate residence, the corporate entity is not entitled to any relief or exemption from tax provided by the Treaty, except as agreed by the competent authorities. Changing from "place of effective management" to mutual agreement between the tax authorities makes it much more difficult for tax advisers advising corporate entities on maintaining their place of residence in a certain jurisdiction.

Articles 5 and 7: Permanent Establishment

Articles 5 and 7 should be looked at together. Article 5 defines "permanent establishment" and Article 7 deals with the taxation of business profits. A permanent establishment (PE) may be found to exist in two circumstances:

1. a fixed place of business; and
2. a dependent agent.

Fixed Place of Business

Article 5(1)–(3) and the related Commentary deal with the concept of "fixed place of business". In order for a fixed place of business to constitute a PE, three factors must be present:

1. there must be a place of business;
2. the place must have some degree of permanence; and
3. the business of the enterprise must be wholly or partly carried on through that place.

Article 5(2) lists examples which, *prima facie*, constitute a PE, e.g. an office or place of management.

Article 5(3) expressly states that a building site or construction or installation project is a PE only if it lasts more than 12 months.

In addition to these specifically mentioned items, the Commentary states that a place of business covers any premises, facilities or installations used for carrying on the business of an enterprise, whether or not they are used exclusively for the purpose. There does not necessarily have to be a formal right to use that place.

The degree of permanence required to constitute a PE has not been determined by the OECD and the Commentary admits that the practices followed by member countries have not been consistent. As a guide, a period of less than six months has generally been taken as not giving rise to a PE.

In order for a fixed place of business to be a PE, the enterprise must carry on its business activity wholly or partly through it. This is often determined by the presence of employees at the fixed place of business. However, the lack of employees does not mean that there is no PE, as a PE can arise without personnel if the activities involve running gaming or vending machines, or leasing plant and equipment.

Dependent Agent

In the absence of a fixed place of business, a PE may exist under Article 5(5) where a dependent agent has, and habitually exercises, authority to conclude contracts in the name of the enterprise in a state.

This is determined by considering the agent's authority and the repeated use of that authority. The Commentary states that the phrase "authority to conclude contracts in the name of the enterprise" is not confined to an agent who enters into contracts literally in the name of the enterprise, but applies equally to an agent who concludes contracts that are binding on the enterprise even if those contracts are not actually in the name of the enterprise.

Under Article 5(6), an agent will not constitute a PE where they are:

1. independent of the enterprise both legally and economically; and
2. acting in the ordinary course of their business.

Therefore, an employee is unlikely to be considered an "independent agent".

As noted previously, the Model Treaty definition of a permanent establishment is likely to change due to the BEPS project, including changes to prevent the situation whereby a company can structure its operations in such a way that it avoids creation of an overseas permanent establishment by relying on the "independent agent" exclusion.

Preparatory or Auxiliary Activities

Even if there is a fixed place of business through which the business of the enterprise is carried on, or a dependent agent, a PE will not exist if the activities undertaken are limited to those set out in Article 5(4). The common feature of these activities is that they are generally preparatory or auxiliary.

In distinguishing between activities that have a preparatory or auxiliary character and those that do not, the Commentary states that the decisive criterion is whether or not the activity forms an essential and significant part of the activity of the enterprise as a whole.

Business Profits

The importance of the definition of PE becomes clear when looking at Article 7 on business profits. This Article was significantly revised in the 2010 version of the Model Treaty to clarify that the profits to be attributed to a PE should be calculated as if the PE were a completely separate enterprise. Article 7(1) states that the profits of an enterprise of a Contracting State shall be taxable **only** in that state unless it carries on business in the other Contracting State through a PE. Where there is a PE, only the profits attributable to that PE can be taxed in the other state.

Example 2.2

White Ltd is resident in State A and manufactures and sells its products there. It also has a fixed place of business in State B, through which it sells its products. It also sells its products in State C, but it does not have a fixed place of business or dependent agent in State C.

States A and B, and States A and C, have DTTs based on the OECD Model Treaty.

State A, as the State of residence, is entitled to tax the profits of White Ltd, wherever arising.

As there is a PE in State B, it can tax the profits attributable to that PE.

The profits arising through the sale of products in State C cannot be taxed by State C because White Ltd does not have a PE there.

State A will grant relief to White Ltd in respect of the profits taxed by State B so that double taxation does not arise.

Article 7(4) means that other Articles of the Treaty apply in preference to Article 7. This means that if there is another Article dealing with the specific type of income or gains in question (e.g. Article 6 on rental income), it will apply instead of Article 7.

Example 2.3

Northern Ltd manufactures office furniture and sells it wholesale to distributors of office products. It currently has operations only in its home State of Razkavia. The company wishes to employ two sales representatives to start selling its products across the border in Ritterwald. It is keen to avoid having a PE in Ritterwald, as the tax rate there is 35%, compared to 25% in Razkavia. There is a DTT between Razkavia and Ritterwald, which is based on the OECD Model Treaty.

You are required to advise Northern Ltd on the activities it could undertake in Ritterwald without being deemed to have a PE there under Article 5 of the Razkavia/Ritterwald DTT.

Solution

Northern Ltd will have a PE in Ritterwald under Article 5 of the DTT if it has a fixed place of business there through which it conducts its activities or if it has a dependent agent there. However, there will be no PE if the activities undertaken in Ritterwald are preparatory or auxiliary activities covered by Article 5(4).

The first step in avoiding a PE is for Northern Ltd not to have premises in Ritterwald. If this is not feasible, any premises should be used only for storage, display or delivery of goods within the meaning of Article 5(4).

Northern Ltd should be aware that it could have a fixed place of business in Ritterwald, even if it does not rent or buy premises there. Care should be taken if the sales representatives employed by the company to sell goods in Ritterwald operate from their homes in that jurisdiction and have home offices (e.g. computer, fax machine). These could be fixed places of business for Ritterwald despite the fact that the company has no right to occupy the property. Similarly, if space is made available for the company's use at a customer's premises on a regular basis, a PE could exist.

continued overleaf

In order to avoid a PE, the company must not have dependent agents with the authority to conclude contracts in Ritterwald. The two sales representatives could create a PE, within the meaning of Article 5(5), if they have, and habitually exercise, authority to conclude contracts in Ritterwald. The sales representatives should be permitted to meet potential customers, discuss the company's products and the standard price list for the products. They should not be permitted to conclude contracts, and the extent to which they can negotiate should be limited. If a customer wishes to buy products, the details should be e-mailed or faxed to the company's office in Razkavia and the sales manager there should conclude the contract. He should not merely 'rubber-stamp' the terms agreed with the sales representatives in Ritterwald as this could allow the conclusion to be reached that they have *de facto* authority to conclude contracts.

As there can be practical difficulties in employing sales representatives in a jurisdiction and trying to avoid a PE being created, Northern Ltd should consider the use of independent agents to initially establish its presence in Ritterwald. It could find a company that acts as a wholesale distributor and could therefore act as an agent to sell Northern Ltd's products in the normal course of its business, within the meaning of Article 5(6).

2.1.7 Chapter III: Taxation of Income

Article 6: Income from Immovable Property

Article 6 deals with income from immovable property (e.g. land and buildings). Article 6(1) states that income derived by a resident of a Contracting State from immovable property situated in the other state may be taxed in that other state. This permits the state where the land is situated (the source state) to tax income arising from that land, but does not prevent the state of residence from also taxing that income.

In order to prevent double taxation, the state of residence will be required to give relief to the taxpayer in relation to the tax paid in the source state. Article 6 is generally considered by tax advisers to apply to 'income' from land (e.g. rent) and not to the proceeds of sale of land. This is not necessarily the view of tax authorities.

Article 10: Dividends

Article 10 covers dividends paid by a company in one state to a resident of the other state. Under Article 10(1), these may be taxed in the state where the recipient is resident.

However, under Article 10(2) the dividends may also be taxed in the state where the company paying the dividends is resident. This is achieved by the state where the payer is resident applying withholding tax (WHT) to the dividend.

Article 10(2) goes on to permit reduced rates of WHT in certain circumstances. It suggests that the rate be reduced to 5% where the beneficial owner of the shares is a company holding at least 25% of the share capital of the company paying the dividend and 15% in all other cases.

Example 2.4

Yellow Ltd, a company resident in State X, declares a dividend of £20 per share. The rate of WHT on dividends under the domestic law in State X is 20%.

1. Orange Ltd, a company resident in State Y, owns 30 shares (30% of the share capital) in Yellow Ltd.
2. Mr Brown, also a resident of State Y, holds 5 shares.
3. Miss Grey, a resident of State Z, also holds 5 shares.

There is a DTT based on the OECD Model Treaty between States X and Y. There is no DTT between States X and Z.

What WHT will be suffered by each of the recipients?

Solution

In the absence of a tax treaty with Z, Miss Grey's dividend of £100 will be subject to WHT at X's domestic rate of 20%, meaning that she only receives £80.

Under the terms of the tax treaty between X and Y, the rate of WHT will be reduced for residents of Y.

continued overleaf

> As a company holding at least 25% of the share capital in Yellow Ltd, the WHT on the dividend paid to Orange Ltd will be reduced to 5%, so that it receives £570 of its £600 dividend.
>
> Mr Brown's dividend of £100 will be subject to WHT at the reduced rate of 15%, meaning that he will receive £85.
>
> The dividends received by Orange Ltd and by Mr Brown will be subject to tax in State Y, but it will be required to grant double tax relief for the tax suffered in X.
>
> State Z will not be required to grant treaty double tax relief to Miss Grey, but its domestic law may allow for unilateral double tax relief.

Articles 11–13: Interest, Royalties and Capital Gains

Article 11 on interest establishes similar principles for interest arising in one state and paid to a resident of the other state. Article 11(1) permits the state of residence to tax the interest. Article 11(2) allows the state where the interest arises to tax the interest, but suggests a reduced WHT rate of 10%.

Article 12 deals with royalties and Article 12(1) states that these should be taxable **only** in the state where the recipient is resident.

Capital gains are dealt with in Article 13. Under Article 13(1), gains derived by a resident of one state from disposing of immovable property (e.g. land, buildings) in the other state may be taxed by the state where the land is situated. This does not prevent the state of residence from also taxing the gain, although it will be required to grant double taxation relief. Article 13(2)–(4) deals with other specific situations. Article 13(5) states that gains arising from property not dealt with in Article 13(1)–(4) are taxable **only** in the state where the person disposing of the property is resident.

2.1.8   Chapter V: Methods for Elimination of Double Taxation

Articles 23A and 23B covers the elimination of double taxation. It gives two alternative forms of wording, which can be used by the Contracting States. One sets out the exemption method (Article 23A) of double tax relief, whereby the state of residence exempts from tax income or gains subjected to tax in the other state. The alternative method is the credit method (Article 23B), generally used by both the UK and RoI, whereby the state of residence grants relief for the tax paid in the other state against tax due on the same income in its state.

2.1.9   Other Articles of the OECD Model Treaty

The other Articles of the OECD Model Treaty are:

- Article 8 – Shipping, inland waterways, transport and air transport;
- Article 9 – Associated enterprises;
- Article 15 – Income from employment;
- Article 16 – Directors' fees;
- Article 17 – Entertainers and sportspersons;
- Article 18 – Pensions;
- Article 19 – Government service;
- Article 20 – Students;
- Article 21 – Other income;
- Article 22 – Capital;
- Article 24 – Non-discrimination;
- Article 25 – Mutual agreement procedure;
- Article 26 – Exchange of information;
- Article 27 – Assistance in the collection of taxes;

- ▦ Article 28 – Members of diplomatic missions and consular posts;
- ▦ Article 29 – Territorial extension;
- ▦ Article 30 – Entry into force; and
- ▦ Article 31 – Termination.

2.2 The UK/Ireland Double Tax Treaty on Income and Capital

The *UK/Ireland Income and Capital Gains Tax Convention*, referred to as the UK/Ireland double tax treaty (DTT), is based on the OECD Model Treaty and therefore the guidance in the Commentary can be used as a guide for the interpretation of the DTT. The discussion below will look at the main Articles of the Treaty and focus on elements that may differ from the OECD Model Treaty. (You should be completely familiar with the application of the provisions of the UK/Ireland DTT, a copy of which can be downloaded from www.gov.uk/government/collections/tax-treaties.).

2.2.1 Legal Status of Double Tax Treaties

It is useful to understand the position tax treaties have under UK law.

Tax treaties are negotiated between the UK government and the government of another state. Once a tax treaty has been negotiated, it does not enter into force until both states have ratified it.

Tax treaties are brought into UK law by means of a statutory instrument, which is a piece of secondary legislation enacted by Parliament. This is permitted by section 2 Taxation (International and Other Provisions) Act 2010 (TIOPA 2010).

Each state is bound by the terms of a tax treaty under public international law. A treaty takes priority over UK domestic law. However, under constitutional law, the current Parliament cannot restrict the ability of a future Parliament to legislate in the way it chooses and, therefore, it is possible for laws to be passed in the UK, after the ratification of a tax treaty, which in some way restrict the operation of that treaty. If this happened, the other party to the treaty would, in theory, be able to seek a remedy under international law.

2.2.2 Introduction to the UK/Ireland Double Tax Treaty

As in the OECD Model Treaty, the terms "Contracting State" and "other Contracting State" are often used in the UK/Ireland DTT. It can be difficult to comprehend the provisions using these terms, so it is best to replace them with "the UK" and "RoI", as appropriate, to understand which jurisdiction has taxing rights in a given situation. This has been done below to aid understanding of the Articles in the DTT.

Article 1 defines the scope of the Treaty and is identical to the OECD Model Treaty. Article 2 states the taxes that are covered by the DTT; for the UK, these are income tax, corporation tax, petroleum revenue tax, capital gains tax and any identical or substantially similar taxes. Note that inheritance tax, stamp duty and VAT are not covered.

Article 3(1) contains definitions of certain terms used in the DTT. Article 3(2) differs slightly from the wording in the current OECD Model Treaty and states that any term not defined shall have the meaning that it has under the laws of either the UK or RoI.

2.2.3 Article 4: Fiscal Domicile

Article 4(1) defines the term "resident". A resident of the UK includes any person who, under the law of the UK, is liable to tax in the UK by reason of his domicile, residence or place of management. As these terms are not defined in the DTT, they have the meaning that they have under UK domestic law.

Article 4(2) contains the tie-breaker clause for individuals who are resident in both the UK and the RoI by virtue of the domestic law in each jurisdiction. This is a possible circumstance due to the different rules that apply to residence in each jurisdiction. The tests are the same as those set out in Article 4(2) of the OECD Model Treaty.

Corporate Residence

Article 4(3) is the tie-breaker clause for corporate residence. It uses the old wording in the OECD Model Treaty and states that where a person, other than an individual, is a resident of both states, that person shall be deemed to be a resident of the state in which its place of effective management is situated.

There is guidance on the meaning of "place of effective management" in the Commentary; its meaning is similar to the UK concept of "central management and control", as set out by the House of Lords in *De Beers Consolidated Gold Mines* ((1906) AC 455).

A company will be resident in the UK under domestic law if its management and control is exercised in the UK or, under section 14 Corporation Tax Act 2009 (CTA 2009), if it is incorporated in the UK. Similar rules are in place in the RoI.

Thus, if a company is incorporated in the UK but its central management and control is exercised in the RoI, both jurisdictions will view the company as resident under domestic law. The tie-breaker test in Article 4(3) of the UK/Ireland DTT will then be applied to determine where the company is resident for the purposes of the Treaty. On the basis that "central management and control" equates to "place of effective management", the company would be deemed to be resident in the RoI only.

Section 18 CTA 2009 would then apply in the UK. This section provides that companies held to be non-UK resident under a DTT will be treated as non-UK resident for all purposes of the Taxes Acts (with an important exception in the controlled foreign company legislation).

2.2.4 Article 5: Permanent Establishment

Article 5 defines the term "permanent establishment" (PE). Note that Article 5(2)(h) states that a building site, construction or installation project that lasts more than six months will be a PE, whereas the OECD Model uses 12 months.

UK domestic law contains a definition of PE in section 1141 Corporation Tax Act (CTA 2010). This definition can be restricted by the terms of a double tax treaty. However, if the presence of a non-resident company in the UK would be a PE under the terms of a double tax treaty but not under the UK domestic law definition, there would be no PE, as a double tax treaty cannot impose a charge to tax in these circumstances.

Example 2.5

Bob Ltd, an RoI resident company, has a contract to build a bridge in Co. Down. It is estimated that the entire construction project will take four months. Bob Ltd has no other contracts in the UK.

Will Bob Ltd have a PE in the UK?

Solution

The first place to look is the UK domestic legislation in section 1141 CTA 2010, as there can be no PE if the activities do not fall within the definition in the domestic legislation. Section 1141(2)(h) provides that there will be a fixed place of business in the UK where there is a building site or construction or installation project. No time limits are given. It would therefore appear that there is a PE under UK domestic law.

The next step is to look at Article 5 of the UK/Ireland DTT. Article 5(2)(h) limits section 1141(2)(h) by stating that a construction project will be a PE where it lasts more than six months. Therefore, provided that the construction of the bridge takes less than six months from start to finish, Bob Ltd will not have a PE in the UK under the terms of the DTT.

2.2.5 Article 6: Limitation of Relief

Article 6 of the UK/Ireland DTT is entitled "Limitation of Relief" and this article is not found in the OECD Model Treaty. Article 6 deals with the remittance basis of taxation (where an individual is taxed on the amount of income remitted to the state rather than the full amount of income arising) and allows a state to restrict relief granted for double tax to the amount remitted.

Article 6 is required because both the UK and the RoI apply the remittance basis of taxation to certain taxpayers, e.g. in the UK, non-domiciled individuals can have their income taxed on a remittance basis if certain conditions are met.

2.2.6 Article 7: Income from Immovable Property

Article 7 of the UK/Ireland DTT equates to Article 6 of the OECD Model Treaty. Article 7(1) gives the state where the immovable property is situated the right to tax income arising from that property.

Non-residents who receive rental income from land or buildings in the UK are subject to tax on that income. Either a withholding tax is applied on the gross rental income or the landlord submits a non-resident landlord tax return and pays UK income tax at the lower rate on the net taxable income. Article 7(1) permits the UK to apply this legislation to Irish residents.

2.2.7 Article 8: Business Profits

Article 8 of the UK/Ireland DTT deals with business profits and equates to the old Article 7 of the OECD Model Treaty.

The profits of a UK resident enterprise are taxable only in the UK unless it carries on business through a PE (within the meaning of Article 5) in the RoI. In that case, only the profits attributable to the PE are taxable in the RoI.

Under Article 8(2), the company and the PE must deal with each other on arm's-length terms. Where a UK enterprise has a PE in the RoI, it should maintain separate accounting records for the PE so that it can easily determine the amount of profit arising in the RoI. The RoI PE will be required to file a tax return and a statutory profit or loss account with the RoI Revenue Commissioners.

Example 2.6

Trainco Ltd is a UK resident company that provides training courses to third parties. It has offices in Belfast and Dublin. The Belfast office provides training courses in Northern Ireland and the Dublin office provides courses throughout the Republic of Ireland. The company maintains separate accounting records for each office. For the year ended 30 June 2016, the Belfast office made a profit of £350,000 and the Dublin office made a profit of £200,000. The accounting profit for each office is equal to the taxable profit.

What amounts are taxable in the RoI and in the UK?

Solution

Under Article 8(1) of the DTT, the Revenue Commissioners can only tax the profits arising in the RoI PE. Therefore, the amount subject to tax in the RoI would be £200,000.

Under UK domestic legislation, a UK resident company is subject to tax on its profits, wherever arising. Article 8(1) does not prevent HMRC from also taxing the profits that arise in the RoI. Therefore, the amount subject to tax in the UK would be £550,000.

The UK would, however, be required to grant double tax relief for the RoI tax suffered.

2.2.8   Article 11: Dividends

Article 11 deals with the taxation of dividends and equates to Article 10 of the OECD Model Treaty. Under Article 11(1), dividends paid by an Irish company to a UK resident may be taxed in the UK. The dividends may also be taxed in the RoI through the imposition of WHT.

Where the recipient of the dividends is a UK company controlling at least 10% of the voting power in the Irish company paying the dividends, the rate of WHT may not exceed 5%. In all other cases, the WHT must not exceed 15%. These provisions apply vice versa where a UK company is paying a dividend to an RoI resident.

The UK does not impose WHT on dividends under domestic legislation. Therefore, although the DTT permits it to apply WHT of 5% or 15%, it does not choose to do so.

The standard domestic rate of WHT on dividends in the RoI is 20%. However, exemption from WHT is available to recipients resident in the EU or jurisdictions with which the RoI has a DTT. This demonstrates that, although the DTT permits the states to tax in certain circumstances, they do not necessarily apply this right through their domestic law.

2.2.9   Articles 12 and 13: Interest and Royalties

Article 12 is the interest article, similar to Article 11 of the OECD Model Treaty. Although Article 11 of the OECD Model Treaty suggests that states apply WHT to interest, the UK and the RoI have decided not to do so. Therefore, Article 12(1) states that interest derived and beneficially owned by a resident of the UK shall be taxable only in the UK, and vice versa for RoI residents.

Under its domestic law, the UK applies a WHT of 20% on interest paid to non-residents, so Article 12(1) provides a good benefit for RoI residents. Where two states are close trading partners, like the UK and the RoI, they often reduce the rates of WHT below those suggested in the OECD Model Treaty. Note that Article 12(4) and (5) contains anti-avoidance provisions in an attempt to prevent the exploitation of the 0% WHT.

Article 13 applies to the payment of royalties and is generally similar to Article 12 on interest. The term "royalties" is defined in Article 13(2) and further information on the definition can be found in the OECD Commentary on Article 12 of the Model Treaty.

2.2.10   Article 14: Capital Gains

Article 14 deals with capital gains and equates to Article 13 of the OECD Model Treaty.

Under Article 14(1), gains derived by a UK resident from the alienation of land or buildings in the RoI may be taxed in the RoI, and vice versa. In addition, under Article 14(2), gains derived from the alienation of shares in a company deriving the greater part of their value from land or buildings may be taxed by the state where the land or buildings are situated.

Generally, the UK domestic tax law does not subject non-residents to capital gains tax in respect of UK situs assets; although Finance Act 2015 introduced an amendment whereby the sale of UK situs residential property on or after 6 April 2016 is now within the charge to UK CGT. An RoI resident disposing of non-residential UK land or buildings in a capital transaction will not be subject to tax in the UK, even though the UK has the right to tax the transaction under Article 14(1).

By contrast, the RoI imposes capital gains tax on non-residents who dispose of any land or buildings situated in the RoI. A UK resident selling RoI land or buildings in a capital transaction will be taxed in both the UK and RoI. As the state of residence, the UK will be required to grant double tax relief.

Under Article 14(3), where a UK resident enterprise disposes of movable property which forms part of the business property of the enterprise's RoI PE, the gain may be taxed in the RoI. Article 14(4) deals with the alienation of ships and aircraft operating in international traffic.

Under Article 14(5), gains from the alienation of property not specifically dealt with in Article 14(1)–(4) are taxable only where the alienator is resident. This paragraph contains a proviso relating to the remittance basis of taxation, similar to that contained in Article 6 of the DTT. Where, under UK law, a UK resident individual is subject to UK tax only on the amount of the gain remitted to the UK, the first sentence of Article 14(5) shall not apply to the amount of the gain not remitted to the UK.

Article 14(6) states that Article 14(5) does not affect the right of the UK to levy, according to its law, a tax on gains from the alienation of any property derived by an individual who is a resident of the RoI and has been a resident of the UK at any time during the three years immediately preceding the alienation of the property, and vice versa.

2.2.11   Other Taxation of Income Articles

Article 15 deals with income from employments, and applies subject to Article 16 on artistes and athletes and Article 17 on pensions. Under Article 15(1), salaries, wages and other remuneration derived by a UK resident shall be taxable only in the UK, unless the employment is exercised in the RoI. If the employment is exercised in the RoI, only the remuneration derived from that employment may be taxed in the RoI.

Article 15(2) provides an exception to Article 15(1) and states that remuneration derived by a UK resident in respect of an employment exercised in the RoI shall be taxable only in the UK if:

1. the recipient is present in the RoI for periods not exceeding 183 days in the fiscal year;
2. the remuneration is paid by an employer who is not a resident of the RoI; and
3. the remuneration is not borne by a PE or a fixed base that the employer has in the RoI.

Article 15(3) applies the provisions of Article 15(1) and (2) to directors of a company as if they were employees of that company.

Article 20 is the 'catch-all' article. It states that income of a UK resident which is of a type not expressly mentioned in earlier Articles, other than income paid out of trusts or the estates of deceased persons, shall be taxable only in the UK. This is similar to Article 21 of the OECD Model Treaty.

2.2.12   Other Articles

Article 21 is the elimination of double tax article, based on Article 23B of the OECD Model Treaty. Under Article 21(2), the UK must, in accordance with its domestic law, grant a credit for tax payable under the laws of the RoI and in accordance with the DTT.

The other Articles of the UK/Ireland DTT are:

- Article 9 – Shipping and Air Transport;
- Article 10 – Associated Enterprises;
- Article 14A – Charities and Superannuation Schemes;
- Article 16 – Artistes and Athletes;
- Article 17 – Pensions;
- Article 17A – Pension Scheme Contributions;
- Article 18 – Government Functions;
- Article 19 – Students;
- Article 22 – Personal Allowances;
- Article 23 – Non-discrimination;
- Article 24 – Mutual Agreement Procedure;
- Article 25 – Exchange of Information;
- Article 26 – Diplomatic and Consular Officials;

- Article 27 – Territorial Extension;
- Article 28 – Entry into Force; and
- Article 29 – Termination.

2.3 The UK/Ireland Double Tax Convention on Estates, Inheritances and Gifts

The UK/Ireland double tax treaty (DTT) covers income tax and capital gains tax amongst other taxes, but it does not cover inheritance tax (IHT). Therefore the two jurisdictions have entered into a separate Convention on "Estates of Deceased Persons and Inheritances and on Gifts", commonly referred to as the UK/Ireland Capital Taxes Treaty. Although the UK has an extensive network of DTTs on income and capital, it has entered into capital taxes treaties with only a limited number of jurisdictions.

As mentioned at **Section 2.1.2**, the OECD also published a draft Convention dealing with taxes on estates and inheritance. The layout is similar to the OECD Model Treaty, and the UK/Ireland Capital Taxes Treaty is based on this draft Convention.

2.3.1 Main Articles of the UK/Ireland Capital Taxes Treaty

Article 1 of the UK/Ireland Capital Taxes Treaty states the scope of the agreement. It can "apply to any person who is within the scope of a tax which is the subject of this Convention, and to any property by reference to which there is a charge to such tax." This differs from the residence requirement in Article 1 of the UK/Ireland DTT on income and capital.

Article 2(1) sets out the taxes covered by the treaty, which at the time of enactment were gift tax and inheritance tax in the RoI and capital transfer tax in the UK. The taxes in both jurisdictions have since changed, with the RoI now having capital acquisitions tax (CAT) and the UK replacing capital transfer tax with inheritance tax (IHT), but they are covered by Article 2(2) which states that the treaty shall also apply to any identical or substantially similar taxes imposed in addition to, or in place of, the existing taxes.

Article 3(1) gives definitions of specific terms. Article 3(2), as in the UK/Ireland DTT on income and capital, states that any term not defined shall have the meaning it has under domestic law.

Article 4 deals with fiscal domicile. Under Article 4(1), whether a person is domiciled in the UK is determined by whether he or she is domiciled in the UK in accordance with UK law, or is treated as so domiciled for the purpose of any tax that is the subject of the treaty. Therefore, where an individual is deemed to be domiciled in the UK for IHT by virtue of being resident in the UK for 17 out of the previous 20 tax years, he or she will be domiciled in the UK for the purposes of the treaty.

Article 4(2) provides a tie-breaker clause to determine whether a person is domiciled in the UK or the RoI where, applying Article 4(1), the person is domiciled in both states. The tests in the tie-breaker follow those for residence of an individual in Article 4(2) of the UK/Ireland DTT on income and capital, using the concepts of "permanent home", "centre of vital interests", "habitual abode and nationality".

Article 5 allocates taxing rights to the jurisdictions. Article 5(2)(a) applies to property, other than settled property, and gives subsidiary taxing rights to the state in which the person is not domiciled under Article 4(2).

Article 6 sets out rules for determining the situs of assets. Under Article 6(1), the situs of property is determined under the law of each state. If applying the law of each state leads to disagreement about the situs of an asset, Article 6(2) states that the situs shall be determined under the law of the state allocated the subsidiary taxing rights under Article 5(2) and, if there is no such state, it must be determined by mutual agreement.

Article 8 deals with the elimination of double taxation. Under Article 8(1), where the UK imposes IHT on property that is situated in the RoI, the UK shall allow a credit against UK tax for the tax imposed in the

RoI. Where both the UK and RoI impose tax on property situated in a third state, the state that was allocated the subsidiary taxing rights in Article 5(2) shall give a credit against its tax equal to the tax paid in the other Contracting State.

2.3.2   Other Articles

The other Articles in the UK/Ireland Capital Taxes Treaty are:

- Article 7 – Deduction of Debts;
- Article 9 – Time Limit;
- Article 10 – Non-discrimination;
- Article 11 – Mutual Agreement Procedure;
- Article 12 – Exchange of Information;
- Article 13 – Diplomatic and Consular Officials;
- Article 14 – Entry into Force; and
- Article 15 – Termination.

2.4   Unilateral Credit Relief for UK Companies

UK resident companies are subject to UK corporation tax on their worldwide income. Where the UK company has income that arises in another country, it is likely to suffer foreign tax on the income.

Therefore, income arising overseas can be subject to double taxation, in both the foreign jurisdiction and the home jurisdiction (i.e. the UK). Double tax relief is intended to alleviate this double taxation on the same source of income.

The rules on double tax relief (DTR) are complex and are now contained in the Taxation (International and Other Provisions) Act 2010. This section sets out the basic principles of unilateral relief for companies. Unilateral relief is the double tax relief provided for by UK domestic legislation; it does not rely on a DTT being in place between the UK and the foreign jurisdiction.

2.4.1   Unilateral Credit Relief

The UK applies a credit system for DTR. The basic principle of this system is that where the tax paid in the foreign jurisdiction on the income is lower than the UK tax on the same income, the company will pay the difference in the UK. Where the foreign tax is higher, relief is restricted to the UK tax on the same income. This leaves no tax liability in the UK in respect of the foreign income. The additional tax paid in the foreign jurisdiction cannot be reclaimed from HMRC but, in certain circumstances, the unrelieved foreign tax may be utilised.

As can be seen from the discussions above on the OECD Model Treaty and the UK/Ireland DTT, foreign source income can arise in a number of ways and the rules for each type of income differ. The types of foreign income that can arise in a UK company include:

- the profits of a permanent establishment (PE) in another jurisdiction, which may suffer corporation tax in the foreign jurisdiction;
- income arising from a bank account held in a foreign jurisdiction or a loan to a foreign company, which may suffer withholding tax (WHT) in the foreign jurisdiction; and

▓ dividends from subsidiaries in foreign jurisdictions. WHT may be suffered on the dividends paid to the UK company and, in addition, these dividends are likely to have been paid from the after-tax profits of the subsidiaries and so have suffered "underlying" tax.

2.4.2 Double Tax Relief on Profits of a Permanent Establishment

Double tax relief (DTR) is available in the UK for foreign tax suffered on the profits of a foreign permanent establishment (PE). As DTR applies on a source-by-source basis, each foreign PE must be looked at separately.

The relief is restricted to the amount of the UK tax on the same income. However, where the profits are taxed as trading income, the unused relief may be carried forward indefinitely, or carried back to accounting periods beginning in the previous three years on a last in/first out basis.

Example 2.7

In the year ended 31 December 2016, Gaskell Ltd, a UK resident company, has the following trading profits:

UK trade – £2,050,000

PE in Northland – £500,000

PE in Southland – £350,000

The tax suffered in Northland was £175,000 and the tax suffered in Southland was £26,250.

Compute the UK corporation tax liability for Gaskell Ltd, after claiming the maximum DTR.

Solution

The UK legislation requires that foreign income is relieved on a source-by-source basis. Therefore, it is best to use a tabular format to calculate DTR.

	UK	Northland	Southland	Total
	£	£	£	£
Trading profits	2,050,000	500,000	350,000	2,900,000
UK tax @ 20%	410,000	100,000	70,000	580,000
DTR for foreign tax	–	(100,000)	(26,250)	(126,250)
UK corporation tax liability	410,000	–	43,750	453,750

Note that £75,000 of the tax suffered in Northland is unrelieved. Due to the requirement to calculate DTR on a source-by-source basis, this cannot be set against the tax payable on the profits arising in Southland. However, it can be carried forward or carried back for 12 months to set against profits of the PE in Northland.

2.4.3 Double Tax Relief on Interest Income

For UK companies, loan interest receivable is generally taxed under the loan relationship rules. The tax payable on loan relationships is always calculated on the net debit or credit arising from all loan relationships. If the interest receivable includes foreign interest, the UK legislation permits non-trading debits on loan relationships to first be set against UK source interest receivable. This maximises the foreign interest income and thereby maximises the DTR.

Example 2.8

Blue Ltd, a UK resident company, has the following loan relationship debits and credits in the year ended 30 September 2016.

- ▓ Interest receivable from UK bank – £5,000

- ▓ Interest receivable from UK subsidiary – £10,000

- ▓ Interest payable to UK parent – £9,000

- ▓ Interest receivable from Eastland subsidiary – £9,000 (net figure after WHT @ 10% applied)

- ▓ Interest receivable from Westland subsidiary – £10,000 (gross figure before WHT @ 35% applied)

Calculate the tax payable on the net loan relationship after DTR, assuming that Blue Ltd pays at the full rate of corporation tax.

Solution

	UK	Eastland	Westland	Total
	£	£	£	£
Loan relationship credits	15,000	10,000	10,000	35,000
Loan relationship debits	(9,000)			(9,000)
Net LR credit	6,000	10,000	10,000	26,000
UK tax @ 20%	1,200	2,000	2,000	5,200
DTR for foreign tax	–	(1,000)	(2,000)	(3,000)
UK corporation tax liability	1,200	1,000	–	2,200

Notes:
1. The gross amount of the interest receivable is taxable in the UK, regardless of the amount of tax withheld at source.
2. The non-trading loan relationship debit arising on the loan payable to the UK parent has been set against the UK interest receivable in order to maximise DTR.
3. The DTR on the interest receivable from Westland is restricted to the UK tax on the same income. The unrelieved foreign tax of £1,500 cannot be used against other interest income or carried back/forward.

2.4.4 Double Tax Relief on Dividend Income

On 1 July 2009, the UK introduced an exemption from tax for dividends received by UK resident companies from UK or overseas companies. The rules are contained in Part 9A of the Corporation Tax Act 2009 (CTA 2009).

Section 931B CTA 2009 sets out the exemption for "small" companies. A "small" company is defined as one with less than 50 employees and whose turnover or gross balance sheet total do not exceed €10 million. The small company dividend exemption will apply where the dividend is paid by a UK resident company or a company resident in a "qualifying territory", subject to anti-avoidance provisions. Under section 931C, a "qualifying territory" is basically one with which the UK has a double tax treaty containing a non-discrimination clause. The UK has a large number of such treaties with other states, including all of the EU Member States.

Chapter 3 of Part 9A contains the rules relating to companies that are not "small". In order to qualify for the exemption, a dividend received by such a company must fall within one of the exempt classes set out in sections 931E–931I. The vast majority of dividends will fall into one of these classes, and thus be exempt from tax when received by a UK company.

The introduction of these exemptions has meant that most dividends received by UK companies are exempt from tax in the UK. This is a type of double tax relief, i.e. giving relief by exemption. As no UK tax is payable in respect of the dividends, no credit can be claimed for foreign tax paid. A company receiving a distribution that would otherwise be exempt may elect for it to be taxable. The election must be made within two years of the end of the accounting period in which the dividend is received.

The UK's general policy is to grant double tax relief through the credit system. The credit system of double tax relief for dividends will still apply where the dividend in question does not qualify for one of the exemptions.

2.5 Unilateral Credit Relief for UK Individuals

The UK also operates a credit system of unilateral DTR for individuals, which operates on a source-by-source basis. The extent to which an individual will be subject to UK tax on income and gains arising in a foreign jurisdiction depends on the domicile and residency status of the individual. UK resident individuals who are also domiciled in the UK are subject to tax on their worldwide income and gains.

The types of foreign income and gains that a UK individual could receive include:

■ the profits of a PE in another jurisdiction, which may suffer income tax in the foreign jurisdiction;
■ foreign investment income – income arising from a bank account held in a foreign jurisdiction or a loan to a foreign company and dividends from non-UK companies, which may suffer withholding tax (WHT) in the foreign jurisdiction;
■ foreign property income – e.g. rental income from a foreign property; and
■ capital gains arising on the sale of chargeable assets situated in a foreign jurisdiction.

In the absence of a tax treaty, unilateral DTR will operate to give a credit against UK income tax or CGT for the foreign tax paid on the same income or gain, restricted to the UK tax payable.

Example 2.9

Lisa is UK resident and domiciled. In the tax year 2016/17, Lisa had the following chargeable gains:

■ Chargeable gain on sale of UK residential rental property in September 2016 – £20,000

■ Chargeable gain on sale of residential rental property in Neverland in January 2016 – £30,000 (This is the gross amount. The tax suffered on the gain in Neverland was £10,000.)

Calculate the CGT payable in the UK by Lisa for 2016/17, after DTR. Lisa is a higher rate taxpayer.

Solution

	UK	Neverland	Total
	£	£	£
Chargeable gains	20,000	30,000	50,000
Annual exemption	(11,100)	–	(11,100)
Net gains	8,900	30,000	38,900
UK tax @ 28%	2,492	8,400	10,892
DTR for foreign tax	–	(8,400)	(8,400)
UK CGT liability	2,492	–	2,492

Notes:
1. The gross amount of the foreign gain is taxable in the UK, regardless of the amount of tax suffered in Neverland.
2. The CGT annual exemption has been set against the UK gain to maximise DTR.
3. The DTR on the Neverland gain is restricted to the UK tax on the same income.

2.6   Corporate Residence

In the UK, the residence of companies was determined by case law until legislation was introduced by section 66 Finance Act 1988. This legislation is now contained in section 14 Corporation Tax Act (CTA) 2009.

Residence status for the purposes of a DTT did not affect residence for UK tax purposes until the introduction of section 249 Finance Act 1994, which is now section 18 CTA 2009.

2.6.1   Case Law

The case law test for determining a company's residence was enunciated by Lord Loreburn in *De Beers Consolidated Mines v. Howe* (1906) (5 TC 198). He stated that: "A company resides … where its real business is carried on … and the real business is carried on where the **central management and control actually abides**." (Emphasis added.)

Determining the place of "central management and control" is a question of fact. HMRC's view is set out in *Company of Residence: Statement of Practice 1/90*. It will look to the highest level of control. The place of central management and control is to be distinguished from the place where the main operations are carried on, although often they will be in the same place.

The place where the board of directors meets is important, but not necessarily conclusive. HMRC outlines the following approach:

1.   It will try to ascertain whether the directors actually exercise management and control.
2.   If they do, then it will seek to establish where it is exercised.
3.   If they do not, then it will seek to establish who does exercise central management and control, and where.

A more recent case on the issue of corporate residence is that of *Laerstate BV v. HMRC* ((2009) TC00162), which provides a useful indication of the factors a court will look at to determine whether a non-UK company is really resident outside the UK. These factors include:

■   whether the board meets regularly to consider all strategic and policy decisions to be made by the company;

■   whether documentation is tabled at board meetings, and information provided to allow all members of the board to properly consider the matters discussed at the meeting and the execution of relevant documentation;

■   whether there are minutes of meetings that accurately record the discussions by the board and any issues or questions raised by its members;

■   whether all meetings are held and all documents signed outside the UK, with attendance by telephone from within the UK being avoided (travel documentation should be kept to evidence attendance at meetings and where documentation is signed); and

■   whether any UK resident directors (or directors conducting business from within the UK) conduct themselves in such a way that may lead third parties to assume that they are authorised to negotiate on behalf of and bind the company (where possible, any duties carried out on behalf of the company, such as the negotiation of documents, should be delegated by the board at a meeting, and the entry into all documentation should remain subject to the board's approval).

2.6.2   Branch or Subsidiary?

When a UK resident company decides to extend its operations overseas, it must decide whether to incorporate a separate company in the overseas territory or trade through a permanent establishment (PE).

Of course, the decision will be impacted by commercial and legal considerations, such as the costs and legal requirements of setting up a subsidiary as compared to those of setting up a branch. Another important commercial consideration is the higher level of commitment to potential customers in the local market illustrated by the incorporation of a local subsidiary.

From a taxation perspective, it is generally accepted that it is better for a loss-making start-up to be taxed as a branch/PE, with incorporation being considered once the business starts to show a profit.

In this way losses incurred in the early days of the overseas business, as it is setting up and building a customer base, can be utilised in the UK. Once the business is established and profit-making, the incorporation of a subsidiary allows the business to take advantage of lower overseas tax rates on its profits.

The foreign profits regime will need to be considered when choosing the appropriate entity. For example, the dividend exemption rules (discussed at **Section 2.4.4** above) mean that dividends payable by an overseas subsidiary to its UK parent will generally be exempt from UK corporation tax.

2.7   Foreign Profits Regime

In the aftermath of ECJ judgments that found the legislation on the taxation of controlled foreign companies (CFCs) and of foreign dividends to be in breach of EU law, it has become necessary to reform these areas.

The reform of the CFC legislation (see **Chapter 10**) is part of a larger scheme to transform the taxation of foreign profits, with the aim of both protecting the UK's competitiveness and protecting its tax base from erosion through the artificial diversion of profits. The regime seeks to adopt a more territorial approach to taxing the profits of foreign subsidiaries.

2.7.1   Dividend Exemption

One of the first steps taken in the reform of the foreign profits regime was the 2009 introduction of an exemption from taxation for dividends received by UK resident companies from UK or overseas companies. This is discussed in further detail at **Section 2.4.4** above.

2.7.2   Taxation of Branches

Legislation was introduced in Finance Act 2011 for accounting periods commencing on or after 19 July 2011 to exempt the profits of foreign permanent establishments (PEs) of UK resident companies from corporation tax, precluding the need for credit relief to prevent double taxation.

The legislation (section 18A CTA 2009) allows a company to make an irrevocable election for all its foreign PEs, located anywhere in the world, to be exempt from corporation tax on their profits. Where a treaty with a non-discrimination article is in place, the exempt income will be the UK measure of the profits of the PE that are taxable by the other state in accordance with the relevant treaty. Otherwise the measure will be based on the OECD Model Treaty (see **Section 2.1**). Exempt profits will include any capital gains attributable to the PE and taxable under the treaty. Where an election is made, no relief is available for the PE's losses, as the profits and gains are not taxable. This also means that no relief is available for foreign tax paid on any profits. Note that it is not possible, therefore, to elect for profitable PEs to be exempt but to exclude loss-making PEs from the exemption – an exemption is "all or nothing".

Certain restrictions prevent abuse whereby profits that would otherwise remain within the charge to corporation tax are diverted to an exempt PE. There is also a transitional rule to ensure that any outstanding loss relief that has been claimed in the six years before the introduction of the new rules is recaptured by HMRC (except in the case of very large losses, which remain in the scope of the transitional rule indefinitely).

2.7.3   Worldwide Debt Cap

Another set of legislation recently introduced in this area of international corporate taxation is the worldwide debt cap rules.

These rules (which can be found in Part 7 of TIOPA 2010) apply for accounting periods that began on or after 1 January 2010. The purpose of the rules is to limit the tax deduction for interest and other finance expense of UK companies in large groups to the external interest and other finance expense of the overall group. The debt cap rules can also apply to wholly UK groups.

The rules apply to large groups if any of the UK members have a net finance expense of £500,000 or more, and a net UK debt of £3 million or more. For the purposes of this legislation, a group is large if it has more than 250 employees or has turnover in excess of €50 million and gross assets in excess of €43 million.

If a group falls within the rules, then the impact may be avoided if it passes a "gateway test", where the aggregate net debt of the UK companies in the group is less than 75% of the group's worldwide gross debt.

The worldwide gross debt is the average of the sum of the group's liabilities (as per the consolidated balance sheet) for the current and prior accounting periods. The UK net debt amount for a particular company is calculated as the average of the net debt and the start and end of the relevant accounting period.

Example 2.10

Alpha Ltd and Omega Ltd are UK resident members of a large worldwide group. The gross debt for the group is £71 million for the year ended 31 December 2015 and £76 million for the year ended 31 December 2016. The worldwide gross debt is, therefore, £73.5 million.

The UK companies' net debt position for the year ended 31 December 2016 is as follows:

	Net debt at 01/01/16	Net debt at 31/12/16	Net debt amount
	£	£	£
Alpha Ltd	£2.5 million	£3 million	£Nil
Omega Ltd	£51 million	£54 million	£52.5 million
Total			£52.5 million

As the net debt amount of Alpha Ltd is below £3 million, it is treated as having a net debt amount of nil.

The total UK net debt is, therefore, below 75% of the worldwide gross debt (£55.125 million) and, as such, the gateway test is passed and the debt cap rules will not apply to the group's UK members for this accounting period.

If the rules apply and the gateway test is not passed, then a disallowance of finance expense across the group will arise where the tested expense amount exceeds the available amount. The difference between these amounts is the "total disallowed amount".

The "tested expense amount" for a period of account of the worldwide group is the sum of the net financing deductions of each relevant group company.

The "available amount" for a period of account of the worldwide group is the sum of the amounts disclosed in the financial statements of the group for that period in respect of:

1. interest payable on amounts borrowed;
2. amortisation of discounts relating to amounts borrowed;
3. amortisation of premiums relating to amounts borrowed;
4. amortisation of ancillary costs relating to amounts borrowed;
5. the financing cost implicit in payments made under finance leases;

6.   the financing cost relating to debt factoring; or

7.   amounts of such other description as may be specified in regulations made by HMRC.

Amounts that represent a dividend payable in respect of preference shares where the shares are recognised as a liability in the financial statements of the group for the period are disregarded. Where the worldwide debt cap rules apply, a return must be submitted to HMRC within 12 months of the end of the period of account, giving details of the tested amount and the total disallowed amount, as well as the companies to which the provisions apply and the amounts to be disallowed in respect of each.

In the UK Chancellor's Budget speech in March 2016, it was announced that with effect from April 2017, the tax deductibility of interest incurred by UK tax resident companies will be restricted to 30% of tax EBITDA. These rules are currently the subject of consultation, but it is envisaged that the application of the worldwide debt cap rules will be limited when the 30% cap is introduced.

Questions

Review Questions

(See Suggested Solutions to Review Questions at the end of this textbook.)

Question 2.1

Permanent Establishment
Highways Ltd is a UK resident company engaged in road construction. It has won a contract to work on the upgrade and repair of the main road from Carlow to Kilkenny, which is scheduled to take 10 months. Highways Ltd has never before worked on a contract in the RoI.

The company has written to the Revenue Commissioners to become registered in the RoI under the equivalent to the UK Construction Industry Scheme, to ensure it meets all its obligations in that jurisdiction.

The Revenue Commissioners responded that the company will be required to file corporation tax returns in respect of the profits arising on the RoI contract, as the work to be performed on the road brings an RoI PE into existence, under RoI domestic legislation.

Gerry, the finance director of Highways Ltd, has only limited understanding of the concept of PE. He understands that there has to be a fixed place of business and, as Highways Ltd will be continuously moving along the road, he argues that there is no such fixed place of business.

Requirement
Based on the UK/Ireland DTT and the Commentary on the OECD Model Treaty, advise Gerry on this issue.

Question 2.2

Capital Gains Tax
John is domiciled and resident in the UK and is a higher rate taxpayer. He has never been resident in the RoI. In the tax year 2016/17, he disposes of the assets listed below (all of which he had held as investments for a number of years).

1.   20 August 2016 – a vintage motor car, which he bought in 2002 for £20,000 and sold for £50,000. He bought the car in Belfast and always kept it in a garage attached to his home in Co. Armagh.

2. 6 November 2016 – shares in Times plc, a UK internet trading company whose shares are listed on the London Stock Exchange, making a taxable gain of £5,000.
3. 1 December 2016 – a holiday home in Donegal, making a taxable gain of £10,000.
4. 19 February 2017 – shares in Skye Ltd, an RoI company engaged in the manufacture and sale of meteorological equipment, making a taxable gain of £5,000.

Requirement

(a) State which jurisdiction(s) may subject the disposals to CGT. Assume that, under its domestic law, the RoI imposes CGT at a rate of 33% on all RoI situs assets, regardless of the residence of the alienator.
(b) State what relief will be granted by the UK where double taxation occurs. Assume that the rules for calculating the amount of the taxable gain are identical in the UK and the RoI.

Question 2.3

Residence

Pierre, a French national, moved to Co. Cork in 2007 to become managing director of the Irish subsidiary of Pineapple Inc. He bought a house in Kinsale, where he lives with his wife and two children.

With effect from 1 April 2016, he was also given responsibility for managing the Northern Irish subsidiary of Pineapple Inc. This requires him to spend a significant amount of time in Belfast and he has therefore rented an apartment in Belfast city centre. As his children attend school in Cork, he retains the house in Cork and his family generally do not travel to Belfast with him.

The UK and RoI have applied their domestic tax rules on individual residence and both consider Pierre to be resident in their jurisdiction.

Requirement

(a) Apply the tests set out in Article 4(2) of the UK/Ireland DTT to determine in which jurisdiction Pierre is resident.
(b) Explain how Article 15 of the DTT could be applied in these circumstances.

Question 2.4

Double Tax Relief

Wade Ltd, a UK incorporated and resident company, had the following income in the year ended 30 September 2016.

- Trading profit arising in the UK – £3,450,000.
- Trading profit arising in the RoI – £750,000.
- Interest receivable from UK bank – £50,000.
- Non-trading debit on UK loan relationship – £10,000.
- Interest receivable on loan to company in Isle of Man – £16,000 (net of 20% WHT).

The tax suffered by the RoI PE was £100,000.

Requirement

Compute Wade Ltd's UK corporation tax liability for the year ended 30 September 2016, after DTR.

Challenging Questions

(Suggested Solutions to Challenging Questions are available through your lecturer.)

Question 2.1

Permanent Establishment

DubAir Ltd is an RoI incorporated and resident company. It is wholly owned by a German company, Radio GmbH, which owns a number of subsidiaries operating in the entertainment sector. DubAir Ltd is engaged in the operation of a digital radio station in the RoI.

Radio GmbH also owns a UK incorporated and resident company, Play Ltd, whose headquarters are in Newry, Co. Down. Play Ltd is engaged in the distribution and hire of gaming machines in the UK.

DubAir Ltd wishes to sell airtime for advertising to customers based in the UK and has entered into a solicitation agreement with Play Ltd. Under the agreement, Play Ltd solicits orders for radio advertising and passes them to DubAir Ltd for acceptance or rejection. The agreement specifically states that Play Ltd is not authorised to conclude contracts on behalf of DubAir Ltd.

Requirement

Discuss whether DubAir Ltd has a PE in the UK by virtue of its relationship with Play Ltd.

Question 2.2

Capital Gains Tax

Simon, who is UK resident and domiciled, has been engaged for many years in property development and investment through a number of companies, of which he is the sole shareholder.

One company, Si(RoI) Ltd, is an RoI incorporated and resident company, whose only asset is development land in Co. Cavan zoned for commercial development. Simon has received an offer to sell the shares in the company for £1 million.

Before he makes a decision about the offer, he wishes to understand the CGT consequences in the UK and RoI.

Requirement

Assuming that the RoI applies CGT at 33% on all RoI situs assets and that the rules for computing chargeable gains are identical in the UK and RoI, you are required to advise Simon on the tax consequences in both jurisdictions of disposing of the shares in Si(RoI) Ltd. It is September 2016 and Simon is a higher rate taxpayer.

HMRC Enquiries, Investigations and Powers, and Significant Recent Developments in Taxation

Learning Objectives

After studying this chapter you will understand:

- The various methods and powers available to HMRC, including enquiries, investigations, requests for assistance, information powers and seizure powers, etc.
- Specific HMRC initiatives, such as the duties of senior accounting officers of qualifying companies and the introduction of online filing under iXBRL.

3.1 Conduct of Enquiries and Investigations

Tax returns for individuals and companies are submitted on a self-assessment basis. This means that the taxpayer is responsible for calculating the tax due. HMRC enters the information contained in the return into its system, but does not check all returns. HMRC decides to open an enquiry into certain returns, usually based on a risk assessment of the taxpayer. It must do so within the time limits prescribed by the legislation.

HMRC divides enquiries into two types: full enquiry (covering the entire return) and aspect enquiry (dealing with one or more aspects of the return but falling short of a full enquiry).

Following a review of HMRC's powers, deterrents and safeguards, Finance Act 2008 (FA 2008) introduced new provisions on information powers, record-keeping, time limits, penalties and failure to notify chargeability to tax. These new legislative measures came into effect on 1 April 2009.

The legislation in this area has also been amended and supplemented in subsequent Finance Acts.

3.1.1 Compliance Checks

Finance Act 2008 aligned the regime for compliance checks (audits, inspections and enquiries) for income tax, corporation tax, CGT, VAT, PAYE and SDLT.

HMRC has developed a *Compliance Handbook Manual* to explain to its staff how to apply the new regime for compliance checks (see www.gov.uk/hmrc-internal-manuals/compliance-handbook). HMRC guidance on opening, conducting and concluding compliance checks can be found in the Enquiry Manual at www.gov.uk/hmrc-internal-manuals/enquiry-manual.

These are useful reference guides for tax advisors whose clients are undergoing a compliance check, though with two caveats:

1. Parts of the manuals are not made available to the general public, as HMRC can take advantage of certain exemptions in the Freedom of Information Act 2000. Therefore, a tax advisor will not have access to all of the information given to HM Inland Revenue (as it was then).
2. This is HMRC's view of the legislation. Tax practitioners and the UK Courts may apply a different interpretation.

3.1.2   HMRC Enquiries

The first step in an enquiry into a self-assessment return is generally for HMRC to write to the taxpayer, and to the taxpayer's advisor where a Form 64-8 (authorising an agent) has been filed, stating that it is opening an enquiry, under which powers the enquiry is being opened and the nature of the enquiry. If the tax advisor believes that HMRC is outside the time limits for opening an enquiry, they should inform HMRC of this fact and state their reasons.

HMRC will usually open a full enquiry only where it suspects that the records used to prepare the return are inadequate or that the taxpayer has been involved in fraud. The majority of enquiries are aspect enquiries, where HMRC chooses one or more aspects of the return and requests additional and/or back-up information.

HMRC carries out a risk assessment and chooses the aspects of the tax return where it considers there could be a potential loss of tax revenue. The types of issue into which HMRC often enquires include:

■   the closing stock figure of an unaudited business, as a higher closing stock figure will reduce the profits for the year and thereby reduce the tax liability;
■   loans to participators in close companies;
■   the breakdown of accruals and deferred income, as these items can reduce the taxable profit for the year;
■   the accounting treatment of an unusual transaction;
■   transactions with connected parties;
■   the use of valuations, particularly for CGT purposes;
■   whether capital expenditure qualifies for a certain type of capital allowance;
■   whether there is any capital expenditure included in the profit and loss account;
■   R&D tax credit claims;
■   whether expenditure has been "wholly and exclusively" incurred for the purposes of the business; and
■   the employment status of an individual.

Where a taxpayer has undertaken a disclosable tax-planning scheme during the year and hence put the scheme disclosure number on the tax return, HMRC will open an enquiry. The enquiry will look at the technical merits of the disclosed scheme and will focus on the implementation of the scheme by the taxpayer, as incorrect implementation can often cause a scheme to fail.

3.1.3   Provision of Information

When opening an enquiry, HMRC will request the taxpayer to provide information within a specified period. Where the taxpayer considers that it will not be possible to provide the requested information within the timeframe, the taxpayer or the advisor should immediately apply to HMRC for an extension, setting out the reasons for the delay.

Where the information requested is onerous, the taxpayer can approach HMRC with an alternative suggestion. For example, if HMRC requests all invoices included within repairs and maintenance for a large business, the taxpayer could suggest that HMRC select a random sample from a list of expenditure and/or that HMRC accept all invoices over a certain amount.

Where a tax advisor is happy that HMRC is not exceeding its information-gathering powers, the advisor should encourage the client to cooperate fully with HMRC and make full disclosure of any errors or uncertain tax positions. As explained below at **Section 3.3**, this will help to mitigate any penalties HMRC can impose. The taxpayer can make amendments to the tax return during the enquiry period.

Where a tax advisor becomes aware during an enquiry that a client has engaged in tax evasion or fraud, the advisor should bear in mind obligations imposed by the Proceeds of Crime Act 2000, the Terrorism Act 2000 and the Money Laundering Regulations 2007.

3.1.4 Closing an Enquiry

An enquiry may not reveal any errors or mistakes in the taxpayer's return. Where adjustments are required, it is usually possible to reach agreement with HMRC on the additional amounts assessable. HMRC will then issue a closure notice.

Where additional tax is payable, interest will be due for late payment of tax, calculated using HMRC's official rates. Where, during an enquiry, it appears that additional tax is payable, the tax advisor should advise the client to make an additional payment to mitigate the interest charged. Doing so should be weighed against the possibility of prejudicing the position being taken by the taxpayer where a technical argument for a certain treatment is being advanced.

It is also possible for HMRC to issue a closure notice where agreement has not been reached. HMRC will do so where the taxpayer persists in refusing to supply information and it has already exhausted all the other formal powers available or has already obtained some information (whether from the taxpayer or his advisor or from third parties) that would enable it to arrive at a conclusion as to the amount that should be included in the taxpayer's self-assessment, and the taxpayer or the tax advisor is not cooperating.

HMRC is unable to ask any more questions about the return once the closure notice has been issued. It will therefore consider the timing of its issue carefully, to ensure it has sufficient evidence to draw soundly based conclusions.

The closure notice will state HMRC's view of the current position and make any amendments needed. If the taxpayer does not agree with the closure notice, an appeal must be made within 30 days.

At any time during the course of an enquiry, the taxpayer may apply to the Tax Tribunal for a direction that HMRC should issue a closure notice. Unless the Tribunal is satisfied that HMRC has reasonable grounds for not giving a closure notice, it will give a direction in favour of the taxpayer, specifying a date by which HMRC must issue a closure notice.

Where no agreement can be reached on the conclusion of an enquiry, either HMRC or the taxpayer can request that the matter be heard by a Tax Tribunal.

3.2 HMRC Powers

Schedule 36 FA 2008 contains the statutory framework for compliance checks in respect of income tax, corporation tax, CGT and VAT. These rules came into force on 1 April 2009.

3.2.1 Basic Powers

Paragraph 1 sets out the basic power for an HMRC officer to obtain information and documents from a taxpayer. It states that an HMRC officer may, by notice in writing, require a taxpayer to provide information or produce a document where the information or document is reasonably required to check the taxpayer's tax position. Paragraph 1 differs from the previous information powers, as it allows HMRC to inspect records before a return is filed.

The type of information and documentation requested by HMRC typically include:

- copies of invoices for certain expenditure, e.g. the acquisition of a fixed asset, legal and professional fees;
- a detailed breakdown of certain items in the profit and loss account, e.g. repairs and maintenance expenses, consultancy expenses, to determine if any capital items have been expensed;
- copies of valuations of assets or shares in companies where these have been used in preparing a tax return;
- copies of minutes of board meetings as evidence of transactions undertaken by companies; and
- copies of bank statements and other documents originated by third parties but held by the taxpayer as independent evidence.

Paragraph 2 grants a similar power to allow HMRC to obtain information from a third party to check the tax position of another person. However, under paragraph 3, a notice cannot be issued to a third party without the agreement of the taxpayer or the approval of the First-tier Tax Tribunal. Paragraph 4 requires that the taxpayer must receive a summary of the reasons for a third-party notice, unless the First-tier Tribunal rules that this could prejudice the assessment or collection of tax.

Paragraph 7 deals with the taxpayer's obligations in respect of complying with an information notice. The information or document must be provided within the time period specified and by the means and form set out in the notice. Paragraph 8 allows copies of documents to be supplied, although HMRC may subsequently request the originals.

3.2.2 Other Powers

Paragraphs 10–14 set out HMRC's powers to enter and inspect business premises, and business assets and documents contained therein. These powers do not give HMRC the right to force entry or to search premises. Inspection visits should be arranged with the taxpayer at least seven days in advance, although unannounced visits can be made in certain circumstances.

Paragraph 15 gives HMRC the right to copy documents. Under paragraph 16, an officer may remove a document and retain it for a reasonable period of time.

3.2.3 Restrictions on HMRC Powers

Tax advisors should ensure that they are familiar with Part 4 (paragraphs 18–28) of Schedule 36, which sets out restrictions on HMRC's powers.

Paragraph 18 states that an information notice only requires a person to produce a document if it is in the person's possession or power. For example, if a taxpayer has implemented a tax planning scheme sold to him by an accountancy firm, but the accountancy firm has not released the detailed technical analysis behind the scheme, the taxpayer cannot be required to produce such documentation.

Paragraph 18 excludes three types of document from being required under an information notice:

1. information related to the conduct of a pending tax appeal;
2. journalistic material; and
3. personal records.

Pending Tax Appeal

A document that relates to the conduct of a pending appeal is a document that has been brought into existence as part of the preparation for the presentation of a tax appeal. It does not cover information or documents that may be used in presenting the appeal, but which existed before the appeal process began.

HMRC's Compliance Handbook illustrates this by an example of an appeal on the qualifying cost of an asset for capital allowances. HMRC cannot require production of documents drawn up to analyse the legal arguments about what sort of costs can be claimed. However, it can require production of invoices as evidence of the asset's cost.

Journalistic Material

"Journalistic material" is defined in section 12 of the Police and Criminal Evidence Act 1984 as material acquired or created for the purposes of journalism.

Material is journalistic material only if it is in the possession of a person who acquired or created it for the purposes of journalism, or is unsolicited material sent to a person with the intention of it being used for journalism.

For example, if a journalist has obtained copies of bank statements for a politician's offshore bank account and intends to use the information to expose the politician as a tax evader for not declaring the offshore interest income in his tax returns, HMRC cannot require the journalist to submit copies of the bank statements.

Personal Records

The term "personal records" is defined in section 12 of the Police and Criminal Evidence Act 1984 and means records concerning any individual's physical, mental, spiritual or personal welfare.

HMRC can require a person to produce records which contain personal and other information, by omitting the personal element of the records. For example, a doctor operating a private clinic may keep information on a patient's medical condition and the amounts paid by the patient to the doctor in the same document. HMRC cannot require the doctor to disclose details of a patient's medical condition. However, it could require the doctor to produce the document containing the financial and medical details, with the medical details blacked out, for the purposes of checking the doctor's tax return.

Other Restrictions

Under paragraph 20, where the whole of a document is more than six years old, the document does not have to be produced, unless this provision is disapplied with the agreement of an authorised officer. Such agreement may be given where HMRC is investigating a deliberate understatement of a tax liability and can look into the last 20 years of the taxpayer's affairs.

Paragraph 21 provides that a notice may not be issued to check the tax position for a period for which income tax, CGT or corporation tax has already been made, with the following exceptions:

1. where a self-assessment notice of enquiry has been issued under the relevant legislation and is still in progress in respect of that return;
2. where HMRC has reason to suspect that there has been a loss of tax; or
3. where it relates to taxes other than income tax, corporation tax or CGT, such as VAT or PAYE.

Paragraph 22 states that an information notice given for the purpose of checking the tax position of a person who has died may not be given more than four years after the person's death. (Previously, the limit was six years.)

Privileged Information

Paragraph 23 gives protection to privileged information. Information or a document is privileged if a claim to legal professional privilege could be maintained in respect of it in legal proceedings.

Legal and professional privilege applies to communications between a taxpayer and legal advisors, but not auditors or tax advisors. Limited protection for auditors and tax advisors is contained in paragraphs 24–26.

Paragraph 24 states that an information notice does not require an auditor to:

1. provide information held in connection with the performance of the person's functions; or
2. produce documents which are the auditor's property, and which were created by the auditor or on the auditor's behalf in connection with the performance of those functions.

Paragraph 25 states that an information notice does not require a tax advisor to provide information about relevant communications or to produce documents belonging to the taxpayer and consisting of relevant communications.

Relevant communications are communications between a tax advisor and a client, or another tax advisor of a client, whose purpose is the giving or obtaining of advice about the client's tax affairs. Note that this protection applies only to relevant communications in the hands of the tax advisor. An information notice can require such communications where they are held by the taxpayer.

Both paragraph 24 and paragraph 25 are subject to the restrictions set out in paragraph 26. Under paragraph 26, auditors or tax advisors can be required to provide explanatory material provided to a client in relation to any information or document which they assisted in preparing for, or delivering to, HMRC.

Paragraph 27 provides that, where parts of a document contain privileged information, the taxpayer can be required to produce the parts not containing such information. Paragraph 28 confirms that HMRC may only inspect documents that could be required by an information notice.

Paragraphs 29–33 set out the rights of appeal against information notices and the procedures for appeals. Paragraphs 34–38 deal with rules relating to special cases.

Under paragraph 39, failing to comply with an information notice, or obstructing an HMRC officer carrying out an inspection, leads to a penalty of £300. Where this continues after the penalty is imposed, paragraph 40 imposes a daily penalty of £60 until the default is remedied.

These penalties will not apply where HMRC is satisfied that there is a reasonable excuse, as detailed in paragraph 45.

Where the failure or obstruction continues after the fixed penalties are imposed, paragraph 50 permits HMRC to apply to the Upper Tribunal for the imposition of an additional tax-geared penalty.

3.3 Appeals and Penalties

3.3.1 Appeals

Prior to 1 April 2009, the first level of appeals for direct tax matters was the General Commissioners or the Special Commissioners, and for VAT it was the VAT Tribunal. On 1 April 2009, the Tribunals Courts and Enforcement Act 2007 came into force. This Act established a Tax Chamber, which deals with appeals for all taxes, including income tax, corporation tax, CGT, IHT, VAT and stamp duty. The Tax Chamber is split into the First-tier Tribunal and the Upper Tribunal.

Generally, an appeal made by HMRC or a taxpayer will initially be heard by the First-tier Tribunal. Such cases may then be appealed by either party to the Upper Tribunal. In certain circumstances, the initial appeal may be heard by the Upper Tribunal.

Tax cases are no longer referred to the High Court and any cases appealed on a point of law from the Upper Tribunal will be heard by the Court of Appeal. Judgments of the Court of Appeal can be appealed to the House of Lords, which will make a final decision on the application of the law.

3.3.2 Penalties

The current penalty regime also came into force on 1 April 2008. The legislation is contained in Schedule 24 of Finance Act 2007. Schedule 24 applies to income tax, CGT, corporation tax and VAT. The regime was extended to other taxes and duties, including stamp duties and inheritance tax, by Schedule 40 Finance Act 2008. This came into force on 1 April 2009.

Taxpayer's Behaviour

The penalty regime focuses on the behaviour of the taxpayer. Where a taxpayer has made a mistake in a return submitted to HMRC, but has taken reasonable care in the preparation of that return, no penalty will be applied by HMRC.

In its Compliance Handbook, HMRC states that appointing a tax advisor does not automatically mean that the taxpayer has taken reasonable care in the preparation of a return. The tax advisor should be competent and qualified, but the taxpayer still bears responsibility for the return and is expected to, within their ability and competence, make sure that the return being signed is correct.

Example 3.1

Davy is a self-employed car mechanic. He has never previously been required to file a self-assessment tax return. He complains to Jack, one of his customers, that he does not know the first thing about tax. Jack, a retired plumber, tells him not to appoint an accountant as they cost too much. He offers to complete Davy's tax return in exchange for repairs to his car, as he has been preparing his own return for years. Jack prepares the return and Davy signs the return without even reading it.

Clearly, Davy has not taken reasonable care and will be liable for a penalty if there are any mistakes in his return.

Under paragraph 3 of Schedule 24, the categories of behaviour where penalties will be imposed are as follows:

1. careless (failure to take reasonable care);
2. deliberate but not concealed (the inaccuracy is deliberate, but there are no arrangements to conceal it); and
3. deliberate and concealed (the inaccuracy is deliberate and there are arrangements to conceal it).

Once HMRC has categorised the behaviour of the taxpayer, the potential lost revenue (PLR) will be computed. The penalty imposed is based on a percentage of PLR. Paragraph 5 states that the PLR is the additional amount of tax due or payable as a result of correcting the inaccuracy.

Paragraph 4 sets out the maximum percentage penalty that will apply to each type of behaviour.

However, paragraph 10 sets out reductions which may be applied where the taxpayer has disclosed the inaccuracy. Disclosure is split into two types – unprompted and prompted – with greater reductions being given where the taxpayer makes a disclosure that has not been prompted by HMRC.

HMRC states in its Compliance Handbook that a disclosure is unprompted if it is made at a time when the person making it has no reason to believe that HMRC has discovered, or is about to discover, the inaccuracy.

The ranges of percentage penalties which will be applied by HMRC to the PLR, based on the behaviour of the taxpayer and the extent of the disclosure, are summarised in the table below.

Behaviour	Careless	Deliberate but not Concealed	Deliberate and Concealed
Minimum penalty with unprompted disclosure	0%	20%	30%
Minimum penalty with prompted disclosure	15%	35%	50%
Maximum penalty	30%	70%	100%

Example 3.2

HMRC discovers an arithmetical error in Davy's tax return for 2015/16. The PLR is calculated to be £500. Davy had not checked the tax return prepared by Jack and so was not aware of the error. He has been careless in the preparation of his tax return and was not able to disclose the error to HMRC before HMRC discovered it. Because the error was arithmetical, it was within his competence and ability to find it. HMRC may impose a penalty of 30% of £500, i.e. £150.

Penalties may also be imposed where the taxpayer has failed to inform HMRC of an under-assessment of tax.

HMRC may suspend penalties for a certain period where it is satisfied that the taxpayer is taking steps to address the non-compliance.

Example 3.3

For each of the scenarios below, state whether the taxpayer has:

- taken reasonable care;
- failed to take reasonable care;
- taken deliberate but unconcealed steps; or
- taken deliberate and concealed steps.

1. Nadine is the personal representative of her deceased father's estate. Her father owned a house in Belfast, but Nadine makes no attempt to establish its market value at the date of her father's death. When completing the IHT account, Nadine uses an estimated value based on the amount her father paid for the house 15 years earlier, even though she knows that it is worth much more.

2. Marian runs a newsagents. She replaces her old van with a new estate car. She uses the estate car partly for business purposes (e.g. trips to the cash and carry) and partly for personal purposes. When completing her VAT return for the quarter, Marian is unsure what input tax can be reclaimed on the purchase of the car. She is in a hurry to complete the return and decides to reclaim all the input tax, without contacting her accountant or HMRC for advice.

3. Hazel contacted HMRC by telephone for advice when completing her self-assessment tax return. She gave them full details, but was given inaccurate advice.

4. Chloe is the personal representative of her deceased husband's estate. Her husband had a number of bank accounts, but Chloe cannot locate any recent bank statements. When she is completing the IHT account, Chloe estimates the bank balances at the date of her husband's death, rather than contacting the bank to find out the balances.

5. Andrea is the personal representative of her deceased mother's estate. Five years before her death, Andrea's mother gave her a valuable painting. Andrea knows that, as her mother died within seven years of making the gift, she should include the gift of the painting in the IHT account. Andrea does not include the gift, thereby reducing the IHT payable. During a HMRC enquiry, Andrea produces a Deed of Gift, which she has altered to suggest that the gift of the painting was made more than seven years before her mother died.

Solution

1. Nadine has taken deliberate steps, as she has used a value for the house that she knows to be incorrect. However, she has not taken any steps to conceal her actions. Therefore, a penalty of between 20% and 70% of the PLR could be imposed.

continued overleaf

2. Marian has failed to take reasonable care in completing her VAT return for the quarter and could be liable for a penalty of up to 30%.

3. Hazel has taken reasonable care by contacting HMRC for advice and fully disclosing the facts to an officer. She would not be liable for a penalty due to any errors in her tax return resulting from the inaccurate advice.

4. Chloe has failed to take reasonable care, because she estimated the balances, and would be liable for a penalty of up to 30%.

5. Andrea has taken deliberate steps and then attempted to conceal her actions. She would be liable to a penalty of between 30% and 100% of the PLR.

3.4   Tax Agents: Dishonest Conduct

Finance Act 2012 introduced measures that allow HMRC to obtain working papers from tax agents who engage in dishonest conduct, to impose penalties on them and to even publish their details.

Under the legislation, HMRC can issue a tax agent with a "conduct notice" if it has been determined that the agent has engaged in dishonest conduct. The agent can appeal the notice.

HMRC can apply to the First-tier Tribunal for approval to issue a "file access notice" requiring tax agents found to have engaged in dishonest conduct to produce their working papers. Where the agent no longer has the working papers, HMRC can request them from a third party.

A tax agent, for these purposes, is an individual who, in the course of business, assists other persons with their tax affairs (i.e. clients). These terms are widely defined in the legislation but, as the assistance should be provided in the course of business, will not include those who provide general tax assistance to friends or family.

An individual has engaged in dishonest conduct if, in the course of acting as a tax agent, he does something dishonest with a view to bringing about a loss of tax revenue. A loss of revenue does not have to actually occur for the legislation to be triggered.

There is a civil penalty for dishonest conduct of between £5,000 and £50,000. In cases where a full disclosure is not made, HMRC can publish details of the tax agent if the agent is charged a penalty for dishonest conduct of more than £5,000.

The legislation has effect on dishonest conduct occurring on or after 6 April 2013.

3.5   Significant Recent Developments in Taxation

3.5.1   Senior Accounting Officers

Finance Act 2009 introduced requirements for Senior Accounting Officers (SAOs) of large companies. The main duty of an SAO, as set out in Schedule 46 Finance Act 2009, is to "take reasonable steps to ensure that the company establishes and maintains appropriate tax accounting arrangements". As part of this duty, SAOs must monitor the company's tax accounting arrangements and identify where they fall short of any requirements.

According to HMRC guidance, the steps an SAO must take to ensure the company meets its tax accounting requirements include:

- establishing and monitoring processes;
- ensuring staff and businesses to whom work is outsourced are appropriately trained and qualified to undertake their functions; and
- instituting improvements where shortcomings have been found in the tax accounting arrangements.

The SAO must perform the main duty throughout the period of his responsibility, not just at the year end.

A qualifying company under this legislation is a UK incorporated company which, either standing alone or when its results are combined with other UK group companies, has relevant turnover in the previous financial year of more than £200 million and/or a balance sheet (gross assets) total of more than £2 billion.

The SAO must provide a certificate to HMRC after the end of a financial year of a qualifying company, stating that either:

- the company had appropriate tax accounting arrangements throughout the financial year; or
- the company did not have appropriate tax accounting arrangements throughout the financial year and give details about the respects in which the arrangements were not appropriate.

The SAO must provide a certificate for each financial year in which the company is a qualifying company. They can include more than one company for which they are SAO on a certificate. The certificate must be provided to HMRC before the filing date for the accounts with Companies House.

If the SAO does not comply with this duty, there is a penalty of £5,000. Likewise, if a certificate is not provided, or if it contains a careless or deliberate inaccuracy, the penalty is £5,000.

Each company gets to nominate a suitable "officer" or "director" as the SAO.

3.5.2 iXBRL

All company tax returns must be filed online with accompanying financial statements and computations in Inline eXtensible Business Reporting Language (iXBRL) format.

iXBRL is an electronic format for business information, which is expected by HMRC to provide benefits in the preparation, analysis and communication of business and financial data. With iXBRL format there is an XML document which has standard barcodes within it. The barcodes or "tags" effectively convert everybody's financial statements and computations into a standard machine-readable template.

3.5.3 Capital Allowances

These have been covered in detail elsewhere in your studies, but you should ensure that your information is up-to-date, particularly with regard to the changing rates of annual investment allowances, writing down allowances and first year allowances. Special attention should also be given to the business premises renovation allowances (BPRA), although it should be noted that it was announced in Budget 2016 that these allowances will end, as originally legislated, at 5 April 2017 for income tax purposes and 31 March 2017 for corporation tax purposes.

3.5.4 R&D Expenditure and Intangible Fixed Assets

R&D expenditure and intangible fixed assets (IFAs) were covered in the CA Proficiency 2 syllabus. The tax treatment of intangible fixed assets has not undergone any significant changes since 2002, but it is worth ensuring that you have up-to-date information on the tax relief available on research and development (R&D) expenditure, as this relief was amended as a result of Finance Act 2013 (FA 2013) with further minor amendments introduced by Finance Act 2015.

The main change introduced to this area by FA 2013 was new legislation that permitted large companies (broadly defined as being part of a group with either more than 500 employees or turnover greater than €100 million and gross assets greater than €86 million) to claim an "above the line" (ATL) credit in respect of qualifying R&D expenditure.

The ATL treatment was phased in between 2013 and 2016, replacing the old 'super-deduction' treatment, whereby large companies received an additional 30% deduction in computing taxable profits in respect of qualifying R&D expenditure. From 1 April 2016 onwards, large companies must apply the ATL method and the super-deduction method is no longer available.

Qualifying expenditure for ATL credit is quantified in the same way as qualifying expenditure for existing R&D claims. It includes expenditure on directly attributable staffing costs, software and consumable items, as well as qualifying expenditure on externally provided workers.

The ATL credit is then quantified as 11% of the qualifying R&D expenditure and is netted off against this expenditure in the company's profit and loss account. The ATL credit is then allowed as a deduction from the company's corporation tax liability. This is illustrated in **Example 3.4**.

Example 3.4

Backstreets Limited has incurred expenditure of £1 million that qualifies for the ATL credit. Backstreet Ltd is a large company for R&D purposes. Its profit and loss extract for the year ended 31 March 2017 is as follows:

	£000
Turnover	10,000
R&D expenditure	1,000
Other expenditure	7,000
Profit	2,000
Tax	420
Profit after tax	1,580

Relief is given for qualifying expenditure as follows:

	ATL credit
	£000
Turnover	10,000
R&D expenditure	(1,000)
ATL credit	110
Other operating expenses	(7,000)
Taxable profit	2,110
Tax @ 20%	422
Less: ATL credit	(110)
Tax payable	312

Loss-making Companies

In the case of a loss-making company that has made a claim for the ATL credit, the company is still entitled to payment of the credit, albeit that corporation tax is effectively withheld from the payment. This differs substantially from the existing super deduction system, in which large loss-making companies can only increase their carried forward loss by making an R&D relief claim.

The amount of the payable credit is limited to the amount of the company's PAYE/NIC liability of the period. It is then offset against any other corporation tax liabilities of the company relating to other accounting periods. Any remaining payable credit can be surrendered to other group companies, if the company so chooses. Next, any remaining credit is used to settle any other HMRC liabilities that the company may have. Finally, any further remaining credit is paid to the company, provided that the company is a going concern at the time that payment is due to be made.

As mentioned above, corporation tax is effectively withheld from the payable credit for loss-making companies. This is illustrated in **Example 3.5**.

Example 3.5

Instead of having other operating expenses of £7 million, Backstreets Limited now has operating expenses of £10 million, and a pre-tax loss of £890,000 instead of a pre-tax profit of £2,110,000. Assuming that it has no outstanding tax liabilities with HMRC, no other group companies and a PAYE/NIC liability for the period of greater than £110,000, it will be entitled to the following payable ATL credit for the year ended 31 March 2017:

	£000
ATL credit as before	110
Corporation tax withheld @ 20%	22
ATL credit payable now	88

The withheld element (£22,000) will then be available for offset against future corporation tax liabilities of the company.

Time Limits

The time limit for making an ATL claim is two years from the end of the company's accounting period, which is the same time limit that applies for most claims and elections applicable to companies. However, given that a company's statutory accounts need to be filed with Companies House within nine months of the end of its period of account, it will be beneficial for a company to have quantified, and effectively finalised, its claim within the same time period.

3.5.5 Patent Box

The "patent box" was introduced by Finance Act 2012 and allows companies to elect to apply a 10% rate of corporation tax from 1 April 2013 to all profits attributable to qualifying patents.

The regime also applies to other qualifying intellectual property rights, such as regulatory data protection (also called "data exclusivity"), supplementary protection certificates (SPCs) and plant variety rights.

Other non-qualifying profits in these companies continue to be taxed at the main rate. The Patent Box will potentially benefit a wide range of companies that receive patent royalties, sell patented products, or use patented processes as part of their business.

The full benefit of the regime was phased in from 1 April 2013. Companies apply an appropriate percentage to the profits they earn from their qualifying patents. The appropriate percentages for each financial year are:

- 1 April 2013 to 31 March 2014: 60%.
- 1 April 2014 to 31 March 2015: 70%.
- 1 April 2015 to 31 March 2016: 80%.
- 1 April 2016 to 31 March 2017: 90%.
- from 1 April 2017: 100%.

In order to benefit from the patent box, a company must either own a patent or hold an exclusive license to exploit the patent. The patent must be granted by the UK Intellectual Patent Office (IPO), the European Patent Office, or the relevant body in various other countries in the EU.

It is also necessary for the claimant company, or another group company, to have undertaken qualifying development for the patent by making a significant contribution to either the creation or development of the patented invention, or to a product incorporating the patented invention.

Profits that qualify for patent box relief (referred to as "relevant IP profits") include profits that derive from the following type of income:

- selling patented products (or products incorporating the patented invention);
- licensing out patent rights; or
- selling patented rights.

In order to calculate the profits that benefit from the patent box, i.e. the relevant IP income, there are three stages to follow:

1. Identify the profits attributable to income arising from exploiting patented inventions.
2. Remove a routine profit, which recognises that the business would be expected to make a profit even if it didn't have access to patent IP. The routine profit is equivalent to 10% of certain costs.
3. Remove the profit associated with other intangible assets (e.g. brands) so that income from other forms of IP is not rewarded.

It is important to note that the patent box is intended to be a generous relief. For example, if a company manufactures and sells a car that includes a patented windscreen wiper, then the whole proceeds of the car will potentially qualify for the effective 10% rate.

Finance Act 2016 introduced new rules in respect of patent box. These new rules broadly seek to restrict the potential patent box relief in circumstances where the underlying R&D/development is carried on by a related person rather than the claimant company. The new rules work by applying a 'Nexus fraction' to qualifying patent box expenditure. As part of the new rules, claimant companies will also be required to 'track and trace' their turnover, expenditure and R&D to enable the calculation of the Nexus formula. 'Grandfathering' provisions will apply until 30 June 2021, which will enable companies to continue to apply the old rules in certain circumstances (although track and trace will become mandatory even if claimant companies are relying on the grandfathering provisions).

3.5.6 Cap on Unlimited Tax Reliefs

Legislation limiting the income tax reliefs that can be claimed by high earners was introduced by Finance Act 2013. This measure introduced a cap on certain currently unlimited income tax reliefs that may be deducted from income under section 24 of the Income Tax Act 2007 (ITA 2007). The cap is set at £50,000, or 25% of income, whichever is greater. The primary reliefs affected will be trade and property loss reliefs, which can be relieved against general income and qualifying loan interest relief. A small number of other reliefs will also be affected. The limit will not apply to charitable reliefs.

3.5.7 Introduction of the General Anti-abuse Rule

In Finance Act 2013, HMRC introduced the General Anti-abuse Rule (GAAR). The GAAR has been introduced as part of the UK Government's stated commitment to tackling tax avoidance.

The GAAR came into effect in respect of any tax arrangements entered into on or after 17 July 2013. The GAAR is wide-reaching and covers the following taxes (among others):

- income tax;
- corporation tax;
- capital gains tax;
- inheritance tax; and
- stamp duty land tax.

A tax arrangement is defined as any arrangement that, considering all the circumstances, can reasonably be viewed as having the intention of obtaining a tax advantage as its main purpose, or one of its main purposes.

A tax advantage includes: relief from tax; repayment of tax; avoidance or reduction in a charge to tax; avoidance of an assessment (or possible assessment) to tax; deferral of a tax payment or acceleration of a tax repayment; and avoidance of an obligation to deduct or account for tax.

A tax arrangement is considered to be abusive if it constitutes an arrangement that cannot reasonably be regarded as a reasonable course of action in relation to the relevant tax legislation, having regard to all the circumstances (including the existence of any contrived or abnormal steps, and the intention to exploit shortcomings in the tax legislation).

The legislation includes examples of situations that are likely to constitute "abuse" (in circumstances where such an outcome is not the anticipated result of the legislation in question):

1. arrangements that result in an amount of income/gain/profits for tax purposes that is significantly less than the amount for economic purposes;
2. arrangements that result in deductions or losses of an amount for tax purposes that is significantly greater than the amount for economic purposes; and
3. arrangements that result in a claim for a tax repayment/credit that has not been paid, and is unlikely to be paid.

Counteracting the Tax Advantages
In situations where tax arrangements are found to be abusive, the GAAR operates by counteracting the tax advantages that would otherwise arise, with the making of just and reasonable adjustments. HMRC must notify the taxpayer, in writing, as to why it considers that a tax advantage has arisen from tax arrangements that are abusive and the nature of the counteraction.

HMRC must also explain that the taxpayer has 45 days from the date of issue of the notice in which to respond with written representations.

If the taxpayer makes representations within 45 days, the case must be referred to the GAAR Advisory Panel. The GAAR Advisory Panel will then consider all the facts and make a final decision as to whether abusive tax arrangements are in place, and whether counteraction is required in respect of them. The GAAR Advisory Panel is an independent advisory panel of persons, created specifically to approve HMRC GAAR guidance and to provide opinions on cases where HMRC considers the GAAR may apply.

Finance Act 2016 contains a provision to apply a penalty of 60% in all cases where a counteraction notice has been served by HMRC and is not appealed or is unsuccessfully appealed. This 60% penalty will be in addition to penalties imposed under Schedule 24 Finance Act 2007, although the total penalty will be limited to 100% (other than in cases involving offshore arrangements).

3.5.8 Diverted Profits Tax

The diverted profit tax (DPT) rules were introduced by Finance Act 2015 and came into force on 1 April 2015 in respect of accounting periods ended on or after that date. The purpose of the DPT rules is to deter and counteract contrived arrangements used by large multinational groups that divert profits from the UK, resulting in the erosion of the UK tax base.

There are three possible cases in which a company is regarded as having taxable diverted profits, and hence potentially be within the charge to DPT:

1. Where a UK resident company ('C') enters into a transaction with another "person" ('P') that has "insufficient economic substance" resulting in an "effective tax mismatch", and both C and P are not small or medium-sized enterprises. This corresponds to section 80 FA 2015.
2. Where a UK permanent establishment of a non-UK resident company ('C') enters into a transaction with another "person" ('P') that has insufficient economic substance and which results in an effective tax mismatch, and both C and P are not small or medium-sized enterprises. This corresponds to section 81 FA 2015.
3. Where a non-UK resident trading company ('F') makes a supply of services, goods or other property to a "person" ('A') carrying on activity in the UK; and

   (a) it is reasonable to assume that the activity is designed to ensure that F does not have a PE in the UK;
   (b) the "mismatch" condition and/or the "tax avoidance" condition is met; and
   (c) F and A are not small or medium-sized enterprises.

   This corresponds to section 86 FA 2015.

Section 86 does not apply to the foreign company for an accounting period if one or both of the following conditions are met:

1. For the accounting period, the total of:

    (a) the UK-related sales revenues of the foreign company, and
    (b) the UK-related sales revenues of companies connected with the foreign company, does not exceed £10,000,000; and/or

2. the total of:

    (a) the UK-related expenses of the foreign company incurred in the accounting period; and
    (b) the UK-related expenses of companies connected with the foreign company incurred in that period, does not exceed £1,000,000.

Each of these sections is looked at in more detail below.

Sections 80 and 81

There are a number of conditions that must be met for section 80 to apply:

1. The UK resident company (C) is UK resident in the period.
2. Provision has been made, or imposed, between C and a "person" (P) (whether or not P is UK resident) by means of a transaction or series of transactions ("the material provision").
3. The participation condition is met in relation to C and P. This condition is met if either C or P indirectly participates in the management, control or capital of the other, or if the same person or persons indirectly participates in the management, control or capital of each of C and P.
4. The "material provision" results in an effective tax mismatch between C and P. There is an effective tax mismatch if, broadly, the additional tax payable by P in respect of the material provision (i.e. the payment of the insurance premium) is less than 80% of the tax reduction in C as a result of the material provision.
5. The effective tax mismatch outcome is not an excepted loan relationship.
6. The "insufficient economic substance" condition is met (see below).
7. C and P are not small or medium-sized enterprises for the period. The definition of small and medium-sized enterprises for this purpose is largely based on the definition contained in the Annex to Commission Recommendation 2003/361/EC, issued by the European Commission in May 2003. Broadly, an enterprise is medium-sized under this definition if it has less than 250 employees and either annualised turnover of less than €50 million or gross balance sheet assets of less than €43 million. Where an enterprise forms part of a group, these criteria are applied at group level.

"Insufficient Economic Substance"

The insufficient economic substance condition is met if there is an effective tax mismatch and it is reasonable to assume that the transaction was designed to secure the tax reduction, unless at the time that the material provision was made, it was reasonable to assume that the non-tax benefits referable to the transaction would exceed the financial benefit of the tax reduction.

In this definition, the legislation also clarifies that it may still be reasonable to assume that a transaction (or transactions) was designed to secure a tax reduction, despite it also being designed to secure any commercial or other objective.

The onus is therefore on C to clearly demonstrate that the commercial (non-tax) financial benefits achieved by the material provision exceed the financial tax benefits from a UK tax perspective.

Section 81 operates in the same way as section 80. In a situation where a non-UK resident company (I) carries on a trade in the UK through a permanent establishment, a DPT charge will apply to the UK PE if it meets the conditions above, replacing references to a UK resident company with references to a UK PE of a non-resident company.

Section 86

For the purposes of section 86, the mismatch condition is met where:

1. in connection with the supplies made by a non-UK resident trading company (F) in the course of its trade, there is a transaction between F and A (a "person" carrying on activity in the UK) that has insufficient economic substance (see above) and the transaction results in an effective tax mismatch (as above); and
2. at the time of the transaction, F participates in the management, control or capital of A, or vice versa, or a third person participates in the management, control or capital of both F and A.

The tax avoidance condition is met where, in connection with the supply of services, goods or other property made by F in the course of its trade, there are arrangements in place the main purpose of which is to reduce or avoid a charge to UK corporation tax.

Calculation of Diverted Profits

Sections 80 and 81

Assuming that no transfer pricing adjustments are required, the DPT charge is determined by identifying what transaction the company would have reasonably entered into (if any) with a connected company had tax not been a relevant consideration. This is referred to as the "relevant alternative provision". The DPT charge is calculated by reference to the re-characterised arrangements, i.e. by comparing the taxable profits under the actual arrangements to the hypothetical taxable profits if the relevant alternative provision was used instead of the actual arrangements.

Section 86

In section 86 cases, the diverted profits will be based in applying transfer pricing principles. In other words, in the absence of the arrangements in place to prevent a UK PE from existing (i.e. if a UK PE did actually exist), what profits would be attributable to the UK PE under transfer pricing principles?

DPT Charge

Once the diverted profits have been calculated, the DPT charge will be equivalent to 25% of the diverted profits. In addition, an amount of 'true up interest' is calculated based on applying a 3% rate to the amount of the DPT charge for the period of time between six months after the end of the company's accounting period and the date HMRC issue a "charging notice". 'True up interest' offsets or removes the advantage that could be obtained where the DPT charge is delayed.

Notification Requirements

A company has a duty to notify HMRC if it is potentially within the charge to DPT. In considering whether a company is potentially within the charge to DPT, the subjective conditions (i.e. whether or not there is sufficient economic substance and whether or not arrangements are designed to avoid a UK PE) are replaced with objective conditions that focus on whether there is a tax advantage gained by the arrangements, and if this is "significant" relative to the non-tax benefits.

Therefore, unless a company can sufficiently state that any financial benefit of the arrangements is not significant, it will be required to notify HMRC.

Further to this, a company is not required to notify HMRC its potential DPT liability if it falls within one of the specifically exempt situations listed in the rules. One of these exemptions is that "it is reasonable to assume that, although a company is potentially within the scope of DPT, no charge to DPT would arise for the current period." Therefore, if a company is confident that the non-tax benefits of the arrangements outweigh the tax advantage, it might conclude that the risk of a DPT charge is sufficiently low to not require notification to HMRC.

The deadline for notifying HMRC of potentially being within the scope of DPT is three months from the end of the accounting period to which the potential charge applies. This deadline is extended to six months from the end of the accounting period for the first period in which DPT potentially applies. There can be tax-geared penalties in the event that notification is not made on time, and the deadline by which HMRC can impose a DPT charge is also extended from two years to four years in these circumstances.

Questions

Review Questions

(See Suggested Solutions to Review Questions at the end of this textbook.)

Question 3.1

State whether HMRC is entitled to request the following, with reference to the powers set out in Schedule 36 Finance Act 2008:

(a) Copies of all VAT invoices with VAT amounts greater than £1,000 in respect of the input VAT figure on the VAT return for the quarter ended 31 October 2016.

(b) Copies of all invoices for amounts included in repairs and maintenance in the profit and loss account for the year ended 31 March 2016. The corporation tax return was submitted on 30 September 2016 and no enquiry has been opened by HMRC under paragraph 24 of Schedule 18 Finance Act 1998.

(c) Working papers created by a company's auditors, and held on the audit file, to substantiate the amount of a bad debt provision in the company's accounts for the year ended 31 May 2016. The corporation tax return was submitted on 28 November 2016, and HMRC has opened an aspect enquiry under paragraph 24 of Schedule 18 Finance Act 1998.

(d) Copies of all invoices for amounts greater than £2,000 included in fixed asset additions in the accounts of a partnership for the year ending 31 August 2017.

(e) Copies of a letter from Add-up & Co. (tax advisors) to Valerie, advising her on the CGT treatment of a transaction occurring in the tax year 2016/17, where:

    (i) the letter is held on the files of Add-up & Co.; and

    (ii) the letter is held by Valerie.

Question 3.2

With reference to HMRC's *Compliance Handbook*, state whether HMRC is likely to consider the following as prompted or unprompted disclosure:

(a) In preparing a company's VAT return for the quarter ended 31 December 2016, Sean, the company accountant, notices that the amount of output tax in the return for the quarter ended 30 September 2016 was understated and computes that additional VAT of £15,000 should have been paid by the company to HMRC.

    (i) Sean makes full disclosure to HMRC the day after he finds and quantifies the error.

    (ii) Sean does not notify HMRC until 23 February 2017. He received notice of a compliance visit by a HMRC VAT Inspector on 19 February 2017.

(b) In preparing for the visit by the VAT Inspector, Sean realises that client entertaining expenses incurred during the year ended 30 June 2016 were incorrectly coded to postage and stationery expenses in the profit and loss account. He investigates and discovers that, while the expenses have been treated correctly for VAT, they have not been disallowed in the company's corporation tax return for the year, which was filed on 8 February 2017. He contacts the company's tax advisors to inform them of the error and the tax advisors prepare a letter fully disclosing the error to HMRC.

Challenging Questions

(Suggested Solutions to Challenging Questions are available through your lecturer.)

Question 3.1

Your firm has taken on a new client, Bart Ltd, a company operating a successful online retail business. The company is equally owned by Jim and Rosie Bart, who are also the directors. The company was incorporated on 1 October 2014 and prepared its first set of statutory accounts to 30 September 2015, showing a profit after tax of £200,000. Prior to 1 October 2013, the business operated as a partnership, with Mr and Mrs Bart as equal partners.

Bart Ltd's tax return was submitted on 30 September 2016 by the previous accountants and tax advisors, Arthur Daly & Co. An aspect enquiry into this tax return has been opened under Schedule 18 Finance Act 1998. One of the areas into which HMRC is enquiring is amounts withdrawn from the company by Jim and Rosie.

At a meeting with you, Jim explains what happened:

"From the time we incorporated the company, Rosie and I withdrew £3,000 each per month in cash from the company. We had done this when the business was a partnership and I continued to record the cash withdrawn as drawings in the books. We did not realise that we were not entitled to do this.

In mid-July 2016, when Arthur Daly was preparing our accounts for the year to September 2014, he noticed the cash withdrawals. He explained that this money belonged to the company and when we withdrew it, it was either salary, dividend or a loan. If it was salary, we should have been paying PAYE and NIC each month. Arthur said that if the money was a loan from the company to us, we would have to pay something called 455 tax, and that this would be 25% of the amount withdrawn. We were horrified as the company had a cash shortage at the time and there was no way that it could pay £18,000 in tax.

Arthur explained that this amount would not have been due if we had repaid the £72,000 to the company before 1 July 2016. It was already past that date and, anyway, we didn't have the cash. Arthur told us that we wouldn't have needed the cash as the loan could have been repaid by the company declaring a dividend of £72,000 to us.

Arthur suggested that we could create documents to show that a dividend had been declared before 1 July and he could reflect in the accounts that the loan was cleared by the dividend. He drafted board minutes and dividend vouchers to reflect that a dividend of £80,000 had been paid on 27 September 2015. We signed the documents on 31 July 2016, but dated them 27 September 2015. Arthur explained that we would have to pay income tax on the dividends and we were happy as long as the company did not have to pay that 455 tax. Now we have this letter from HMRC and we don't know what to do. We're worried about the consequences for us and the company, especially having to pay penalties to HMRC. Could you advise us what we should do?"

The last letter from HMRC requested the following information from Bart Ltd:

1. details of all cash sums withdrawn by the directors from the company in the year;
2. copies of board meetings, dividend vouchers, etc. supporting the declaration of the dividend on 27 September 2015; and
3. copies of any correspondence between the company and Arthur Daly & Co. on the company's tax position.

Requirement
Write Jim and Rosie a letter dealing with the issues outlined above.

Residence, Domicile and Situs of Assets: Liability to CGT, IHT and Stamp Duty

Learning Objectives

In this chapter you will learn to do the following:

▪ Apply the territoriality provisions in the capital taxes, particularly in relation to where assets are situated, and the administrative issues arising therefrom, including capital transactions with foreign resident/foreign domiciled individuals.

4.1 Concepts of Residence, Domicile and Situs of Assets in UK Tax Law

The scope of the charge to taxation on income and capital is dependent on the residence and domicile status of the recipient. The location of the source of the income or captial can also affect chargeability. The impact of residency status and the location (situs) of assets on chargeability to tax is referred to as the territorial provisions in the relevant legislation.

Therefore, as a first step to examining how business decisions trigger a potential charge to capital taxes from a business and individual perspective, it is important to understand the territorial provisions of the charge to tax, in order to advise clients on how best to comply with and minimise tax in the UK.

The detailed rules applying in this area can be found at **Chapters 13, 14** and **21** of *CA Proficiency 2: Taxation 2 (NI) 2016–2017*:

▪ situs of assets for capital gains tax (CGT) (**Section 13.10**);
▪ residence and domicile for UK CGT (**Section 13.5** and **Chapter 14**); and
▪ domicile and situs of assets for UK inheritance tax (IHT) (**Section 21.3**).

4.1.1 Situs of Assets

The situs of assets becomes important when the person in question is non-UK resident, non-UK domiciled or both. The majority of UK-based individuals are, and always have been, UK resident and domiciled. These taxpayers are subject to IHT and CGT on their worldwide assets.

The legislation on the situs of assets is contained in section 275 of the Taxation of Chargeable Gains Act 1992 (TCGA 1992). This legislation applies for both CGT and IHT purposes.

4.1.2   Residence and Domicile

Residence and domicile are key concepts when determining the extent of a person's liability to UK CGT and/or IHT. It is vital that you understand the difference between the concepts.

Residence and domicile are referred to in international tax law as "connecting factors", as they connect a taxpayer with a certain jurisdiction. It is important to recognise when advising on a transaction that may have CGT and IHT consequences that the connecting factors for the two taxes may be different.

You should bear in mind the principles outlined in **Chapter 2** regarding the interaction of UK domestic tax law with double tax treaties (DTTs). An individual or company may be resident in the UK under domestic law but be treated as non-resident due to the operation of a DTT. This can also apply to domicile where there is an IHT Treaty in place, such as the UK/Ireland Double Tax Convention on Estates, Inheritances and Gifts (see **Section 2.3**).

4.2   Recap of the Concepts of Residence and Domicile for Individuals

An individual's residence and domicile status will determine their liability to UK taxation.

4.2.1   Residence

The term "residence" was not defined in UK tax legislation prior to Finance Act 2013. Taxpayers had to rely on factors established in case law and guidance provided by HMRC.

An individual's residence status was determined by reference to a tax year. An individual was always resident in the UK if they were physically present in the UK for 183 days or more. There were no exceptions to this rule.

Previously, days of arrival in, or departure from, the UK were ignored in calculating the number of days present in the UK. This rule has now been amended and an individual will be counted as being present in the UK if they are in the UK at midnight on that day.

4.2.2   Statutory Residence Test

The statutory residence test (SRT) was introduced from 6 April 2013 with the intention of providing more certainty regarding the residence status of those individuals with complex circumstances. HMRC's Guidance Note RDR3 provides guidance on the changes introduced by the SRT (see www.gov.uk/government/collections/tax-on-foreign-income-rules-from-6-april-2013). Under the SRT, the basic rule is that an individual is resident in the UK for a tax year and at all times in that tax year (except under split-year treatment), if they do not meet any of the automatic overseas tests and they do meet either the automatic UK tests or the sufficient ties test. RDR3 includes the following flowchart to show how these rules should be applied:

The statutory residence test – an overview

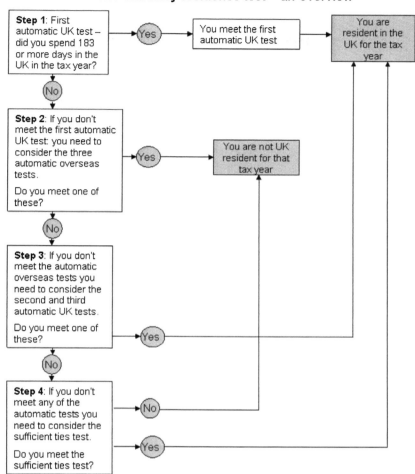

If an individual meets any of the automatic overseas tests for a tax year, they are automatically non-resident for that year. Consideration should therefore be given to these tests first when determining residence, because if an individual meets any one of them they will not need to consider any of the other parts of the test.

The first automatic overseas test is where an individual was resident in the UK for one or more of the three tax years preceding the tax year, and spent fewer than 16 days in the UK in the tax year. If an individual dies in the tax year then this test does not apply.

The second automatic overseas test is where an individual was resident in the UK for none of the three tax years preceding the tax year, and spent fewer than 46 days in the UK in the tax year.

The third automatic overseas test is where an individual works full time overseas over the tax year, without any significant breaks during the tax year from overseas work, and:

■ they spend fewer than 91 days in the UK in the tax year; and
■ the number of days in the tax year on which they worked for more than three hours in the UK is less than 31.

The third automatic overseas test does not apply to individuals who have a relevant job on board a vehicle, aircraft or ship at any time in the relevant tax year, and at least six of the trips they make in that year as part of that job are cross-border trips that:

- begin in the UK;
- end in the UK; or
- begin and end in the UK.

If an individual does not meet any of the automatic overseas tests, then consideration should be given to the automatic UK tests. If they meet any of the automatic UK tests, they are resident in the UK for the tax year. If they do not meet any of the automatic UK tests, they will need to consider the "sufficient ties" test.

The first automatic UK test is where an individual spends 183 days or more in the UK in the tax year. The second automatic UK test is relevant if they have or had a home in the UK during all or part of the tax year. An individual will meet this test if there is at least one period of 91 consecutive days, at least 30 days of which fall in the tax year, when:

- they have a home in the UK in which they spend a sufficient amount of time, and either they:
  - have no overseas home, or
  - have an overseas home or homes in each of which they spend no more than a permitted amount of time.

The third automatic UK test is where an individual works full time in the UK for any period of 365 days, with no significant break from UK work and:

- all or part of that 365-day period falls within the tax year;
- more than 75% of the total number of days in the 365-day period when they do more than three hours of work are days when they do more than three hours of work in the UK; and
- at least one day in the tax year is a day on which they do more than three hours of work in the UK.

The third automatic UK test does not apply if the individual has a relevant job at any time in the relevant tax year and at least six of the trips they make in that year as part of that job are cross-border trips that:

- begin in the UK;
- end in the UK; or
- begin and end in the UK.

If any one of the automatic UK tests applies to an individual for a particular tax year, and none of the automatic overseas tests apply, then they are UK resident for tax purposes for that tax year.

If an individual does not meet any of the **automatic overseas tests** or any of the **automatic UK tests**, they should use the "sufficient ties" test to determine their UK residence status for a tax year. They will need to consider their connections to the UK, called "ties", and determine whether their ties, taken together with the number of days they spend in the UK, are sufficient for them to be considered UK resident for tax purposes for a particular tax year.

If an individual was not UK resident for any of the three tax years before the tax year under consideration, they will need to consider if they have any of these UK ties:

- a family tie;
- an accommodation tie;
- a work tie; and
- a 90-day tie.

If they were resident in the UK for one or more of the three tax years before the tax year under consideration, they will also need to consider if they have a country tie.

Under the SRT, an individual is either UK resident or non-UK resident for a full tax year and at all times in that tax year. However, if during a year they either start to live or work abroad or come from abroad to live or work in the UK, the tax year will be split into two parts if their circumstances meet specific criteria:

- a UK part for which they are charged to UK tax as a UK resident;
- an overseas part for which, for most purposes, they are charged to UK tax as a non-UK resident.

An individual must be UK resident for a tax year under the SRT to meet the criteria for split-year treatment for that year. They will not meet the split-year criteria for a tax year for which they are non-UK resident under the SRT.

Split-year treatment in the context of the SRT applies only to individuals. It does not apply to individuals acting as personal representatives. It applies in a limited way to individuals acting as trustee of a settlement in determining the trustees' residence status:

- if the individual becomes or ceases to be a trustee of the settlement during the tax year;
- provided that the period they are a trustee falls within the overseas part of the tax year for that individual.

Split-year treatment will not affect whether an individual is regarded as UK resident for the purposes of any double taxation arrangement.

4.2.3   Treaty Non-residence

The introduction of the SRT makes it much easier to determine whether or not a taxpayer is UK tax resident under domestic law. As discussed in **Chapter 2**, where an individual is considered to be resident in two states under their domestic laws, the provisions of a DTT between the two states will apply to determine the individual's place of residence for the purposes of the DTT.

Where, for example, an individual is resident in both the UK and RoI under their domestic laws, but is treated as resident in the RoI by virtue of Article 4(2) of the UK/RoI DTT, that individual is said to be "treaty non-resident" in the UK.

4.2.4   Domicile

The term "domicile" is not defined in UK tax legislation. It is a general law concept, rather than a tax-specific concept.

The guidance on domicile now set out at section 5 of RDR1 is much more in-depth than the guidance previously given.

HMRC states that there are many things that affect domicile. Some of the main points to be considered are:

- an individual cannot be without a domicile;
- an individual can only have one domicile at a time;
- an individual is normally domiciled in the country where they have their permanent home;
- an existing domicile will continue until a new one is acquired; and
- domicile is distinct from nationality or residence, although both can have an impact on domicile.

There are three types of domicile relevant to income tax and CGT:

1. domicile of origin;
2. domicile of choice; and
3. domicile of dependence.

Domicile of Origin

A person normally acquires a domicile of origin at birth from their father or, if the parents are not married, from the mother.

A domicile of origin may change as a result of adoption and is not easy to displace, although this does occur. If an individual leaves the country of their domicile of origin, they will continue to be domiciled there until they acquire a domicile of choice elsewhere.

The fact that someone is born in the UK does not automatically mean that they are domiciled in the UK. For example, they might have been born in the UK to a non-UK domiciled father and then moved to another country.

Domicile of Choice

An individual has legal capacity to acquire a new domicile at the age of 16.

In order to acquire a domicile of choice, an individual must leave their current country of domicile and settle in another country.

HMRC's view is that a person will need to provide strong evidence that they intend to live in that other country permanently or indefinitely. They consider the following factors to be relevant, though not exhaustive:

- the person's intentions;
- the person's permanent residence;
- the person's business interests;
- the person's social and family interests;
- the person's ownership of property; and
- the form of any will that the person has made.

Domicile of Dependence

Until an individual has the legal capacity to change it, their domicile will follow that of the person on whom they are legally dependent. If the domicile of that person changes, they will automatically acquire the same domicile, in place of their domicile of origin.

Before 1974, married women automatically acquired their husband's domicile. A married woman who married before 1974 would retain her husband's domicile until she legally acquired a new domicile.

However, a woman who married on or after 1 January 1974 does not necessarily have the same domicile as her husband. Her domicile will be decided in the same way as any other individual who is able to have an independent domicile.

4.3   Charging Sections for Capital Gains Tax

The UK legislation on CGT for individuals, partnerships, companies and trusts is set out in TCGA 1992. **Chargeable gains realised by a UK resident company form part of the company's profits subject to corporation tax** and tax will be paid at the rate paid by the company (currently 20%).

The general rule for CGT is contained in section 2 TCGA 1992. This states that a person is chargeable to CGT in respect of gains accruing in a tax year during any part of which the residence condition is met.

Example 4.1

Red Ltd, a UK incorporated and resident company, sells a commercial property in London, realising a gain of £1.5 million. Pink BV, a company incorporated and resident in the Netherlands, sells the neighbouring commercial property and realises a gain of £1.8 million.

State whether the companies are chargeable to CGT on the disposal of the buildings.

Red Ltd is resident in the UK and therefore its gain of £1.5 million will be included in its profits chargeable to corporation tax.

Pink BV is not resident in the UK and therefore has no liability to UK tax on the disposal of its commercial property in London.

However, with effect from 6 April 2015, CGT has been extended to non-residents disposing of UK residential property (see **Section 4.6**).

4.3.1 Individuals

Under section 2(1A)(a), the residence condition is met in the case of an individual where they are resident in the UK for the year in question.

The SRT allows the tax year to be split between the times before and after arrival in, or departure from, the UK in limited circumstances. Under section 2(1B), where the year is a split year, the individual is not chargeable to CGT in respect of chargeable gains accruing to them in the overseas part of that year.

Section 10 TCGA 1992 is an exception to the general rule in section 2. It provides that a person who is non-resident in the UK but who is carrying on a trade in the UK through a UK branch or agency is chargeable to UK CGT on the disposal of:

1. assets situated in the UK and used in the trade at or before the time when the capital gain accrued; or
2. assets situated in the UK and used for the purposes of the branch or agency before the disposal, or assets acquired for use by or for the purposes of the branch or agency.

Section 12 TCGA 1992 deals with individuals who are not domiciled in the UK and who realise foreign chargeable gains, i.e. gains from the disposal of an asset situated outside the UK. Where such individuals are being taxed under the remittance basis in a tax year, CGT will be charged on the amount of the foreign chargeable gains remitted to the UK in that tax year. The rules on what constitutes a remittance are complex but, at a basic level, this would include bringing the cash realised on the disposal into the UK or using the cash to buy an asset that is then brought into the UK.

Example 4.2

Carlos is resident but not domiciled in the UK and for the 2016/17 tax year has elected to be taxed on the remittance basis in the UK. On 9 July 2016 he sells a villa in Portugal and realises a gain of €0.5 million. He uses the proceeds to buy a boat in Portugal. He sails to the UK and moors the boat permanently at the marina in Carrickfergus from 31 July 2016.

Carlos has remitted the full proceeds to the UK and will be subject to UK CGT on the gain of €0.5 million.

Since the changes to the rules on non-UK domiciled individuals came into force on 6 April 2008, tax planning for non-UK domiciled individuals who have been long-term resident in the UK and have substantial unremitted income and gains has included consideration of whether or not the individual should elect for the remittance basis of taxation, and pay the appropriate remittance basis charge (of up to £90,000), where applicable, in a given tax year.

Note that individuals are not subject to a deemed disposal rule when they become non-UK resident. Individuals are instead subject to the temporary non-residence rule, described below.

4.3.2 Individuals: Temporary Non-residence for CGT

Section 10A TCGA 1992 prevents **UK resident individuals** from avoiding UK CGT by becoming non-resident for a short period of time.

Where an individual leaves the UK and subsequently returns, they will be charged to CGT on gains arising on assets owned prior to departure and alienated during the period of non-residence where:

1. they satisfy the residence requirement in the year of return;
2. they were UK resident for four out of seven years of assessment prior to the year of departure; and
3. the period of non-UK residence was less than five complete tax years.

Therefore, where an individual who has always been resident in the UK wishes to leave the UK and become resident in another jurisdiction to avoid tax on a chargeable gain, he will need to remain outside the UK for five full tax years to avoid paying UK tax on a gain that arises when he is non-resident.

Example 4.3

Sinead is a UK domiciled and resident individual. She has collected art for many years and now has a very valuable collection. She is considering selling part of her collection, and could realise a gain of approximately £5 million.

Sinead was chatting to an acquaintance at an art gallery recently and he told her that she could avoid paying any UK tax on the gain by moving to the Isle of Man for a year.

Sinead is seeking your advice.

Solution

The tax advice given to Sinead by her acquaintance is incorrect. If she only left the UK for one year, any gains realised from the sale of her art collection during that year would be taxable in the UK. Also, where an individual leaves the UK for such a short period, it can be difficult to demonstrate that non-UK residence has actually been achieved.

If Sinead wishes to avoid paying UK tax, she will have to leave the UK for five full tax years. This will be a major change in lifestyle and Sinead will have to decide if she is willing to make this change in order to save a maximum of £1 million in tax.

Sinead could end up paying more tax if she becomes resident in a jurisdiction with a higher rate of CGT than the UK, as she may be subject to CGT in that jurisdiction.

The reducing differential in the rates of income tax (maximum 45%) and CGT (maximum 20%, other than in the case of certain residential properties for which the rate is 28%) has made it less attractive for individuals to leave the UK to avoid CGT, especially with regard to residential property. If the individual wishes to pay no tax on a proposed gain, it will be necessary to find a jurisdiction that does not subject the gains in question to tax.

Unless an individual is planning to leave the UK for other, non-tax reasons, the amount of the proposed gain would need to be substantial before it is likely to be worthwhile to interrupt the individual's family and personal life by becoming non-resident for at least five years.

Where an individual is willing to become non-UK resident to avoid UK CGT, the advice would be to clearly leave the UK on or before 5 April one year and return on or after 6 April five years later. The individual should retain evidence of the dates of leaving and returning to the UK (e.g. airline boarding passes).

Care will have to be taken where the individual visits the UK during a period of non-residence. The individual will have to maintain a careful record of days spent in the UK in each tax year, remembering that presence in the UK at midnight counts as being present for one day.

4.3.3   Capital Transactions with Foreign Resident or Domiciled Individuals

The UK does not charge withholding tax where an asset is sold by a non-resident individual. This is due to the fact that the UK did not historically subject non-UK residents to CGT on the disposal of a chargeable asset, regardless of where it was situated, although this has now changed in respect of UK situs residential property (see **Section 4.4**).

4.3.4   Trusts

The rate of CGT payable by trustees is 28% for residential property and 20% for other assets. Trusts cannot qualify for the 18% /10% rates of CGT.

Section 69 TCGA 1992 sets out the rules for determining the residence of a trust. Under section 69(1), the trustees of a settlement are deemed to be a single person. This deemed person will be resident in the UK when **either** of the following conditions is met:

1.   Condition 1 is that all the trustees are resident in the UK.
2.   Condition 2 is that:
    (a)   at least one trustee is resident in the UK;
    (b)   at least one trustee is not resident in the UK; and
    (c)   a settlor in relation to the settlement was resident, ordinarily resident or domiciled in the UK at the time of his death where the settlement arose on his death or, in other cases, at the time when the settlement was made.

Therefore, where the aim is to create a non-UK resident trust, it would be advisable that none of the trustees be UK resident, to avoid being caught by condition 2 above.

Care must be taken when using professional trustees, as section 69(2D) provides that a non-resident trustee will be treated as if they were resident in the UK at any time when they act as trustee in the course of a business carried on in the UK through a branch, agency or permanent establishment.

There is a danger if the trust becomes UK resident, by virtue of the residence of its trustees, even for a short period of time. Section 80 TCGA 1992 states that, where the trustees of a settlement become neither resident nor ordinarily resident in the UK, the settlement is deemed to have disposed of all assets constituting settled property at market value and immediately reacquired them. So, if a trust becomes resident and then loses resident status, a charge to tax will be triggered. There is an exception for assets situated in the UK and used for the purposes of a trade carried on in the UK through a branch or agency.

Example 4.4

Claire and Michael, who are non-UK residents, are the trustees of a non-UK resident trust. On 6 April 2012, they moved to the UK to take up permanent employment and so became UK resident. They continued to be the only trustees of the trust. On 30 September 2016, they permanently left the UK and are no longer UK resident.

The trust did not dispose of any assets in the period between 6 April 2012 and 30 September 2016.
On 30 September 2016 the trust held the following assets, with the original costs and market values shown:

	Original Cost	Market Value at 6 April 2011	Market Value at 30 September 2015
	£	£	£
Office building in Milan	750,000	850,000	1,000,000
Shares in British Airways plc	25,000	55,000	40,000
Painting displayed in the Louvre	1,200,000	1,350,000	1,500,000

Calculate the UK chargeable gain arising under section 80 TCGA 1992.

continued overleaf

Solution

No uplift to market value is given when the trust became resident in the UK on 6 April 2012. Therefore, each gain is calculated by reference to the original cost of the asset.

As the trust is UK resident, the situs of the assets is irrelevant.

	UK Chargeable Gain
	£
Office building in Milan	250,000
Shares in British Airways plc	15,000
Painting displayed in the Louvre	300,000
Total chargeable gain	565,000

4.4 Anti-avoidance Legislation

It is important to have an awareness of the anti-avoidance legislation contained in sections 13, 86 and 87 TCGA 1992.

4.4.1 Section 13 TCGA 1992

Section 13 TCGA 1992 is designed to prevent UK resident individuals and companies from avoiding UK CGT by holding an asset, and realising a chargeable gain, in a non-UK resident company.

Section 13 applies where a **chargeable gain accrues to a company that is not resident in the UK and which would be a close company if it were UK resident**.

Every UK resident or ordinarily resident person who is a shareholder in the company at the time when the gain accrues is attributed part of the gain equating to their percentage shareholding. This does not apply where the total percentage of the gain attributable to the person, and persons connected with them, does not exceed 10%.

Example 4.5

Island Ltd is a company incorporated and resident in the Isle of Man. On 1 October 2016 it realises a gain of £1 million on the sale of a shopping centre in Berlin. All the UK shareholders are higher rate taxpayers.

On that date, its shareholders are:

	No. of Shares
Mr Black (UK resident)	20
Mrs Black (UK resident)	5
Mr Gray (resident and ordinarily resident in the Isle of Man)	15
Taste Ltd (UK resident)	30
Smell Ltd (RoI resident)	25
Ms Brown	5
Total	100

Calculate the gain attributable to each shareholder under section 13 TCGA 1992.

continued overleaf

Solution

Island Ltd is not UK resident and can therefore fall within section 13. If it were UK resident, it would be a close company as it is controlled by five or fewer participators. Therefore, section 13 applies to attribute gains to UK resident or ordinarily resident shareholders.

Mr Black is UK resident and owns 20 shares. He is attributed 20% of the gain, i.e. £200,000, and will be subject to CGT at 20% on the gain.

Mrs Black is UK resident but owns less than 10% of the shares. However, her shares must be added to those owned by her husband in determining if she can avail of the exception in section 13(4). As the aggregate amount is greater than 10%, part of the gain is attributed to Mrs Black: £50,000 of the gain will be attributed to her.

None of the gain is attributed to Mr Gray, as he is not resident or ordinarily resident in the UK.

Taste Ltd is UK resident and owns 30 shares, therefore 30% of the gain will be attributed to the company. The £300,000 so attributed will be included in the company's profits, subject to corporation tax.

Smell Ltd is not UK resident and therefore no gain will be attributed to it under section 13.

Provided that Ms Brown is not connected with any of the other shareholders of Island Ltd, none of the gain will be attributed to her as she holds less than 10% of the shares.

4.4.2   Sections 86 and 87 TCGA 1992

There are similar anti-avoidance provisions in sections 86 and 87 TCGA 1992, which deal with the **use of non-resident trusts to avoid UK CGT**.

Section 86 assesses gains of a non-resident settlement on a UK resident settlor if he, or his family, are capable of benefitting from the settled property.

Section 87 assesses gains of a non-resident settlement on UK resident beneficiaries who receive capital payments from the settlement.

These sections should be considered when advising individuals who are planning to become resident in the UK. Such individuals may already be shareholders in non-UK resident companies or be a settlor/beneficiary of a non-resident trust.

4.5   Companies: Residence and CGT

UK resident companies are subject to tax in the UK on their worldwide income.

Non-resident companies will be chargeable to UK corporation tax only if they are carrying on a trade in the UK through a permanent establishment.

4.5.1   Legislation

Legislation relating to residence is contained in section 14 Corporation Tax Act 2009 (CTA 2009). This section states that a company which is incorporated in the UK will be regarded as resident in the UK for tax purposes.

However, as most double tax treaties apply "the place of effective management" as the determining factor in establishing corporate residence, it is possible for a company to be resident in the UK under section 14 by virtue of its incorporation and also resident elsewhere by virtue of its place of effective management.

Section 18 CTA 2009 provides for such "treaty non-resident" companies to be treated as non-UK resident for all tax purposes. The one exception is in relation to a controlled foreign company, as discussed in **Chapter 10**.

4.5.2 CGT

UK resident companies are subject to corporation tax on chargeable gains on all chargeable assets, wherever situated.

Non-resident companies are subject to tax on capital disposals in the UK where the chargeable asset belongs to a UK permanent establishment (PE); section 10B TCGA 1992 contains a similar rule in section 10 for non-UK resident companies trading in the UK through a PE.

Example 4.6

Pink BV, a company incorporated and resident in the Netherlands, sells a building in London and realises a gain of £1.8 million. Pink BV used the building in London as premises for its UK branch.

State whether Pink BV is chargeable to CGT on the disposal of the building.

Solution

The £1.8 million gain realised on the sale of the building would be chargeable to UK tax under section 10B.

4.6 Non-residents Disposing of UK Residential Property

Finance Act 2013 introduced a CGT charge on properties on which an "annual tax on enveloped dwellings" (ATED) is due, irrespective of the residence status of the seller. (For full details of ATED see **Section 4.11**.) The chargeable amount is the lower of:

- the full ATED-related gain; and
- 5/3rds times the difference between the consideration for the disposal and the threshold amount for that disposal.

In addition, Finance Act 2015 introduced a charge to CGT on gains on the disposal of UK residential property interests by non-UK residents. The charge applies mainly to non-resident individuals, non-resident trustees, personal representatives of a non-resident deceased person and some non-resident companies.

Residential property is property suitable for use as a dwelling. Certain types of residential property will be exempt from the charge, including:

- care or nursing homes;
- purpose-built student accommodation;
- building land, provided no residential building is under construction – this does not include disposals of rights to acquire UK residential property 'off plan';
- hospitals or hospices;
- military accommodation; and
- prisons.

The rate of tax charged on non-resident individuals will be the same as for UK resident individuals, i.e. 18% or 28% depending on total UK income and gains. The annual exemption (currently £11,100) will also be available. Trustees and personal representatives of a non-resident deceased person will be charged at 28%.

Non-resident corporates will pay tax at 20% on their chargeable gains and will have access to limited indexation allowance. Group companies can enter into pooling arrangements to aggregate gains and losses. Only non-resident companies and funds not meeting the genuine diversity of ownership test will be subject to the "non-residents capital gains tax" (NRCGT) charge. This means that, generally, only 'close' companies will be caught.

The following type of company is exempt from NRCGT:

- qualifying diversely-held company;
- qualifying unit trust scheme;
- qualifying open-ended investment company;
- life assurance companies holding the property as part of their portfolio of investments to provide policyholder benefits, and not otherwise exempted as diversely-held companies.

The chargeable gain will be based on growth in the value of the property from 6 April 2015. This means that the property will be rebased at its market value at 6 April 2015 and only gains from that date will be charged to tax. HMRC provide examples to illustrate the different approaches that can be used to calculate the difference in value. **Examples 4.7** to **4.9** replicate HMRC's examples, showing the calculations for the disposal of a residential property purchased in January 2001 for £750,000, with incidental acquisition costs of £40,000, and disposed of in June 2016 for £1,250,000, with incidental disposal costs of £30,000. The value of the property at 6 April 2015 was £1,000,000.

Example 4.7: **Default HMRC approach**
Rebasing calculation – gain from 5 April 2015 to disposal:

Disposal proceeds	£1,250,000
Incidental disposal costs	£30,000
Net disposal proceeds	£1,220,000
Market value at 5 April 2015	£1,000,000
Enhancement costs	£0
Total cost	£1,000,000
Gain over period from 5 April 2015 market value	£220,000

Alternatively the taxpayer can elect to apportion the gain on a straight-line basis.

Example 4.8: **Straight-line time apportionment**
Total ownership 65 months, period from 6 April 2015 to disposal was 14 months, 21.53% (14/65 x 100) of ownership relates to period from 6 April 2015 to disposal.

Disposal proceeds	£1,250,000
Incidental disposal costs	£30,000
Net disposal proceeds	£1,220,000
Acquisition cost	£750,000
Incidental costs of acquisition	£40,000
Enhancement costs	£0
Total acquisition cost	£790,000
Gain over period of ownership	£430,000
Time-apportioned post-5 April 2015 gain @ 21.53%	£92,579

The taxpayer can also elect not to apportion a gain/loss.

Example 4.9: **Gain over whole period of ownership**

Disposal proceeds	£1,250,000
Incidental disposal costs	£30,000
Net disposal proceeds	£1,220,000
Acquisition cost	£750,000
Incidental costs of acquisition	£40,000
Enhancement costs	£0
Total acquisition cost	£790,000
Gain over period of ownership	£430,000
Time-apportioned post-5 April 2015 gain @ 21.53%	£92,579

The gain accruing after April 2015 will be time-apportioned if necessary where the property is only used as a dwelling for part of the period.

Any UK residential property losses will be ring-fenced and only available to set against current and future gains on UK residential property.

A property may be subject to both ATED-related CGT and NRCGT. If both charges apply:

- ATED-related CGT will take precedence;
- any ATED-related gain will be subject to ATED-related CGT at 28%; and
- any remaining gains made after 5 April 2015 will be subject to NRCGT at 20%.

It should be noted that the principal private residence (PPR) nomination has been changed as a result of this new legislation. From April 2015 a person's residence will not be eligible for PPR for a tax year unless the person making the disposal was tax resident in the same country as the property for that tax year or spent at least 90 days in the property (i.e. was in the property at midnight on 90 days).

4.7 Charging Sections for Inheritance Tax

Under section 1 of the Inheritance Tax Act 1984 (IHTA 1984), IHT is charged on the value transferred by a chargeable transfer.

Chargeable transfer is defined by section 2 IHTA 1984 as a transfer of value that is not an exempt transfer.

Generally, by virtue of section 3 IHTA 1984, a transfer of value is a disposition made by a person (the transferor), as a result of which the value of his estate immediately after the disposition is less than it would be but for the disposition, and the amount by which it is less is the value transferred by the transfer.

Section 6 IHTA 1984 states that property situated outside the UK is excluded property where the person beneficially entitled to it is domiciled outside the UK. Therefore it is important to understand the situs of property rules. Where an individual is not domiciled in the UK, he will be subject to UK IHT only on assets situated in the UK.

Example 4.10

Maria, who has always been domiciled and resident in Italy, dies holding the following assets:

1.   Apartment in Rome.
2.   Apartment in Edinburgh.
3.   Shares in Spanish company.
4.   Euro bank account in Milan.
5.   Sterling bank account in London.

Which of these assets is chargeable to IHT in the UK?

Solution

As Maria is not domiciled in the UK, only the apartment in Edinburgh and the Sterling bank account in London are chargeable to UK IHT.

Section 48(3) IHTA 1984 treats settled property situated outside the UK (but not a reversionary interest in the property) as excluded property, unless the settlor was domiciled in the UK at the time the settlement was made.

   Note that **the main connecting factor applied for IHT is domicile**. This contrasts with the CGT rules outlined above, where residence is the main connecting factor. An individual can be subject to UK IHT even if he has never visited the UK.

   Domicile is not necessarily the connecting factor for similar taxes in other jurisdictions. For example, capital acquisition tax (CAT) in the RoI is based on the residence of an individual. Therefore, there could be scope for an individual domiciled in the RoI but resident in the UK to escape IHT and CAT on assets situated outside both jurisdictions.

4.8   Deemed Domicile for Inheritance Tax

Under section 267 IHTA 1984, there are two circumstances where an individual who is not domiciled in the UK can be deemed to be domiciled for IHT purposes.

   The first circumstance is where an individual who was previously domiciled in the UK continues to be treated as UK domiciled for IHT purposes for the three years after losing their UK domicile.

Example 4.11

Mary, who had a domicile of origin in the UK, acquires a domicile of choice in the RoI, with effect from 1 January 2017.

Mary will be treated as being UK domiciled for IHT purposes until 1 January 2020. If she dies between 1 January 2017 and 31 December 2019, her entire estate, regardless of the situs of the assets, will be chargeable to UK IHT.

The second circumstance is where a non-UK domiciled individual who has been resident in the UK for 17 out of the last 20 tax years is treated as being UK domiciled for IHT purposes.

Example 4.12

Chuck came to live in the UK on 6 April 1999 and has been UK resident since that date. He maintains his domicile of origin in Texas, USA.

He will be deemed to be domiciled in the UK for IHT purposes for the 2016/17 tax year onwards, as he has now been resident in the UK for 17 out of the last 20 years of assessment.

The deemed domicile rules above apply for IHT purposes only and do not affect a person's domicile for CGT or income tax purposes.

From a planning perspective, where a non-UK domiciled individual is approaching 17 years of residence in the UK and has substantial non-UK situs assets, consideration should be given to breaking UK residence for at least four full tax years. This will prevent the deemed domicile rule from applying and keep the non-UK assets outside the charge to UK IHT.

4.9   Capital Transactions with Foreign Resident or Domiciled Individuals

Where an individual is UK domiciled and their spouse or civil partner is not, section 18 IHTA 1984 imposes a limit on exempt transfers of value from the UK domiciled spouse up until 5 April 2013. Only the first £55,000 of value was exempt from IHT.

Every person, UK domiciled or not, is entitled to the full nil rate band that can be set against their UK assets. On the death of a non-domiciled spouse or civil partner, the nil rate band will be used only against UK assets and the unused nil rate band can be transferred to the UK domiciled surviving spouse or civil partner.

Legislation was introduced in Finance Bill 2013 to reform the IHT treatment of transfers between UK-domiciled individuals and their non-UK domiciled spouse or civil partners in two ways:

- the cap has been increased to the level of the prevailing nil rate band level (currently £325,000); and
- under a new election regime, individuals domiciled other than in the UK and who are married or in a civil partnership with a UK-domiciled person will be able to elect to be treated as UK domiciled for IHT purposes. The legislation will allow individuals who have become UK domiciled to make a retrospective election to cover an earlier period when they were non-UK domiciled. There is also provision for individuals whose marriage or civil partnership has been dissolved to make a retrospective election to cover the period they were married or in civil partnership with a UK-domiciled person.

Where an individual chooses not to elect for UK domicile treatment their overseas assets would now be exempt from IHT, but any transfers from their spouse or civil partner would be subject to the increased cap. Individuals who choose to make an election would benefit from uncapped IHT-exempt transfers from their spouse or civil partner, but subsequent disposals by them would be liable to IHT (subject to their own nil rate band), irrespective of the location of the assets.

The lifetime limit on the amount that can be transferred exempt from IHT to a spouse or civil partner domiciled outside the UK (or treated as such for IHT purposes) has been increased from its previous level of £55,000. Initially the cap has been raised to £325,000. Going forward, its level will be linked to any future changes in the nil rate band.

The election will only affect an individual's treatment for IHT purposes. The election will need to be made in writing to HMRC and may be made at any time after marriage or registration of the civil partnership. Elections that follow a death will only be valid if they are made within two years of the death, or such longer period as an HMRC officer may allow in the particular case; and only where death occurs on or after 6 April 2013. The personal representatives of non-domiciled individuals will be able to make a death election on their behalf.

Electing spouses making either a lifetime or death election will be able to choose a date the election applies from going back up to a maximum of seven years, so that any lifetime gifts during that period are covered by the election. The earliest date that can be specified is 6 April 2013. Where no date is specified, a lifetime election has effect on the date it is made and a death election will be treated as taking effect immediately before any transfer as a result of a disposition on the death of a UK domiciled individual.

Elections will be irrevocable while the electing individual continues to remain resident in the UK. An election will cease to have effect if the electing person is resident outside the UK for more than four full consecutive tax years.

4.10   Charging Sections for Stamp Duty and Stamp Duty Land Tax

There are three separate types of stamp duty in the UK, all of which are payable by the purchaser.

1. Stamp duty land tax (SDLT) – imposed on transactions involving land and buildings.
2. Stamp duty – imposed on documents transferring shares and marketable securities (at 0.5%) and on the issue of bearer instruments (at 1.5%).
3. Stamp duty reserve tax (SDRT) – imposed on transactions in shares.

4.10.1 Stamp Duty Land Tax

Stamp duty land tax (SDLT) was introduced by Finance Act 2003 (FA 2003) and replaced stamp duty in respect of land transactions.

Under section 42 FA 2003, SDLT is charged on land transactions. Section 43 FA 2003 defines "land transaction" as any acquisition of a chargeable interest.

A chargeable interest is defined by section 48(1) FA 2003 as:

1. an estate, interest, right or power in or over land in the UK; or
2. the benefit of an obligation, restriction or condition affecting the value of any such estate, interest, right or power.

However, under section 48(2) FA 2003, the following are exempt interests, and their acquisition will not be charged to SDLT:

1. security interest;
2. a licence to use or occupy land; and
3. in England, Wales and Northern Ireland, a tenancy at will or an advowson, franchise or manor.

The key point that makes a land transaction subject to SDLT is that the land or building is situated in the UK. Unlike CGT and IHT, the residence or domicile of the vendor or purchaser is irrelevant.

Under the old stamp duty legislation relating to land transactions, there were means of avoiding the stamp duty liability, for example by executing the sale contract outside the UK. Using such methods does not avoid SDLT, as section 42(2) FA 2003 specifically states that the tax is chargeable:

1. whether or not there is any instrument effecting the transfer;
2. if there is such an instrument, whether or not it is executed in the UK; and
3. whether or not any party to the transaction is present, or resident, in the UK.

Land Transactions

There are two legal steps in a land transaction. The first step is that a written contract is entered into between the vendor and the purchaser. The second step is the conveyance of the legal title to the land to the purchaser, known as completion.

Under the old stamp duty legislation on land transactions, the liability to stamp duty arose on the second step, i.e. the conveyance of the property. In order to avoid stamp duty under the old rules, some land contracts were not completed, in that the purchaser simply paid the purchase price and took possession of the land without legal title passing.

Section 44 FA 2003 prevents this method being used to avoid SDLT. If a contract for a land transaction is entered into but not completed, the SDLT will be due when the contract is substantially completed. Substantial completion occurs when the purchaser takes possession or when a substantial amount of the consideration is paid.

Rates of SDLT

The current rates of SDLT for England, Wales and Northern Ireland (which were introduced by Finance Act 2016 and took effect from 16 March 2016) are set out in the tables below. (SDLT no longer applies in Scotland, where the land and buildings transaction tax is paid instead.)

Residential Property Freehold Sales and Transfers	Rate of SDLT (on band of consideration)
Purchase price/lease premium or transfer value:	
Up to £125,000	Zero
£125,001 to £250,000	2%
£250,001 to £925,000	5%
£925,001 to £1,500,000	10%
£1,500,001 and over	12%

On the purchase of a new residential leasehold, where the total rent over the life of the lease (known as the 'net present value' (NPV)) is more than £125,000, a further SDLT charge of 1% is due on the portion over £125,000, unless the purchase is of an existing ("assigned") lease.

Higher rates of SDLT are applied on the purchase of a second residential property, i.e. where as a result of the purchase the new owner will hold more than one residential property. In such cases, an extra 3% SDLT will be charged on top of the normal SDLT rates.

Non-residential/Mixed-use Property Freehold Sales and Transfers	Rate of SDLT (on band of consideration)
Purchase price:	
Up to £150,000	Zero
£150,001 to £250,000	2%
£250,001 and over	5%

On the purchase of a new non-residential or mixed-use leasehold, SDLT is charged on both the:

- purchase price of the lease (the 'lease premium') using the rates above; and
- the value of the annual rent (the 'net present value' (NPV)).

These are calculated separately and then added together. The NPV is based on the total rent over the life of the lease, with SDLT charged as follows:

NPV	SDLT Rate
Up to £150,000	Zero
£150,001 to £5,000,000	1%
£5,000,000 and above	2%

An SDLT charge of 15% is applied where a non-natural person (e.g. a company or trust) purchases a residential property for consideration of £500,000 or more.

SDLT and VAT

An important point to note is that where the sale of the property is subject to VAT, SDLT is charged on the VAT-inclusive price. Where the purchaser is registered for VAT and can fully reclaim the input VAT, the VAT charged on the acquisition of the land is merely a cash flow issue. However, the SDLT on the VAT element is a real cost for the purchaser.

Example 4.13

Martin is selling a plot of land to Sarah for £1 million. Martin had opted to tax the land for VAT and therefore must charge VAT on the sale. At a VAT rate of 20%, the VAT-inclusive consideration is therefore £1,200,000.

SDLT is payable by Sarah at £49,500, i.e. £150,000 at 0%, £100,000 at 2% and £950,000 at 5%.

Chargeable Consideration

SDLT is levied on the **chargeable consideration** given for the property, which includes money or money's worth.

Where the purchaser assumes an existing liability of the vendor or transferor (e.g. an existing mortgage), this forms part of the chargeable consideration for SDLT purposes. This can apply where a property is being distributed *in specie* from a company to its shareholder and the shareholder takes over the company's debt secured on the property. The shareholder will be charged to SDLT on the value of the debt.

The terms used in section 48 FA 2003 and other parts of the SDLT legislation are property law terms. Therefore, where a client is undertaking a transaction in land, it is advisable that they consult a solicitor on the SDLT consequences. However, a tax advisor should be aware of the type of transaction that will attract SDLT and possible reliefs from SDLT.

4.10.2 Stamp Duty and Stamp Duty Reserve Tax

Stamp duty is a duty on documents (instruments) transferring shares or marketable securities. Where there is a written instrument by which shares are transferred, a stamp duty charge will normally arise.

Instruments are subject to stamp duty if they relate to UK shares or securities or are executed in the UK.

Some instruments, for example instruments transferring shares by way of a gift where there is no consideration, are not stampable provided that the appropriate exemption certificate is completed.

An instrument transferring shares on a sale carries *ad valorem* duty at 0.5% of the consideration paid by the purchaser to the vendor. Stamp duty is payable by the purchaser. Stamp duty is not payable where the value of the transfer is £1,000 or less and the transfer does not form part of a larger transaction or series of transactions. This should be certified on the reverse of the stock transfer form but does not need to be presented to HMRC for stamping.

Note that stamp duty is not payable when a company issues new shares. However, where a company buys back its own shares, stamp duty at 0.5% is payable.

Stamp duty reserve tax (SDRT) operates alongside stamp duty. It is also levied at the rate of 0.5% and is aimed mainly at subjecting paperless transactions for the sale of shares to duty. **Where stamp duty has been paid on a share transaction, SDRT will not also be payable.**

4.11   Annual Tax on Enveloped Dwellings

The annual tax on enveloped dwellings (ATED) was introduced with effect from 1 April 2013 and is payable by companies that own UK residential property valued above a certain amount. An ATED return must be completed in respect of UK residential property owned wholly or in part by a corporate entity (i.e. a company, a partnership where one of the partners is a company or a collective investment vehicle, e.g. a unit trust) that was valued at more than £1 million on 1 April 2012 or at acquisition (the threshold was £2 million for 2013 and 2014 returns). The chargeable period runs from 1 April to 31 March.

For 2016/17 the rates of ATED are as follows:

	ATED – annual chargeable amount		
Property value	**2014/15**	**2015/16**	**2016/17**
More than £500,000 but not more than £1 million	N/A	N/A	£3,500
More than £1 million but not more than £2 million	N/A	£7,000	£7,000
More than £2 million but not more than £5 million	£15,400	£23,350	£23,350
More than £5 million but not more than £10 million	£35,900	£54,450	£54,450
More than £10 million but not more than £20 million	£71,850	£109,050	£109,050
More than £20 million	£143,750	£218,200	£218,200

The "property value" is the market value on the last previous valuation date. The first valuation date is 1 April 2012 (or date of acquisition if later) and then on 1 April every five years thereafter.

Some buildings which could be said to be residential property are considered not to be dwellings and so are not included under ATED. These are:

- Hotels
- Guest houses
- Boarding school accommodation
- Hospitals
- Student halls of residence
- Military accommodation
- Care homes
- Prisons

There are exemptions from ATED, such as for charitable companies using residential property for charitable purposes.

Relief from ATED is available in some circumstances, such as where the property is let to a third party on a commercial basis or is part of a property trading business and isn't occupied by or available for occupation to anyone connected with the owner. Reliefs can be claimed in the ATED return.

Questions

Review Questions

(See Suggested Solutions to Review Questions at the end of this textbook.)

Question 4.1

State whether the following transactions would be subject to stamp duty or to SDLT in the UK, and calculate the amount of the duty payable.

(a) Ash Ltd, a Jersey incorporated and resident company, buys an office building in Manchester for £2 million plus VAT at 20%.
(b) Beta Ltd, a UK incorporated and resident company, buys an office building in Paris for £3 million.
(c) Capital Ltd, a UK incorporated and resident company, enters into a contract to acquire a plot of land for £5 million. The contract has not yet been completed, but Capital Ltd has paid £4.75 million to the vendor.
(d) Daisy buys 100 shares in Elephant Ltd, a UK incorporated and resident company, for £500.
(e) Fiona buys 1,000 shares in Gamma Inc., a US incorporated and resident company, for £10,000. The instrument to acquire the shares is executed in the UK.
(f) Harry buys 2,000 shares in Indigo SA, a company incorporated and resident in France, for £15,000. The instrument to acquire the shares is executed in Lyon.
(g) Jet Ltd buys the entire share capital of Klaxon Ltd, a UK incorporated and resident company, for £5 million. The only asset of Klaxon Ltd is land in the UK with a current market value of £6 million.

Question 4.2

The individuals (a)–(f) each die while owning the assets listed. State the extent to which each asset is within the charge to UK IHT on each individual's death:

▥ an apartment in Northern Ireland;
▥ a holiday home in France; and
▥ a euro bank account held at an Ulster Bank branch in Dublin.

(a) Laurence, who was resident and domiciled in the UK, leaves his entire estate to his daughter.
(b) Mary, who was resident and domiciled in the UK, leaves her entire estate to her husband, who is also resident and domiciled in the UK.
(c) Nuala, who had been resident in the UK for four years but was domiciled in the RoI, leaves her entire estate to her son.
(d) Owen, who was neither resident nor domiciled in the UK, leaves his entire estate to his niece.
(e) Paula, who was resident and domiciled in the UK, leaves her entire estate to her civil partner. Her civil partner is resident but not domiciled in the UK. Paula's civil partner has not elected to be treated as UK domiciled for IHT purposes.
(f) Quincy, who had been resident in the UK for the last 20 years but was domiciled in the USA, leaves his entire estate to his nephew.

Challenging Questions

(Suggested Solutions to Challenging Questions are available through your lecturer.)

Question 4.1

Maeve is UK domiciled and has always been resident in the UK. She is considering moving to Australia for four years on a secondment with her current employer. After four years, she intends to return to the UK.
    Maeve currently owns the following assets as investments:

1.   A house in Belfast, which she intends to let out while living in Australia.
2.   A painting that she bought in 2004 for £15,000. She has been advised that the painting is now worth £25,000. The painting is currently in Belfast, but she intends to take it to Australia, as she might sell the painting once she is there.
3.   A house in Portstewart, bequeathed to her by her grandmother. The market value at the date of her grandmother's death was £50,000. The house is now estimated to be worth £0.5 million. The house is empty at present and Maeve uses it very rarely.

In addition, Maeve is a trustee of a trust settled by her UK domiciled uncle on his death. The other trustee is Maeve's brother, who is resident in Germany. The only asset held by the trust is a small retail park in Omagh. This was acquired by the trust in 2004 for £100,000 and has a current market value of £600,000.

Requirement
You are required to advise Maeve on the tax implications of her change of tax residence in respect of her investment assets listed above and her position as a trustee. She would also like to know whether you can suggest any tax planning ideas. It is January 2017 and Maeve is a higher rate taxpayer.

Question 4.2

Bill owns the entire share capital of Sawyer Ltd, a special-purpose vehicle whose only asset is an office building in Belfast. The company was incorporated in the UK by Bill in 2005 and has always been resident in the UK. It acquired the office building in 2005 for £0.4 million. The current market value of the office building is £1.2 million.
    Bill wishes to sell the building. His accountant has advised him to sell the shares in the company.
    Kevin, who is resident and domiciled in the RoI, is considering acquiring the building for £1.2 million. Bill has suggested that Kevin buy the shares in Sawyer Ltd for £1.2 million instead, as this will mean that Kevin pays stamp duty at 0.5% rather than SDLT at up to 5%. Kevin thinks that this sounds like a good plan, saving him £43,500, i.e. SDLT of £49,500 (0% on the first £150,000, 2% on the next £100,000 and 5% on the next £950,000) as opposed to stamp duty of £6,000 (£1.2 million × 0.5%).

Requirement
Kevin has come to your firm for UK tax advice on the transaction. Advise Kevin on the tax implications of purchasing the shares in Sawyer Ltd as compared with those of purchasing the office building, assuming that any debt in Sawyer Ltd would be repaid before the shares were purchased.

Valuation Rules and Gifts of Assets

5.1 Valuation of Assets for CGT

5.1.1 Section 17 TCGA 1992: Transactions Not at Arm's Length – Market Value

Section 17(1)(a) TCGA 1992 treats certain disposals and acquisitions of assets as being made for a consideration equal to the market value of the asset. These are transactions not made by way of a bargain at arm's length. Such transactions are specifically stated to include:

■ gifts or transfers into a settlement by a settlor; and
■ distributions from a company in respect of shares in the company.

There is no definition of a bargain made at arm's length. To determine whether or not a transaction represents a bargain at arm's length, HMRC uses the "subjective intention test", which it describes at CG14542 of the *Capital Gains Manual* as follows:

> "Where one of the parties to a transaction has the intention of conferring a gratuitous benefit on another party to the transaction then the transaction is otherwise than by way of a bargain made at arm's length and the market value rule applies."

HMRC looks for the following objective factors which, among others, may indicate the actual intentions of the parties (*Capital Gains Manual* at CG14545):

■ presence or absence of real negotiations between the parties as to the terms of the deal;
■ comparability of the deal's terms with those in similar commercial transactions;
■ separate legal and professional representation of the parties;

- independent advice received by the parties;
- character of comparable prior dealings between the parties;
- links to other transactions between the same parties; and/or
- the relationship of the parties outside the transaction in question.

Market value is imposed by section 17(1)(b) where an asset is acquired or disposed of wholly or partly for consideration that cannot be valued or in connection with an office or employment.

Section 17(2) states that section 17(1) does not apply to the acquisition of an asset if:

1. there is no corresponding disposal of it; and
2. there is no consideration in money or money's worth, or the consideration is lower than the market value of the asset.

5.1.2 Section 18 TCGA 1992

Section 18 TCGA 1992 applies to transactions between connected persons. Section 18(2) states that transactions between connected persons will be treated as being transactions not made by way of a bargain at arm's length. This means that market value will be imposed under section 17(1)(a) for all transactions between connected persons.

"Connected" is defined by section 286 TCGA 1992. An individual is connected with his or her spouse, his or her relatives and the relatives of his or her spouse. For this purpose a relative includes brothers and sisters, ancestors and lineal descendants.

5.1.3 Exchanges of Assets

You should be aware of a quirk where there is an exchange of assets as a result of a bargain otherwise at arm's length. The outcome will depend on whether or not the parties to the transaction are connected.

Example 5.1

In 2007, Holly acquired a necklace for £10,000 and its market value is now £16,000. In 2009, Emily acquired a bracelet for £10,000 and its market value is now £13,000.

Holly and Emily are cousins. They agree that Emily will acquire Holly's necklace in exchange for Emily's bracelet.

Compute Holly's and Emily's chargeable gain.

Solution

Holly and Emily are not connected, as cousins are not included in the definition of relatives at section 286(8). However, this appears to be a bargain not made at arm's length, so market value will be substituted by virtue of section 17(1)(a).

The deemed consideration is equal to the market value of the asset received.

Holly's Chargeable Gain

	£
Proceeds = Market value of bracelet received	13,000
Less: cost	(10,000)
Chargeable gain	3,000
Base cost of bracelet	13,000

continued overleaf

Emily's Chargeable Gain

	£
Proceeds = Market value of necklace received	16,000
Less: cost	(10,000)
Chargeable gain	6,000
Base cost of necklace	16,000

Emily has a larger chargeable gain because she has received a more valuable asset.

Example 5.2

As above, but Holly and Emily are sisters, not cousins.

Compute Holly's and Emily's chargeable gain.

Solution

Holly and Emily are connected as sisters are included in the definition of relatives at section 286(8). This is deemed by section 18 to be a bargain not made at arm's length, so market value will be substituted by virtue of section 17(1)(a).

The deemed consideration is equal to the market value of the asset **surrendered**.

Holly's Chargeable Gain

	£
Proceeds = Market value of necklace surrendered	16,000
Less: cost	(10,000)
Chargeable gain	6,000
Base cost of bracelet	16,000

Emily's Chargeable Gain

	£
Proceeds = Market value of bracelet surrendered	13,000
Less: cost	(10,000)
Chargeable gain	3,000
Base cost of necklace	13,000

In this case, Holly has a larger chargeable gain, even though she is the person who has made the worse bargain.

5.1.4   Market Value

"Market value" for CGT is defined by sections 272–274 TCGA 1992. Section 272(1) defines market value as the price the assets might reasonably be expected to fetch on a sale in the open market.

Listed Shares

The rules for the valuation of listed shares are contained in section 272(3) and (4).

Under section 272(3), the market value of quoted shares (i.e. shares or securities that appear in the Stock Exchange Daily Official List) is generally the lower of:

1. the lower of the two prices shown in the quotations for the shares or securities listed in the Stock Exchange Daily Official List on the relevant date plus one-quarter of the difference between those two figures ("the quarter-up" value); or
2. halfway between the highest and lowest prices at which bargains, other than bargains done at special prices, were recorded in the shares or securities for the relevant date (the "mid-market price").

If no bargains were recorded for the relevant date, then the value arrived at under 1. will apply as it will be lower.

Example 5.3

Shauna gifts shares in Alphabet plc, a quoted company, on 30 July 2016. For that day, the shares are quoted in the Stock Exchange Daily Official List at £250–260. No special bargains were recorded.

For the purpose of computing Shauna's chargeable gain, the value of the shares will be the lower of:

1. the lower price (£250) + one-quarter of the difference between the two prices (1/4 × 10 = 2.5) = £252.5; and
2. half of the difference between the highest and lowest prices: (£250 + £260)/2 = £255.

The market value of the shares will therefore be £252.50.

The method of valuation set out above does not apply to:

- shares or securities for which the stock exchange provides a more active market than on the London trading floor; or
- listed shares and securities where special circumstances mean that the quoted prices are not a proper measure of the value.

Under section 272(4), where the London trading floor is closed on the relevant day, the market value is ascertained by reference to the latest previous date or earliest subsequent date on which it is open, whichever results in the lower market value.

Unquoted Shares and Securities

Section 273 deals with the valuation of unquoted shares and securities.

Section 273(3) states that, for the purposes of the open market postulated by section 272(1), it shall be assumed that there is available to any prospective purchaser of the shares or securities all the information a prudent prospective purchaser might reasonably require if he were proposing to purchase them from a willing vendor by private treaty and at arm's length.

The hypothetical open market was summarised by Plowman J. in *Re Lynall* ((1969) 1 WLR 984, at page 1058), who said that:

"… it is common ground that the shares must be valued on the basis of a hypothetical sale … in a hypothetical market between a hypothetical willing purchaser, on the hypothesis that no one is excluded from buying and that the purchaser would be registered as a holder of his shares but would then hold them subject to the articles of association of the company, including the restrictions on transfer …"

The valuation of unquoted shares is complex and should be undertaken by specialists. As it is based on hypotheses, assumptions have to be made.

It is first appropriate to value the entire company. As this can be done on different bases, e.g. price earnings ratios or net assets, it may be appropriate to use a number of these bases when valuing a company for tax purposes. It is then likely to be a case of reaching agreement with HMRC's Share Valuation Division on the basis to be used.

Once a valuation for the entire share capital of the company has been completed, it will be a matter of agreeing a minority discount where the disposal is of less than 50% of the shares in the company. As there is a very restricted market for minority holdings in unquoted companies, the minority discount can be very significant, e.g. 50–75%.

CGT and IHT
There is an uplift to market value where assets are transferred on death, so that the beneficiary's acquisition cost for CGT purposes is the market value at the date of the donor's death.

Section 274 TCGA 1992 states that where the value of an asset forming part of the deceased's estate has been ascertained for the purposes of IHT, that value shall be taken for CGT purposes as the market value of the asset at the date of death.

Veltema Disclosure
Following the tax case *Langham (HMIT) v. Veltema* ((2004) BTC 156), the following information should be included in the white space for additional information where a valuation has been used in a self-assessment return (this is to prevent HMRC being able to make a discovery assessment once the enquiry window has closed):

- that a valuation has been used in computing the figures in the return;
- by whom the valuation has been carried out; and
- that it was carried out by a named independent and suitably qualified valuer, if that was the case, on an appropriate basis.

5.2　Valuation of Assets for IHT

Section 1 Inheritance Tax Act 1984 (IHTA 1984) charges IHT on transfers of value that are chargeable transfers.

Section 3(1) IHTA 1984 defines a transfer of value as a disposition made by a person (the transferor) as a result of which the value of his estate immediately after the disposition is less than it would be but for the disposition; and the amount by which it is less is the value transferred by the transfer. This is the **"loss to the donor" principle**.

The key point is that it is the loss to the transferor's estate that is important, and not the gain to the transferee. The two amounts may not be the same.

This will be the case where other assets in the transferor's estate lose value as a result of the transfer. This commonly occurs where a transfer of shares in a company results in the transferor no longer having a controlling shareholding in the company.

Where a chargeable lifetime transfer is made and the donor wishes to pay the IHT due on the transfer, the value of the transfer of value must be increased by the amount of the IHT payable.

Section 4 IHTA 1984 applies the loss to the transferor's estate concept to transfers on death. IHT is charged as if, immediately before death, the deceased had made a transfer of value equal to the whole value of the estate.

Under section 5(3) IHTA 1984, liabilities must be taken into account when valuing a person's estate, whether or not such liabilities are attached to a particular asset. However, section 5(5) provides that liabilities are taken into account only to the extent that they are either imposed by law or incurred for consideration in money or money's worth. This prevents the value of an asset being artificially reduced by burdening it with a liability incurred for less than full consideration.

5.2.1 Basis of Valuation of Assets

The basis of valuation of assets is set out in section 160 IHTA 1984.

Section 160 states that the value of any property at any time shall, for the purposes of IHT, be the price that the property might reasonably be expected to fetch if sold in the open market at that time. It also states that the price shall not be assumed to be reduced on the grounds that the whole property is to be placed on the market at the same time.

Section 161 IHTA 1984 relates property in a person's estate to property in the estate of that person's spouse or civil partner for the purposes of valuing assets under section 160.

Section 168 IHTA 1984 deals with the valuation of unquoted shares and securities. This section is similar to section 273(3) TCGA 1992, discussed above. **Sales are deemed to take place in a hypothetical open market and the case law definition as set out above applies**.

Relieving Provisions

There are relieving provisions for certain types of asset, where a lower value is realised on the sale of the asset within a certain period following death. These include the following:

1. Section 176 IHTA 1984 provides relief in respect of property valued at the death under the related property provisions, or in aggregate with other property, and which is **sold within three years of death at a lower price** than that adopted as the value at the date of death.
2. Section 179 IHTA 1984 provides that, where the estate of a deceased person includes **quoted securities** (i.e. shares or securities quoted on a recognised stock exchange) which are **sold within 12 months of the death** by the person or persons liable for the tax attributable to the value of these investments, then a claim may be made that the total of the sale prices should be substituted for the death value of the investments sold. Such a claim must cover all investments sold, whether they were sold at a gain or a loss.
3. Section 191 IHTA 1984 provides for the situation where land or buildings forming part of a deceased person's estate are sold by the person liable for the tax on such **land or buildings within three years of the death** and, in certain cases, in the fourth year after death. It can be claimed that the lower sale price should be substituted for the value at the death.

5.3 Valuation of Assets for Stamp Duty and Stamp Duty Land Tax

Unlike CGT, there is **no general substitution of market value for stamp duty and SDLT**.

Stamp duty is charged on consideration in money or money's worth given for the acquisition of shares or securities in UK companies. Where no consideration is given or the transaction is not at arm's length, the general rule is that stamp duty is payable on the actual consideration, not market value.

5.3.1 Exchanges of Shares

Where two share transfers are executed to effect an exchange of shares, both documents are liable to *ad valorem* stamp duty under section 55 Stamp Act 1891. Each document is chargeable to duty by reference to the value of the shares transferred by the other document.

The shares are to be valued at the date of execution of the transfer document. The CGT basis of valuation set out in section 272(3) TCGA 1992 is also used for stamp duty purposes.

5.3.2 SDLT

SDLT is charged on the chargeable consideration for a transaction relating to UK land.

Schedule 4 Finance Act 2003 deals with the term "chargeable consideration". Paragraph 1 states that chargeable consideration is, except as otherwise provided, any consideration in money or money's worth given, directly or indirectly, by the purchaser or a person connected with him.

Paragraph 2 states that the **chargeable consideration includes VAT**.

Where there is postponed consideration, paragraph 3 provides that no discount for postponement is given in calculating the chargeable consideration.

Under paragraph 8, where the chargeable consideration includes the satisfaction/release of debt due to the purchaser or owed by the vendor, or the assumption of existing debt by the purchaser, **the amount of the debt will form part of the chargeable consideration**.

Where consideration for UK land is given in money's worth, the chargeable consideration for SDLT purposes will be the market value of the asset given as money's worth, as set out in paragraph 7.

Exchanges of Land

Paragraph 5 deals with exchanges of UK land. In this case, the chargeable consideration for the acquisition is the market value of the subject-matter of the acquisition.

Example 5.4

Mr Blue has a house with a market value of £600,000. Mrs White has a house with a market value of £700,000.

They exchange houses, with Mr Blue paying Mrs White £100,000.

The chargeable consideration on the acquisition by Mr Blue is £700,000.

The chargeable consideration on the acquisition by Mrs White is £600,000.

Deemed Market Value Rule

There is a deemed market value rule for SDLT in section 53 FA 2003.

Section 53 applies **where the purchaser is a company** and:

1. the vendor is connected with the purchaser; **or**
2. some or all of the consideration for the transaction consists of the issue or transfer of shares in a company with which the vendor is connected.

Where section 53 applies, the chargeable consideration for the transaction shall be taken to be not less than the market value of the subject-matter of the transaction as at the effective date of the transaction.

For these purposes, the definition of connected persons in section 1122 CTA 2010 applies.

Section 54 FA 2003 provides three exemptions, listed below, from the application of the deemed market value rule in section 53.

Case 1 Where, immediately after the transaction, the purchaser company holds the property as trustee in the course of a business carried on by it that consists of, or includes, the management of trusts.

Case 2 Where, immediately after the transaction, the purchaser company holds the property as trustee and the vendor is connected with the company only by virtue of section 1122(b) CTA 2010.

Case 3   Where the vendor is a company and the transaction is, or is part of, a distribution of the assets of that company (whether or not in connection with its winding up), and it is not the case that:

1.   the subject-matter of the transaction, or
2.   an interest from which that interest is derived,

has, within the period of three years immediately preceding the effective date of the transaction, been the subject of a transaction in respect of which group relief was claimed by the vendor.

"Market value" is defined at section 118 FA 2003. It is to be determined in accordance with sections 272–274 TCGA 1992, as discussed above.

The market value of an asset does not include VAT, even if VAT is chargeable on the transfer of the asset. This is because market value is based on a hypothetical transaction, not on the actual transaction.

Linked Transactions

In determining the rate of SDLT payable, linked transactions must be aggregated.

Transactions are linked under section 108 FA 2003 if they form part of a single scheme, arrangement or series of transactions between the same vendor and purchaser or, in either case, persons connected with them.

5.3.3   General

Where it is necessary to determine the market value of land for CGT, IHT or SDLT purposes, an **independent valuation in writing should be obtained from a qualified professional**.

If HMRC has doubts about the valuation, it will refer the matter to the district valuer, who will undertake his own valuation. It will then be a matter of reaching agreement, which can often come down to negotiation between the taxpayer (or their advisors) and HMRC.

5.4   Disposal by a Company at Nil or Undervalue

Where a company disposes of an asset at nil or undervalue, it will be deemed to have disposed of it for market value where the transaction is not a bargain made at arm's length, under section 17(1)(a) TCGA 1992.

Where the disposal is to a connected person, it will be viewed as a bargain not at arm's length by virtue of section 18(2). This does not apply to intra-group transfers, under section 171 TCGA 1992, which take place at no gain/no loss. Refer to **Section 5.5** below for special considerations for close companies.

Corporate bodies other than close companies cannot make transfers of value for IHT purposes. Close company considerations are discussed in **Section 5.5** below.

5.5   Close Company Considerations

5.5.1   Section 125 TCGA 1992

Where a close company transfers an asset at an undervalue and it is not a bargain made at arm's length, section 125(1) TCGA 1992 permits the undervalue to be apportioned to holders of the close company's issued share capital.

A close company is defined by Part 10 of CTA 2010 and must therefore be UK resident for these purposes.

Where applicable, the amount apportioned under section 125 is effectively regarded for chargeable gains purposes as a return of the original investment, in order to reduce the allowable expenditure on a disposal of the shares. If the amount is apportioned to a close company, it is sub-apportioned among the holders of that company's issued share capital, etc.

5.5.2 Section 13 TCGA 1992

Section 13 TCGA 1992 is anti-avoidance legislation applying to disposals of chargeable assets by non-UK resident companies that would be close if they were resident in the UK.

The gains realised by the non-resident company are apportioned to its UK resident shareholders. This is discussed in detail in **Chapter 4**.

5.5.3 IHT

Under section 3(1) IHTA 1984, a close company is capable of making a transfer of value. However, it is incapable of making a chargeable transfer under section 2(1) IHTA 1984 because only an individual can make a chargeable transfer. Without specific provision, a transaction effected by a close company, as a result of which the value of its shares was reduced, would not be chargeable to tax.

The solution adopted by sections 94–102 IHTA 1984 is to treat any transfer by a close company as having been made by the participators in the company, in proportion to their holdings immediately before the transfer. Similarly, an alteration in the company's share or loan capital is treated as a disposition by the participators.

Section 102 states that a close company is one that is close under section 439 CTA 2010, or which would be close if it were resident in the UK. Special rules apply where the participator in a company is a trustee.

Under section 94 IHTA 1984, where a close company makes a transfer of value, IHT is charged as if each UK resident participator in the close company had made a transfer of value of a fraction proportionate to its share in the company. If any of the participators is itself a close company, further apportionments are made until all individual shareholders are made liable for IHT.

Where an amount is apportioned to a participator whose estate is more than it would be but for the company's transfer, the apportioned amount must be reduced by such an increase.

Close companies are disadvantaged in comparison with individuals, in that they are incapable of making potentially exempt transfers. The same applies to alterations in the company's share or loan capital. Therefore, any transfer is chargeable at the time when it is made and, although no extra tax becomes payable on a death within seven years, the transfer can never be exempt from IHT.

There are a number of exceptions and *de minimis* provisions relieving dispositions that would otherwise be chargeable. The most important is that no apportionment is made of the value of payments which are chargeable to income tax or corporation tax in the hands of the recipient. The majority of transfers by close companies will, in practice, be so chargeable.

Liability for tax on amounts apportioned on participators falls in the first instance on the company, in accordance with section 202(1) IHTA 1984. Where any tax remains unpaid after it ought to have been paid, liability also falls on persons upon whom apportionments have been made, and on any individual the value of whose estate has been increased by the transfer.

When calculating the IHT payable by the close company, regard is given to chargeable transfers made by each participator in the previous seven years.

Questions

Review Questions

(See Suggested Solutions to Review Questions at the end of this textbook.)

Question 5.1

Jack and Jill are siblings. They each own 50% of two companies, Pail Ltd and Hill Ltd. The shares were left to them on the death of their mother four years ago. They have tried running the companies jointly, but they find it difficult to reach agreement.

They have now decided to swap their shareholdings. Jack will acquire Jill's 50% share of Hill Ltd in exchange for his 50% share in Pail Ltd. They consider that 50% of Hill Ltd is worth more than 50% of Pail Ltd, so Jack will also pay Jill £10,000.

They undertake the exchange of shares and then ask the companies' auditors to value the shares in the company. The auditors conclude that a 50% shareholding in Hill Ltd has a market value of £150,000, while a 50% shareholding in Pail Ltd has a market value of £120,000.

Requirement
Compute the deemed CGT consideration for the disposals by Jack and Jill, on the basis that the exchange took place on 21 May 2016, and the amount of stamp duty payable by each of them.

Question 5.2

Rain Ltd is a trading company with an issued share capital of 10,000 £1 shares. Mary owns 7,000 shares, her sister Jane owns 2,000 shares, and her husband John owns 1,000 shares. All shareholders acquired their shares for nominal value when the company was incorporated in 1997.

Mary wishes to gift 1,500 shares to her son, Joe. The values of the shares are:

Holding	Value
0 – 24%	£100 per share
25% – 50%	£150 per share
50% – 74%	£300 per share
75% – 100%	£500 per share

Requirement
Outline to Mary the amount of chargeable gain to be deferred (on the basis that section 165 holdover relief is available) and the value of the potentially exempt transfer for IHT as a result of the gift to Joe.

Challenging Question

(Suggested Solutions to Challenging Questions are available through your lecturer.)

Question 5.1

Jackson Ltd is a close company whose shares are held by Áine, Brian and Caoimhe in the following proportions:

> Áine – 50%
> Brian – 33.33%
> Caoimhe – 16.67%

In May 2016, the company made a transfer of value of £90,000 in favour of Áine's son, Declan.

At this time, the three shareholders had made the following gross chargeable transfers within the previous seven years:

> Áine – £350,000
> Brian – £200,000
> Caoimhe – £400,000

Each is UK resident and domiciled and had the 2016/17 annual exemption available to utilise against any apportioned transfer of value.

Requirement
(a) Compute the IHT payable by Jackson Ltd as a result of the transfer of value to Declan.
(b) State how your answer would differ if the transfer of value had been made to Áine, rather than to her son.

Capital Transactions and Reliefs Available

6.1 Relief for the Transfer of a Business to a Company

In the absence of relieving provisions, where a sole trader transfers their business to a limited company and thereafter trades as a limited company, they are said to have incorporated. This is a disposal by the individual for capital gains tax (CGT) purposes, which will be deemed to have been conducted at market value. This could be an acceptable outcome where the gain is small and can be sheltered by the annual exemption or where the individual has capital losses to set against the gain arising.

However, where there is a gain on which CGT would be payable, the individual is disadvantaged in that they have received no cash with which to pay any CGT due and so may wish to rely on the available reliefs. Details of these reliefs are covered in **Section 19.1.3** of *CA Proficiency 2: Taxation 2 (NI) 2016–2017*. The following is an overview from a planning perspective.

6.2 Incorporation Relief

Under section 162 TCGA 1992, gains are deferred to the extent that consideration is received in the form of shares in the company.

The deferred gain on the disposal of the chargeable assets is deducted from the base cost of the shares acquired. The gain becomes chargeable on the eventual disposal of the shares in the company.

Conditions for the relief include the following:

- the business being transferred must be a going concern;
- all assets of the sole trade must be transferred; and
- the consideration paid to the individual must be wholly or partly in shares.

It is important to remember that **section 162 TCGA 1992 applies automatically** on the transfer of assets to a company. Where a taxpayer does not wish the relief to apply, the conditions can be broken or an election can be made under section 163 TCGA 1992 to disapply section 162.

The gain to be deferred will be restricted to the extent that consideration other than shares is received from the company.

Under Extra-Statutory Concession D32, HMRC will not treat liabilities taken over by the company on the transfer of the business as being consideration for the purposes of section 162.

It is possible to calculate non-share consideration to ensure that the chargeable gain equals available capital losses plus the annual exemption.

6.2.1 Disadvantages of Section 162

The disadvantage of section 162 is that it requires all the assets of the business (except cash) to be transferred to the company. This can have adverse tax consequences.

For instance, the taxpayer may wish to hold the business premises outside the company. This will prevent an SDLT charge arising on the transfer to the company and will ensure that future capital appreciation will be subject to CGT at 10% or 20% in the hands of the individual, rather than accruing in the company where corporation tax would be payable on disposal and an additional tax charge would be payable if the shareholder wished to extract the proceeds.

6.2.2 Other Tax Considerations

There is no relief from SDLT on the transfer of land or property from an unincorporated entity to a company. Where the business holds a high value of land (particularly where it is a property development business holding land or buildings as stock), the SDLT costs of incorporation can be prohibitive.

Stamp duty will only arise on incorporation if the business holds stocks, shares or marketable securities and these are transferred to the company. This scenario is unlikely to arise.

As a transfer of business assets to a company with the same ownership is not a transfer of value, no IHT liability should result.

However, there will be an impact on business property relief (BPR) where land or buildings used in the business are not transferred to the company. Land or buildings held by and used in a sole trade are entitled to 100% BPR.

By contrast, land or buildings held by an individual and used in a company controlled by the individual are only entitled to 50% BPR. This reduction in BPR should be weighed against the CGT and SDLT benefits of retaining property outside the company.

Subject to certain conditions, the transfer of a business to a company should be a transfer of a going concern (TOGC) and therefore outside the scope of VAT.

6.3 Gift Relief/Holdover Relief

The detailed rules applying in this area can be found at **Section 19.2** of *CA Proficiency 2: Taxation 2 (NI) 2016–2017*. This section provides an overview from a planning perspective.

This section will concentrate on three common scenarios where business asset holdover relief in section 165 TCGA 1992 can be used for capital taxes planning. These scenarios are as follows:

1. Transfer of a business from an unincorporated entity to a company.
2. Gifts of shares in qualifying companies to family members.
3. Gifts of assets immediately chargeable to IHT.

6.3.1 Transfer of a Business from an Unincorporated Entity to a Company

Section 165 TCGA 1992 relieves gifts of assets used in a trade, vocation or profession by the transferor to a company.

The transferor and the company must jointly claim section 165 relief. The relief operates by deducting the gain arising on each asset from the base cost of that asset in the company and thereby defers the gain until the company eventually sells the asset.

The use of this relief, rather than the incorporation relief in section 162, **allows greater flexibility in tax planning on the incorporation of a business**. The individual can **select which assets are to be transferred to the company** and claim section 165 relief where this is advantageous. It should be noted that amortisation for internally generated goodwill and other customer-related intangible assets acquired from a related party is no longer available (with effect from 3 December 2014). Prior to this, amortisation was available in respect of 'new' internally generated goodwill, i.e. goodwill generated after 1 April 2002.

6.3.2 Gifts of Shares in Qualifying Companies

As part of succession planning, the owner of shares in a family company may wish to begin to transfer ownership to the next generation.

Although, where shares qualify for BPR, it can be beneficial from a tax perspective to retain the shares until death (as 100% BPR means that no IHT liability will arise on the shares and there will be an uplift to market value for CGT purposes on death), this may not be suitable from a commercial or practical perspective. If children or grandchildren are working in the family company, gifting shares to them will reward their hard work and incentivise them to create value in the company.

A gift of shares or a transfer at undervalue from a shareholder to a family member will be treated as a disposal at market value under section 17(1)(a) and section 18(2) TCGA 1992. However, it may be possible for the parties to claim CGT holdover relief under section 165 TCGA 1992.

Gift relief must be claimed jointly with both the donor and donee within four years from the end of the tax year in which the transfer was made.

Restrictions

A non-arm's length transfer of unquoted shares in a trading company will normally be eligible for relief under section 165. There are two circumstances where holdover relief cannot be claimed:

1. where the shares are transferred by a company; and
2. where the individual transfers the shares to a "settlor-interested trust".

A settlor-interested trust is one where the individual transferring the shares, or their spouse/civil partner or dependent children, is an actual or discretionary beneficiary of the trust. A dependent child is a child or step-child who is under 18, is unmarried and does not have a spouse/civil partner.

Where a trust becomes settlor-interested within six years of the end of the tax year in which the transfer to the trust was made, any holdover relief claimed will be clawed back.

Trading Company

To qualify for holdover relief, the shares transferred must be **unquoted shares in a trading company or the holding company of a trading group**. The trading company/group definition is now contained in section 165A TCGA 1992.

"Trading company" means a company carrying on trading activities whose activities do not include, to a substantial extent, activities other than trading activities. This is the same definition as previously applied for business asset taper relief.

Section 165A does not define "substantial extent". However, the relief should be available provided that at least 80% of the company/group activities are trading. This is likely to be determined by reference to turnover, gross assets and/or management time.

When looking at a company's gross assets, the value of goodwill should be considered. Goodwill may not appear on the balance sheet, but its value can be included when considering the percentage of trading assets, as it will have a beneficial effect on the calculation.

Holdover relief can also be claimed on quoted shares in a personal trading company or holding company of a trading group. A personal company is one where the individual transferor exercises at least 5% of the voting rights.

Where shares in a non-trading (investment) company are gifted, holdover relief is not available and an immediate CGT liability will be suffered by the transferor.

Operation of Holdover Relief on Shares

Where the shares are transferred for no consideration (i.e. gifted), holdover relief can be claimed to prevent the transferor from having a CGT liability.

The gain held over will be deducted from the transferee's deemed market value acquisition cost.

The held-over gain will become chargeable when the transferee makes a disposal of the gifted shares.

Example 6.1

On 1 December 2016, Amy March gifts her 300 shares in the family trading company, March Ltd, to her daughter, Beth. Amy acquired her 300 shares on the death of her father in February 2007, when their market value was £150,000. The market value of the shares at 1 December 2016 has been agreed with HMRC to be £500,000.

Calculate Beth's base cost of the shares for CGT purposes if holdover relief under section 165 TCGA 1992 is jointly claimed by Amy and Beth. Amy is a higher rate taxpayer.

Solution

	£
Proceeds = Market value @ 01/12/16	500,000
Less: cost (market value @ February 2007)	(150,000)
Gain	350,000
Less: section 165 relief	(350,000)
Chargeable gain	Nil
Beth's base cost:	
Market value @ 01/12/16	500,000
Less: held-over gain	(350,000)
Base cost for CGT	150,000

In most cases, HMRC *Statement of Practice 8/92* will apply to allow a claim for holdover relief to be made without the need to prepare a computation of the capital gain or to agree a formal valuation of the gifted shares. As can be seen from **Example 6.1**, following the abolition of indexation allowance for individuals, Beth takes over her mother's base cost.

This concessionary treatment is not available where the shares are sold for an undervalue exceeding the transferor's base cost. In these circumstances, the gain eligible for holdover relief will be restricted by the amount of the excess consideration. The excess of the actual consideration received by the transferor over the base cost will be chargeable to CGT. This gain may be eligible for entrepreneurs' relief and the annual exemption can be utilised against it.

Example 6.2

As **Example 6.1** above, except Beth provides consideration of £200,000 for the 300 shares transferred to her. Calculate the CGT payable by Amy (on the basis that she has the full annual exemption but has already used her lifetime entitlement to entrepreneurs' relief) and Beth's base cost.

Solution

	£	£
Proceeds = Market value @ 01/12/16		500,000
Less: cost (market value @ February 2007)		(150,000)
Gain		350,000
Less section 165 relief:		
Gain	350,000	
Less: amount restricted (£200,000 − £150,000)	(50,000)	
		(300,000)
Chargeable gain		50,000
Less: annual exemption		(11,000)
Taxable gain		39,000
CGT @ 20% payable by Amy		7,800
Beth's base cost:		
Market value @ 01/12/16		500,000
Less: held-over gain		(300,000)
Base cost for CGT		200,000

Note that Beth's base cost is equal to the consideration paid by her.

Remember that to qualify for section 165 relief, the company must always be a trading company with less than 20% of non-trading activities.

Where the shares are in the transferor's personal company, there is a restriction on holdover relief by reference to the company's chargeable non-trading/investment assets.

Other Tax Considerations

The gift or transfer at undervalue of shares by an existing shareholder to an individual qualifies as a potentially exempt transfer (PET) for IHT purposes.

It should thus be possible to avoid any IHT liability on the transfer. Either the transferor will survive the seven-year period or, if the PET does crystallise on the death of the transferor, BPR may be available. **As the shares will have been transferred before death, BPR will only be available if the transferee has retained the shares and the company continues to meet the qualifying conditions for BPR.**

Where the gift or transfer at undervalue of shares is made by an individual to a relevant property trust, the transfer of value will be immediately chargeable to IHT. However, as most family trading companies will qualify for BPR, it should be possible to transfer these shares to a trust without incurring an immediate IHT liability.

The transfer of shares by gift will require a stock transfer form to be executed and stamped. Gifts are exempt from *ad valorem* stamp duty.

6.3.3 Gifts of Assets Immediately Chargeable to IHT

As noted above, section 165 can only be claimed for business assets. Under section 260 TCGA 1992, holdover relief for gifts of non-business assets is available where the disposal:

1. is immediately chargeable to IHT, or would be but for the fact that it is covered by the IHT annual exemption; or
2. is specifically exempt from IHT under certain specified provisions.

The relief is available in relation to disposals otherwise than at arm's length by either an individual or the trustees of a settlement to either an individual or the trustees of a settlement. Consequently, it applies to both gifts and transfers at undervalue. Relief must be claimed by both the transferor and transferee if the transferee is an individual, or the transferor alone if the disposal is to the trustees of a settlement.

As transfers to relevant property trusts are now immediately chargeable to IHT, gift holdover relief can be claimed in these circumstances. This is subject to the exclusion of settlor-interested trusts, outlined above.

6.4   Rollover Relief

The detailed rules applying to rollover/holdover relief can be found in **Sections 19.1** and **19.2** of *CA Proficiency 2: Taxation 2 (NI) 2016–2017*.

The rollover relief provisions are found in sections 152–159 TCGA 1992 and apply to the **replacement of business assets**. Where the proceeds on the gain of an old asset are reinvested in a new, non-depreciating asset, the gain is deferred and this is referred to as "rollover relief".

Where the proceeds are reinvested in a new, depreciating asset, the gain is held over, and this is generally referred to as "holdover relief". This should not be confused with the holdover relief available under section 165 TCGA 1992.

Rollover and holdover relief are available for chargeable business assets held by a sole trader, partnership or company that fall within the classes of assets listed in section 155 TCGA 1992. Goodwill is one such asset class; however, if a company realises a gain from the disposal of goodwill, then the gain can only be rolled into new intangible assets acquired by the company. This means that a company could not claim rollover relief on the disposal of goodwill by reinvesting the proceeds in, say, a property.

This type of rollover or holdover relief is never available on the disposal of shares in a company.

6.5   Entrepreneurs' Relief

The detailed rules regarding entrepreneurs' relief can be found in **Chapter 18** of *CA Proficiency 2: Taxation 2 (NI) 2016–2017*.

Entrepreneurs' relief (ER) was introduced in Finance Act 2008 as a result of outcry from small business about the abolition of business asset taper relief (BATR), which had reduced the effective rate of CGT on the sale of business assets to 10% after two years of ownership.

Many of the principles of ER are taken from the old legislation relating to retirement relief, which was abolished on 5 April 2003. Therefore, commentators believe that tax cases on retirement relief may be helpful in interpreting how ER applies in practice.

The legislation on ER is contained in sections 169H–169S TCGA 1992. ER applies to **qualifying business disposals made by individuals**.

The lifetime limit for ER was increased from £1 million to £2 million, with effect from 6 April 2010. The limit was further increased to £5 million with effect from 23 June 2010, and to £10 million with effect from 6 April 2011.

Qualifying gains, up to the lifetime limit of £10 million, are taxed at 10%. Remember that the £10 million is a lifetime limit from April 2008, when ER was introduced. Therefore, if an individual claimed the full £5 million in ER available before 6 April 2011, he will only have £5 million of his lifetime limit remaining.

6.5.1 Qualifying Business Disposals

Qualifying business disposals are the disposal (by way of sale, gift, transfer, etc.) by an individual of:

1. all or part of their sole trade business;
2. all or part of an interest in a partnership;
3. certain post-cessation disposals of former business assets;
4. shares or securities in a trading company or the holding company of a trading group that was the individual's personal company for at least 12 months before the disposal; or
5. associated disposals, which are the disposal of chargeable assets owned personally by the individual while used in the business of:

    (a) a partnership of which they were a member, where they are also disposing of their interest in the partnership, or
    (b) a trading company or the holding company of a trading group that was the individual's personal company, where they are also disposing of their shares in the company.

There are a number of potential traps in the ER legislation that can result in the relief being restricted or unavailable. It should be noted that, as a result of measures introduced by Finance Act 2015, with effect from 3 December 2014, ER was no longer available on goodwill or customer-related intangible assets on the incorporation of a business. Finance Act 2016 reintroduced the possibility of obtaining ER on goodwill arising from the incorporation of a sole trade, but only in cases where the claimant holds less than 5% of the ordinary shares and voting powers in the company. In reality, therefore, ER will be unavailable in respect of the disposal of goodwill arising on incorporation in the majority of cases. The new Finance Act 2016 rules have been backdated to take effect from 3 December 2014.

6.5.2 "Personal Company" and "Trading Company"

In order for a company to be an individual's **personal company**, the individual must:

- be an officer (e.g. director, company secretary) or employee of the company; and
- own at least 5% of the company's ordinary shares; and
- be able to exercise at least 5% of the voting rights in the company by virtue of their holding of ordinary shares.

It should be noted that the officer/employee condition does not stipulate a minimum number of hours. Part-time workers will therefore meet this requirement.

Note also that although both the ER legislation and section 165 TCGA 1992 use the same phrase, "personal company", **the tests are not the same**. Section 165 does not require an individual to be an officer or employee, and only refers to 5% of the voting rights, not share capital. This demonstrates the importance of applying the correct tests for each type of relief.

However, the ER legislation does use the section 165A definition of a **trading company**, or the holding company of a trading group.

As discussed above, a trading company for these purposes is one whose activities do not, to a substantial extent, include non-trading activities.

Although "substantial" is not defined in the legislation, HMRC's view is that it means more than 20% (see HMRC's *Capital Gains Manual* CG64090, at www.gov.uk/hmrc-internal-manuals/capital-gains-manual/cg64090). In judging this, HMRC will consider factors such as:

- income from non-trading activities;
- the asset base of the company; and
- expenses incurred, or time spent, by officers or employees of the company in undertaking its activities.

6.5.3 "Associated Disposals"

One of the most complex areas of the ER legislation is the concept of "associated disposals".
Isolated disposals of business property do not qualify for ER.

To qualify, the disposal has to be associated with the disposal of an interest in a partnership or shares in a personal trading company (or holding company of a trading group). For disposals on or after 18 March 2015 they must be associated with a significant material disposal of such an interest, i.e. at least a 5% share in the assets of the partnership or shareholding in the company, and there cannot be arrangements in place to increase the interest again in the future.

ER does not apply to a sole trader who makes a disposal of property held outside the business in association with the disposal of their business.

An important restriction on ER for associated disposals is found in section 169P TCGA 1992. Relief for associated disposals is restricted where:

- the assets concerned have been used for the purposes of the business during only part of the individual's period of ownership;
- only a part of the asset has been so used;
- the individual was a partner, officer or employee for only part of the period in which the assets were used for business purposes; or
- during any part of the period of ownership falling after 5 April 2008 when the asset was in use for the purposes of the business, that use by the partnership or company was dependent upon the payment of rent (or any other form of consideration for its use).

Where these conditions apply, ER is restricted to an amount that is "just and reasonable". In other words, only the just and reasonable part of the gain is to be reduced by the relief and the balance of the gain remains taxable in full.

Personally Owned Business Premises
In practice, this restriction is most likely to apply where an individual personally owns premises that are used in the business of their personal trading company or of a partnership in which they are a partner.

It would be common in these circumstances for the individual to charge full market rent to the company or partnership. If full market rent has been charged after 6 April 2008, ER will not be available on the disposal of the premises in conjunction with the disposal of the shares or the interest in the partnership. Where, for example, rent at 50% of full market value has been charged, ER on an associated disposal of the property would be reduced by one-half.

The potential benefit of ER on the associated disposal of personally owned business premises will have to be weighed against the tax advantages of holding such property personally and charging a market rent.

Charging rent to a company is a tax-efficient means of extracting funds from a company, as the company obtains a corporation tax deduction and no NIC is payable by the company or the individual on the rent.

6.6 Venture Capital Trust, Enterprise Investment Scheme and Seed Enterprise Investment Scheme Reliefs

Venture Capital Trusts (VCTs), the Enterprise Investment Scheme (EIS) and the Seed Enterprise Investment Scheme (SEIS) were covered in detail at CA Proficiency 1. Refer to your *Taxation 1* textbook to refresh your knowledge. Take care not to confuse the CGT deferral for reinvestment into EIS shares with the income tax relief available.

6.6.1 VCT Reliefs

Prior to 6 April 2004, it was possible to defer capital gains by investing the proceeds in VCTs. Although income tax relief is still available for investments in VCTs, it is no longer possible to defer capital gains.

However, the sale of shares in VCTs themselves is exempt from capital gains, so that no chargeable gain arises on a profit and any loss arising is not an allowable loss.

6.6.2 EIS Reliefs

It is possible for individuals or trustees to defer capital gains on the disposal of any asset by subscribing for shares in a company qualifying under the Enterprise Investment Scheme (EIS). It is also possible to obtain income tax relief for EIS subscriptions, but this is subject to limits and additional conditions.

This section looks solely at using EIS for CGT deferral under the rules contained in Schedule 5B TCGA 1992.

All or part of a capital gain can be deferred by investing in one or more qualifying EIS companies within one year before, or up to three years after, the gain arises.

The individual or trustees must subscribe wholly in cash for eligible shares in a qualifying company and be UK resident at that time. Eligible shares are irredeemable shares which do not carry any preferential rights to dividends, assets on a winding up, etc.

Shares issued on or after 6 April 2012 can carry preferential rights and still qualify, provided the amount of dividends and payment date is not dependent on a decision by the company, the holder or anyone else and that the dividends are not cumulative.

If the EIS investment is made in the year before the gain to be deferred arises, the shares must still be owned when the gain is made.

Conditions

EIS deferral relief for CGT is only given in the following circumstances:

1. the individual's share investment is used to finance a **qualifying trade** by the company or its subsidiary;
2. at least 80% of the proceeds from the share issue are used for that trade within 12 months of the share issue date or, if later, 12 months from the commencement of trading;
3. the investee company is a **qualifying company**; and
4. the share issue is made for bona fide commercial purposes and not for tax avoidance.

A **qualifying trade** is any trade except the following excluded activities:

- dealing in land, commodities or futures;
- dealing in shares, securities or other financial instruments;
- dealing in goods other than in the course of an ordinary trade of wholesale or retail distribution;
- banking, insurance, moneylending, debt-factoring, hire-purchase financing or other financial activities;
- leasing (including letting ships on charter, or other assets on hire);
- receiving royalties or licence fees (except in relation to internally generated assets);
- providing legal or accountancy services;
- property development;
- farming and market gardening;
- holding, managing or occupying woodlands, any other forestry activities or timber production;
- operating or managing hotels or comparable establishments, or managing property used as such;
- operating or managing nursing homes or residential care homes, or managing property used as such; or
- providing services or facilities for any of the above trades where a controlling interest in the trade is held by the same person who also has a controlling interest in the company providing the services or facilities.

For shares issued on or after 6 April 2012, the definition of a qualifying business activity excludes acquiring shares in another company and the receipt of feed-in tariffs or similar subsidies for electricity generation.

For shares issued on or after 6 April 2015, further excluded activities include the subsidised generation or export of electricity, the subsidised generation of heat and the subsidised production of gas or fuel.

In order to be a **qualifying company**, the investee company's balance sheet gross assets must not:

- exceed £15 million before the relevant shares are issued; and
- exceed £16 million after the relevant shares are issued.

Also, the number of employees must not exceed 250.

The company must also meet the qualifying conditions, set out below, when the investment is made and in the following three years:

1. the investee company should be an unquoted company, which need not be UK resident, but must have a permanent establishment (PE) in the UK;
2. the company must not be in financial difficulty when the shares are issued; and
3. the company must exist wholly or substantially for the purpose of carrying on one or more qualifying trades or be the parent company of a qualifying trading group. It cannot be a 51% subsidiary of another company or controlled by another company.

Reinvesting in Own Company

Unlike income tax relief for EIS investments, **there is no "connection" test for CGT deferral**. This means that an individual can obtain CGT deferral by subscribing for shares in his own company.

However, no CGT deferral is given if shares are acquired in the company in which the original gain was made or any fellow group company.

Where the investor is a director of the investee company, no more than a reasonable level of remuneration should be paid to him in the first three years to prevent jeopardising the relief.

As can be seen from the list of excluded trades, lower risk activities (often backed by substantial property assets) are excluded from the relief. Many people will be nervous about investing funds in higher risk trading companies.

The relief is most likely to be of use where the investor also has a role in managing the investee company.

Example 6.3

Derek receives proceeds of £500,000 on the sale of an investment residential property in Cookstown in February 2017. He acquired the property for £350,000 in July 2003.

Derek is the sole shareholder in a qualifying trading company, Manhattan Fashions Ltd. After consulting his tax advisor, he decides to defer some of his gain by subscribing £120,000 in cash for the issue of eligible shares by Manhattan Fashions Ltd and claim EIS deferral relief.

Calculate the amount of the gain deferred and the CGT payable in 2016/17 by Derek on the basis that this is his only chargeable disposal, and he is a higher rate taxpayer.

Solution

	£
Proceeds	500,000
Less: cost	(350,000)
Gain	150,000
Less: EIS deferral	(120,000)
Gain remaining chargeable	30,000
Less: annual exemption	(11,000)
Chargeable gain	19,000
CGT @ 28%	5,320

The gain deferred by investing in new shares in Manhattan Fashions Ltd is £120,000.

Advance Clearance Procedure

HMRC operates an advance clearance procedure to confirm whether a potential investee company satisfies the conditions to be a qualifying company and whether the rules for the share issue are met.

This advance clearance procedure should be used to provide assurance that investing in a company will result in EIS deferral of a capital gain.

Operation of the Relief

EIS CGT deferral relief operates by a claim being made to defer a specified amount of the gain by matching it against the investment expenditure on the relevant EIS shares. As the amount specified may be all or part of the gain there is complete flexibility in the amount of relief taken.

The deferred gain is held over, but (unlike section 165 relief) does not reduce the base cost of the EIS shares. Previously, deferred gains were not eligible for ER when the gain crystallised. However, for gains arising on disposals on or after 3 December 2014, ER is now available on the crystallisation of a deferred gain if it would have been eligible for ER at the time of the original disposal.

The **deferred gain will crystallise** as a result of any of the following events:

1. The sale or transfer of the EIS shares at any time (except on the transfer to a spouse or civil partner).
2. Where the individual becomes non-resident within three years of the share issue (except in certain cases where full-time employment is taken overseas).
3. Where the EIS shares cease to be eligible (for example, as a result of the company ceasing to be qualifying) within three years following the share issue or, if later, the commencement of trade.
4. Where the investor receives value from the investee company within one year before and three years after the share issue or, if later, the commencement of trade. This excludes the receipt of reasonable director's remuneration and dividends representing a normal return on the shares.

6.6.3 SEIS Reliefs

The Seed Enterprise Investment Scheme (SEIS) was introduced with effect from 6 April 2012.

The purpose of the scheme is to encourage investment in smaller, early stage companies carrying on, or preparing to carry on, a new business in a qualifying trade.

There are income tax reliefs for investors who subscribe for shares and who have a stake of less than 30% in the company. What is of more interest for the purposes of this chapter, however, is that the scheme provides CGT relief where gains are reinvested in a qualifying SEIS investment, i.e. gains realised on the disposal of assets that are invested through the SEIS will qualify for a 50% relief from CGT.

The legislation for the CGT reinvestment relief is at Schedule 5BB TCGA 1992.

An exemption from CGT is also available on gains on SEIS shares if they are held for more than three years (provided certain conditions are met).

The SEIS will apply to smaller companies (i.e. those with 25 or fewer employees and gross assets of up to £200,000) that are carrying on or preparing to carry on a new business. It will apply to subscriptions for shares, using the same definition of eligible shares as used by the EIS.

There is an annual investment limit for individual investors of £100,000. The investee company can only receive up to a limit of £150,000 through the scheme (this is a cumulative limit, not an annual limit).

A CGT exemption is available in respect of gains made on any other assets disposed of by the investor where the gain (rather than the proceeds) is reinvested in SEIS shares in that same year or the following tax year. This exemption is 50% of the amount of the gain reinvested.

The formula involved in calculating the availability of the CGT reinvestment relief is complex and may result in the relief being less than 50% of the £100,000 annual investment limit.

6.7 Business Property Relief and Agricultural Property Relief for Inheritance Tax

The detailed rules applying in these areas can be found in **Sections 24.1** and **24.2** of *CA Proficiency 2: Taxation 2 (NI) 2016–2017.*

6.7.1 Business Property Relief

Business property relief (BPR) is an important IHT relief that reduces or extinguishes IHT on chargeable lifetime transfers or on death. The legislation is contained in sections 103–114 Inheritance Tax Act 1984 (IHTA 1984).

Be aware that some types of business asset qualify for 100% relief, while others only qualify for 50% relief.

"Relevant Business Property"
BPR applies on transfers of "relevant business property". This is defined by section 105(1) IHTA 1984 as:

"(a)   property consisting of a business or interest in a business;

(b)   securities of a company which are unquoted and which (either by themselves or together with other such securities owned by the transferor and any unquoted shares so owned) gave the transferor control of the company immediately before the transfer;

(bb)   any unquoted shares in a company;

(c)   [repealed];

(cc)   shares in, or securities of, a company which are quoted and which (either by themselves or together with other such shares or securities owned by the transferor) gave the transferor control of the company immediately before the transfer;

(d)   any land or building, machinery or plant which, immediately before the transfer, was used wholly or mainly for the purposes of a business carried on by a company of which the transferor then had control or by a partnership of which he then was a partner; and

(e)   any land or building, machinery or plant which, immediately before the transfer, was used wholly or mainly for the purposes of a business carried on by the transferor and was settled property in which he was then beneficially entitled to an interest in possession."

Assets within section 105(1)(a), (b) and (bb) qualify for **100% relief**, while the others qualify for 50% relief.

"Business"
Note that, unlike the CGT reliefs discussed above, there is no reference in section 105(1) to trading companies or "personal" companies. Although it is often stated that BPR applies to shares in a "trading" company, the legislation refers to a "business" rather than a "trade". **Business is generally wider than trade.**

Section 105(3) states that a business or interest in a business, or shares in or securities of a company, are not relevant business property if the business or, as the case may be, the business carried on by the company, consists wholly or mainly of one or more of the following: dealing in securities, stocks or shares, land or buildings or making or holding investments.

Thus the **legislation excludes certain types of business**. Although dealing in land or buildings is excluded, property development is considered to be a qualifying business activity. Section 105(3) uses a **wholly or mainly test**, rather than the "substantial" test that is used in the CGT reliefs.

"Substantial" requires more than 80% of the activities to be trading activities, whereas "wholly or mainly" only requires more than 51% of the activities to be qualifying. HMRC will look at the turnover, profit and underlying asset values of each activity over a reasonable period before the relevant transfer, to determine if it meets the wholly or mainly test.

Under section 111 IHTA 1984, shares in the holding company of a qualifying group will qualify for BPR. The relief will be restricted to the extent that the value of the holding company's shares derives from any non-qualifying activities carried on by members of the group.

Excepted Assets

BPR is not available on any excepted assets that form part of the relevant business property. **This can occur where the shares in a company qualify for BPR, but the company holds excepted assets.**

An asset is an "excepted asset" where it was not used wholly or mainly for trading purposes in the previous two years, unless it is required for future use in the business. The restriction works by excluding the part of the value transferred that is attributable to the excepted asset.

HMRC will seek to apply the "excepted assets" rule to investments, let property and substantial cash balances.

A business holding large cash balances should be able to demonstrate that the cash is required for the future needs of the business (e.g. a programme of capital expenditure) if it wishes to avoid it being treated as an excepted asset.

There can be a danger where a company makes loans to connected parties, as HMRC may argue that the company is not in the business of making loans and may seek to treat the value of the loan debtors as an excepted asset.

Where possible, planning should be undertaken within companies and groups of companies to minimise the excepted assets and, therefore, to maximise BPR for the owners. For instance, where a holding company owns both trading and investment subsidiaries, it may be tax efficient to undertake a reorganisation to create two groups, i.e. one trading group qualifying for BPR and one investment group that will not qualify. The tax efficiency of this will depend on the percentage of trading versus investment assets.

Lifetime versus Death Transfers

BPR gives shareholders a tax incentive to retain qualifying shares until death, as the value of the shares will be sheltered from IHT.

Although BPR is also available on chargeable lifetime transfers and on all transfers becoming chargeable on the owner's death within seven years, BPR will only be available on death where the donee retains the shares and the shares still qualify for relief at this time.

Unless the shares are transferred to a trust of which the donor is a trustee, the donor will have little control over the shares once transferred and may not be able to prevent the donee disposing of them and thereby increasing the donor's potential IHT liability.

6.7.2   *Agricultural Property Relief*

Agricultural property relief (APR) is similar to BPR. The legislation is found in sections 115–124C IHTA 1984.

Note that the relief is available only on the agricultural value of the land or buildings, which is not necessarily the market value.

6.7.3   Interaction of APR and BPR

Where the market value of the land exceeds the agricultural value of the land qualifying for APR, it may be possible to claim BPR on the non-agricultural value. It is the view of tax practitioners in Northern Ireland that the letting of agricultural land on conacre terms constitutes a business qualifying for BPR.

This view has been successfully challenged by HMRC in *McCall & Another v. Revenue & Customs Commissioners* ((2009) NICA 12). The NI Court of Appeal upheld the Special Commissioners' decision that the letting of agricultural land under conacre was a business consisting of wholly or mainly holding investments within the meaning of section 105(3) and, therefore, the non-agricultural value of the land did not qualify for BPR. However, the facts of this case were particularly favourable to HMRC and there has been no change in the legislation to deal specifically with conacre lettings.

6.7.4   EU Law and APR

Prior to Finance Act 2009 (FA 2009), APR was available only if the agricultural property was situated in the UK, the Channel Islands or the Isle of Man. This provision in the legislation was considered to be incompatible with the freedom of movement of capital contained in the EC Treaty, as it gave favourable tax treatment to UK domiciled individuals who invested in agricultural property in the UK, rather than any other EU Member State.

Similar reliefs in other EU jurisdictions have been found by the ECJ to be incompatible with the EC Treaty.

As a result, on 29 January 2009, the European Commission (EC) formally requested that the UK amend its legislation on reliefs for agricultural and forestry property because the reliefs did not extend to property elsewhere in the European Union (EU) or European Economic Area (EEA). The EC argued that the limited scope of the relief may have dissuaded taxpayers from investing in agricultural or forestry property outside the UK.

The APR legislation was amended by section 121 FA 2009. The relief is now extended to agricultural land in any EEA Member State.

6.8   Other Inheritance Tax Reliefs

Please review the other types of IHT relief available, details of which can be found in *CA Proficiency 2: Taxation 2 (NI) 2016–2017*:

- quick succession relief (**Section 24.3**);
- relief for the surviving spouse of a deceased person (**Section 24.4**);
- fall in value of gift before death (**Section 24.5**);
- growing timber relief (**Section 24.6**); and
- post-mortem relief (**Section 24.7**).

6.8.1   Normal Expenditure Out of Income

In addition to the above reliefs, it should be remembered that there is an exemption from IHT for "**normal expenditure out of income**". This is contained in section 21 IHTA 1984 and exempts transfers of value from IHT where the following three conditions are met:

1. it was made as part of the normal expenditure of the transferor;
2. taking one year with another, it was made out of their income; and
3. after allowing for all transfers of value forming part of their normal expenditure, the transferor was left with sufficient income to maintain their usual standard of living.

Where an individual has a large amount of annual income, e.g. the salary of a managing director of a successful company, a pattern should be established of making regular gifts to, or payments on behalf of, family members with the aim of benefitting from the exemption in section 21.

6.8.2   Relief for the Surviving Spouse/Civil Partner of a Deceased Person

Relief for the surviving spouse of a deceased person takes the form of being able to transfer unused nil rate bands from a deceased spouse or civil partner. This relief was introduced by FA 2008 inserting sections 8A–8C into IHTA 1984, and applies where the death of the surviving spouse occurs on or after 9 October 2007.

   This legislation was very welcome. It is often the case that Wills provide for the entire estate to pass to the surviving spouse or civil partner. Where the recipient is UK domiciled, this will be an exempt transfer for IHT. Prior to the introduction of the new legislation, the downside was that the nil rate band of the deceased spouse was often unutilised and was therefore lost.

   The commencement date of 9 October 2007 applies only to the date of death of the surviving spouse; it is irrelevant when the first death occurred. It is the percentage of the unused nil rate band which can be used by the surviving spouse, based on the nil rate band at the date of the surviving spouse's death.

Example 6.4

Owen died in 1992, leaving his entire estate to his wife, Caroline, and not using any of his nil rate band. Caroline dies in March 2016 without having remarried and having made no lifetime gifts. Her estate, worth £1 million, is left to her daughter.

As Owen did not use any of his nil rate band, Caroline's nil rate band is increased by 100%. The nil rate band applying on her death will be doubled from £325,000 to £650,000, leaving £350,000 of her estate subject to IHT at 40%.

Questions

Review Questions

(See Suggested Solutions to Review Questions at the end of this textbook.)

Question 6.1

David Sharp dies on 10 October 2016, having made no gifts in the previous seven years.

   His wife, Isobel, died in June 2002, leaving a chargeable estate of £121,000 to her son, Charlie. The nil rate band at that time was £242,000.

   David leaves his entire estate to his son, Charlie. His estate is comprised of the following assets:

- Family home valued at £900,000.
- Personal chattels and cash worth £40,000.

■ 51% of the share capital in Sharp Suits plc, a trading company listed on the London Stock Exchange. The value of the shares for IHT purposes is £2 million.

■ The entire share capital in Sharp Retail Ltd, a retailer of accessories through a chain of high-street shops. The shares have been valued for IHT purposes at £1.5 million. The company's assets include £300,000 of cash deposits, which are required neither for working capital nor for the purposes of the business.

■ A warehouse, which is let to Sharp Retail Ltd and used by the company in its trade. The property has been valued at £750,000.

Requirement

Calculate the chargeable value of David's estate.

Question 6.2

It is November 2016 and you are the tax advisor for Massive Bargains Ltd and its shareholders. The company was founded in 2003 by Paul Murphy and Luke Walsh and runs a chain of discount warehouse stores. Paul's wife, Maggie, and Luke's wife, Rachel, also own shares in the company. All the existing shareholders subscribed for their share capital at nominal value in 2003.

Last month, Paul gifted 100 ordinary £0.01 shares to his daughter, Jo, who is the company's sales director. This was done to reward and motivate Jo, who has substantially increased sales since she began working for the company in 2013. Her annual salary is £75,000.

The shareholdings in the company before and after the gift are as follows:

	No. of shares held before gift	No. of shares held after gift
Paul Murphy	720	620
Luke Walsh	680	680
Maggie Murphy	300	300
Rachel Walsh	300	300
Jo McCann	-	100
Total issued shares	2,000	2,000

Paul did not take tax advice before making the gift. His understanding is that there are no tax consequences if a CGT holdover claim is made and Jo has agreed to enter into this claim.

Paul has called to tell you about the gift of shares and to confirm that there are no tax consequences. You have asked him to send through full details, as you do not believe it is so straightforward.

The values of the shares in the company are as follows:

Holding	Value
0% – 20%	£1,000 per share
21% – 50%	£1,500 per share
51% or greater	£3,000 per share

The company does not have any substantial non-trading activities. Paul has not made any CGT disposals in the last three years.

Requirement

Write a letter to Paul explaining the tax issues arising from the gift of shares to Jo.

Challenging Questions

(Suggested Solutions to Challenging Questions are available through your lecturer.)

Question 6.1

Perry runs a boat repair yard and servicing business in Kilkeel. He bought the business in 2002. Initially the business was very profitable, but in 2014 and 2015 it made very substantial losses as a result of the loss of a large contract. Consequently, Perry scaled back the level of activities and so stabilised the trading position. However, he remains confident that there is a good future for the business when trading conditions improve.

Between 2002 and 2008, Perry reinvested the profits made in buying residential property in and around Newcastle, Co. Down, for letting. The residential properties are 1–4 Tullymore Cottages and Block 1 Mourne View Apartments. These properties provide a good rental stream, which has supported the business in recent years.

The business made a profit of £60,000 in the year ended 30 April 2016, but no income tax was payable by Perry due to losses brought forward. At 1 May 2016, Perry had £120,000 of unutilised losses carried forward.

The balance sheet at 30 April 2016 is:

	£	£
Kilkeel repair yard premises at cost	500,000	
Residential properties at cost	750,000	
Plant and machinery at NBV	67,800	
		1,317,800
Work in progress	106,300	
Debtors	725,200	
Cash	8,500	
		840,000
Bank overdraft	(175,000)	
Creditors	(680,900)	
		(855,900)
		1,301,900
Current and capital accounts:		
Brought forward		1,241,900
Profit for the year		60,000
		1,301,900

The current market values of the properties are as follows:

	£
Kilkeel repair yard	700,000
1–4 Tullymore Cottages	800,000
Block 1 Mourne View Apartments	600,000
	2,100,000

The tax written-down value of the plant and machinery pool at 30 April 2016 was £95,683. The plant and machinery has been independently valued at £60,000.

Perry does not believe that the business currently has any saleable goodwill. Perry has previously resisted incorporating the business, but now believes that there is no alternative because of the substantial trading risks concerned. He is also concerned about his trading reputation and wishes to disclose a strong balance sheet. After incorporation, Perry has suggested a share capital of £2 million.

In June 2018, Perry decides that he would like to gift 30% of the shares in the company to a family trust for the benefit of his son, Keith (age 26), and his daughter, Kelly (age 19). At that time, the market value of a 30% holding in the company is £800,000, with the remaining 70% being valued at £2.7 million.

At that time, the company's balance sheet was:

	£	£
Kilkeel repair yard premises at cost	950,000	
Residential properties at cost	1,400,000	
Plant and machinery at NBV	90,800	
		2,440,800
Work in progress	236,300	
Debtors	1,253,200	
Cash	10,500	
		1,500,000
Bank overdraft	(385,000)	
Creditors	(906,900)	
		(1,291,900)
		2,648,900
Share capital		2,000,000
Reserves		648,900
		2,648,900

It is estimated that the value of business goodwill not appearing on the company's balance sheet is £100,000. The market value of the Kilkeel repair yard is estimated to be £1 million and the market value of the residential properties is estimated to be £1.6 million.

Perry has never made a transfer of value and is a higher rate taxpayer.

Requirement
(a) Comment on whether section 162 TCGA 1992 or section 165 TCGA 1992 can apply to the transfer of the business properties into a company on incorporation.
(b) Determine the amount of CGT payable by Perry and the base cost of the shares in the new company on the assumption that section 162 TCGA 1992 applies to the incorporation.
(c) Comment on the potential downsides, from a tax perspective, if the business is incorporated on 1 May 2016 and share capital of £2 million is issued.
(d) Comment on the tax implications of the gift of shares by Perry and calculate any CGT or IHT payable by Perry as a result of the gift. (Assume that 2016/17 rates continue to apply.)

Capital Taxes Planning for Individuals

7.1 Choice of Operating Entity

The main types of entity that can be used to operate a business in the UK are:

■ sole trade;
■ unlimited partnership;
■ limited liability partnership (LLP); and
■ limited company.

The choice of operating entity from an income or corporation tax perspective will be influenced by considerations such as the rate of tax payable on funds withdrawn and retained earnings, loss reliefs, the need for limited liability, etc. It is important to remember that the choice of business entity will also impact on the capital taxes payable.

7.1.1 Sole Traders and Individual Partners

Individuals carrying on a sole trade or acting as a partner in an unlimited or limited liability partnership are subject to income tax on the income profits of the business. They will therefore suffer 40% tax plus 2% NIC on earnings between £43,000 and £150,000, and 45% tax plus 2% NIC on earnings above £150,000. The personal allowance is reduced by £1 for every £2 of income over £100,000. Capital gains arising in the sole trade or partnership will be chargeable to CGT at 10% or 20% on the individual (or 18%/28% if the gain is on residential property or carried interest).

The **main tax advantage** of operating as a sole trade or partnership is that, because there is no additional tax charge on the extraction of cash from the business, no double charge to tax arises.

The **main tax disadvantage** is that a sole trader or partner is taxed according to the taxable profits of the business, not the sums withdrawn, which can cause difficulties where profits are retained in the business for reinvestment or cash flow does not permit profits to be withdrawn.

The introduction of the additional rate of income tax for income exceeding £150,000 on 6 April 2010 (currently 45%) has made operating as a sole trader or partnership less attractive for very profitable businesses.

7.1.2 Companies

A company will pay corporation tax at a rate of 20% on income and capital profits. However, **additional tax will be payable by individual shareholders in a company when cash is extracted**.

A company may be a **more tax-efficient vehicle when income profits are being retained for reinvestment**, due to the lower level of corporation tax compared to income tax.

7.1.3 Sole Trade or Company?

Calculations should be undertaken for each client, looking at the level of the profits generated by the business and the extent to which the profits are to be withdrawn for personal use by the owners. Special attention should be paid to the new rules for the taxation of dividend income introduced by Finance Act 2016, with effect from 6 April 2016.

Example 7.1

Louisa runs a book shop as a sole trade. She wishes to know if it would be more tax efficient for the business to be run through a company. Louisa made taxable profits of £100,000 in the year ended 31 March 2017. If the business was run through a company, Louisa would wish to withdraw £50,000 per annum in dividends from the business.

Assuming that Louisa has no other taxable income and there are no associated companies, compare the tax payable by Louisa as a sole trader with the overall tax payable if she incorporated and withdrew £50,000 in dividends.

Solution

Sole trade

Income tax:	£	£	£
Total income	100,000		
Less: personal allowance	(11,000)		
Taxable income	89,000		
Income tax payable:			
£32,000 @ 20%		6,400	
£57,000 @ 40%		22,800	
			29,200

continued overleaf

Class 4 NIC payable:

£8,060 @ 0%	0
(£43,000 – £8,060) @ 9%	3,145
£57,000 @ 2%	1,140
	4,285
Total payable	**33,485**

Note: Class 2 NICs have been ignored as negligible.

Company

	£	£	£
Corporation tax:			
£100,000 @ 20%			20,000
Income tax:			
Total income	50,000		
Less: personal allowance	(11,000)		
Less: dividend allowance	(5,000)		
Taxable income	34,000		
Income tax payable:			
£32,000 @ 7.5%		2,400	
£2,000 @ 32.5%		650	
			3,050
NIC payable			0
Total payable			**23,050**

As Louisa is retaining a significant percentage of the profits in the business, there is a saving of nearly £10,500 per annum in tax in operating through a company rather than as a sole trade. This saving should be weighed against the additional administration required for a company before any decision is made. Also, as noted at **Section 7.1.2**, the reserves of £30,000 left in the company will be subject to tax on Louisa if they are eventually distributed to her.

In the example above, the new dividend taxation rules introduced by Finance Act 2016, with effect from April 2016, are applied. Prior to April 2016, an effective rate of tax of 25% was applied to dividends falling within the higher rate band. The rate of income tax for dividends falling within the top rate of income tax was 37.5% and a notional tax credit of 10% was attached to the payment, meaning the effective rate was therefore 30.55%. The calculation of these effective rates was illustrated in **Example 7.2** below.

Example 7.2

On 30 April 2015, Peony Ltd pays a dividend of £9,000 each to its three equal shareholders, Liang, Sek and Jung. Liang is a basic rate taxpayer, Sek is a higher rate taxpayer and Jung is a top rate taxpayer. Calculate the income tax payable by each of them on the dividend from Peony Ltd.

Solution

	Liang	Sek	Jung
	£	£	£
Dividend income:			
£9,000 × 10/9	10,000	10,000	10,000
Income tax @ 10%/32.5%/37.5%	1,000	3,250	3,750
Less: notional tax credit (£9,000 × 1/9)	(1,000)	(1,000)	(1,000)
Income tax payable	0	2,250	2,750
Income tax payable as % of dividend received (£9,000)	0%	25%	30.55%

These effective rates were useful as a quick method of calculating the income tax on a dividend based on the dividend received. It is worthwhile to note that dividends falling within the basic rate band did not actually incur any income tax due to the notional tax credit.

7.1.4   Limited Liability Partnership

A limited liability partnership (LLP) is a useful vehicle as it **allows liability to be limited** to the amount of capital invested in the LLP by a member but is **"look-through" for tax purposes**, and thus taxed in the same way as an unlimited partnership.

Companies can be partners in a general partnership or members in an LLP.

An LLP can be used in a structure to combine the tax advantages of operating as a sole trader with those of operating as a company.

Example 7.3

Mark operates a highly successful sole trade and makes taxable profits of £2 million per annum. He has an extravagant lifestyle and withdraws £1 million per annum from the business for personal use.

At present, Mark is paying 45% income tax plus 2% NIC on the profits of the sole trade, equating to £940,000 per annum. (As the numbers are large, the lower tax bands can be ignored for comparison purposes.)

If the business was incorporated, the company would pay 20% corporation tax on profits, being £400,000. Mark would then pay income tax on extracted profits, say 38.1% on a dividend of £1 million, i.e. £381,000. The total tax payable is £781,000, which saves £159,000 per annum compared to operating as a sole trade.

Consider the situation if Mark formed a limited company, of which he was the sole shareholder, and Mark and the limited company formed an LLP to carry on the business. Profits could be shared 50/50.

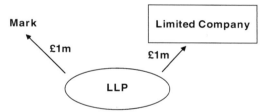

If the LLP makes profits of £2 million, 50% will be allocated to Mark and taxed at 47% (income tax plus NIC), being £470,000. The other 50% will be allocated to the company and taxed at 20%, being £200,000. This reduces the total tax payable to £670,000.

This is achieved by the company receiving the share of profits to be retained in the business, due to the lower rate of corporation tax. Mark receives his personal funds directly, in his capacity as a member of the LLP, and therefore avoids the double tax charge.

There can be a tax cost to creating these structures once the business has been running for some years. This cost should be weighed against the potential future tax advantages. If a high level of profit is expected from the outset, this structure could be created to operate the business.

7.1.5   Partnerships and Land

Care should be taken when holding UK land or property in a partnership as a change in the profit-sharing ratio of a partner in the partnership can trigger a liability to SDLT.

This applies where the partnership is a **property-investment partnership**, as defined by paragraph 14, Schedule 15 FA 2003. A property-investment partnership is one whose sole or main activity is investing or dealing in land or property.

7.2   Methods of Cash Extraction

As discussed above, although rates of corporation tax are generally lower than income tax rates, **there is additional tax to be paid by shareholders in a company when profits are extracted from that company**. The main methods of extracting income from a company are:

- dividends;
- salary/bonus/benefits-in-kind;
- termination payments;
- pension contributions;
- loans to participators; and
- rent of company premises owned personally.

You should be familiar with the tax consequences of each of these methods from your previous studies and therefore the points below will focus on planning, rather than calculation of tax liabilities.

7.2.1   Dividend versus Salary

Due to the dividend allowance (currently £5,000) and lower rates of income tax on dividends in the UK (7.5% for basic rate taxpayers, 32.5% for higher rate taxpayers and 38.1% for additional rate taxpayers), plus the fact that NIC is not charged on dividends, **dividends can be a tax-efficient method of extracting profits from a company**.

The lower income tax rates should be weighed against the corporation tax implications, as a **company pays dividends from post-tax profits and so does not receive a tax deduction for dividends paid**.

Dividends can only be paid where there are sufficient distributable reserves and so may not be suitable in the early years of a company or where the company has been loss-making for a number of years.

Remuneration paid to working shareholders of the company will be **subject to income tax (through PAYE) and employer and employee NIC**. Therefore, the effective rates of tax payable by the individual are higher than for dividends. However, **the company will be able to obtain a tax deduction for the remuneration plus the employer NIC**.

The combined effective rates of tax on dividends versus remuneration should be calculated for each scenario.

Example 7.4

Doone Ltd makes profits of £100,000 in the year ended 31 March 2017. Lorna is the sole shareholder and wishes to extract all the profits by either salary or dividend. Assume that Lorna's entire income is taxed at the 40% rate and that earnings are all in excess of the upper earnings level for NIC purposes.

Calculate the effective total rate of tax on dividends versus salary.

Solution

On the basis that all the profits are used to pay Lorna's salary and related NIC, the effective rate of tax on salary will be the same regardless of the rate of corporation tax:

	£	£	£
Corporation tax:			
Profits before extraction		100,000	
Less: Salary	(87,873)		
Employer NIC @ 13.8%	(12,127)		
		(100,000)	
Profits subject to corporation tax		Nil	

continued overleaf

Income tax:	
£87,873 @ 40%	35,149
Employee NIC:	
£87,873 @ 2%	1,758
Total payable by Lorna	36,907
Gross profits	100,000
Employer NIC	(12,127)
Income tax	(35,149)
Employee NIC	(1,758)
Net received by Lorna	**50,966**

Therefore, £49,034 has been paid in tax, giving an overall effective tax rate of 49.03%.

Where profits are extracted by way of dividend, the effective rate will depend on the rate of corporation tax.

	£
Corporation tax:	
Taxable profits	100,000
Less: corporation tax @ 20%	(20,000)
Profits after tax	80,000
Dividend paid	(80,000)
Retained profits	Nil
Income tax:	
Dividend after £5,000 allowance @ 32.5%	24,375

	£
Gross profits	100,000
Corporation tax @ 20%	(20,000)
Income tax	(24,375)
Net received by Lorna	**55,625**
Overall effective rate of tax	**44.38%**

Therefore, in this example, dividends are the most tax-efficient form of extraction.

It is advisable for shareholders who work in the company to take a small salary, say £10,000 per annum, to utilise the personal allowance and pay a small amount of NIC to secure entitlement to state benefits.

7.2.2 Termination Payments

Where an employment is terminated (e.g. through retirement or redundancy), there may be scope for the employee to receive the first £30,000 of a termination payment tax-free. This is based on the exemption in sections 401–403 Income Tax (Earnings and Pensions) Act 2003.

However, this exemption applies only where the payment is not taxable under the general taxation of employment income rules.

Except in the case of a genuine redundancy payment, where there is a contractual right to the termination payment or a reasonable expectation of receiving a termination payment, then the receipt of the payment will be treated as taxable earnings from the employment and the £30,000 exemption will not be available.

It can be difficult to achieve a tax-free termination payment, particularly where it is made to an employee/director who has a significant shareholding in the company.

7.2.3 Pension Contributions

There is some scope to make tax-efficient pension contributions. From an extraction of funds perspective, it is tax-efficient if pension contributions are made by a company on behalf of an employee or director.

Company contributions to a registered pension scheme can be deducted as a trading expense in the period in which they are paid, provided they are "wholly and exclusively" incurred for the purposes of the company's trade.

The maximum amount that the company can contribute for each employee or director is the annual allowance, which is £40,000 for 2016/17. It should be noted that the annual allowance includes contributions made by the individual. So if, for example, a director makes a personal contribution to their pension scheme of £30,000, then the employer could only make a contribution of £10,000 in the same tax year. In the event that the annual allowance is exceeded, the individual will be subject to an annual allowance charge, taxed at the taxpayer's marginal rate of tax.

From 6 April 2016 the allowance is reduced by £1 for each £2 of income between £150,000 and £210,000. The minimum allowance for those earning £210,000 or more will be £10,000. Unused annual allowances for the preceding three tax years can still be used via the existing carry-forward rules.

Company pension contributions for a working shareholder are an excellent method of reducing the corporation tax liability in a profitable year. **However, as the tax deduction is available only in the year in which the contribution is paid, it is vital that this tax planning takes place before the year end.** The company must have the cash available to make and pay the pension contribution before the year end.

Example 7.5

Harris Ltd is estimating that taxable profits for the year ending 31 March 2017 will be £400,000. The two shareholders of the company are Tom and Julie Harris, both of whom are full-time working directors of the company. The company operates a Small Self-Administered Pension Scheme (SSAS) for the benefit of the directors, but no pension contributions have been made in the year to date. There are no associated companies. Tom and Julie have annual income of under £30,000 each.

It is February 2017 and Tom and Julie have asked for your advice on reducing the corporation tax payable by the company for the year ending 31 March 2017.

The company's corporation tax liability without any planning will be:

£400,000 @ 20% =   £80,000

If the company chooses to pay pension contributions to the SSAS for Tom and Julie before 31 March 2016 totalling £80,000, the corporation tax liability will be reduced by £16,000.

This could also be achieved by paying a bonus to Tom and Julie. This would decrease the corporation tax liability, but would result in income tax and NIC being payable. The pension contribution does not result in any additional tax liabilities.

Each person's pension is subject to a lifetime allowance, which is £1 million for 2016/17. There can be adverse tax consequences if this lifetime limit is exceeded.

7.2.4 Loans to Participators

Loans to participators in close companies are generally regarded as being ill-advised, due to the 32.5% section 455 tax payable by the company if the loan remains outstanding for more than nine months and one day after the end of the accounting period. This rate was increased from 25% by Finance Act 2016 (with effect from 6 April 2016) following the changes to dividend taxation. Transitional rules will apply in respect of accounting periods straddling 1 April 2016, such that loans arising pre-1 April 2016 will be subject to the 25% rate, and loans made on or after 1 April 2016 will be subject to the 32.5% rate.

However, **interest-free loans to directors can be a useful short-term funding option**. No section 455 tax will be payable if the loan is fully repaid in time, although there will be a benefit-in-kind charge payable by the director under the beneficial loan rules.

> **Example 7.6**
> Paddy is the sole shareholder and managing director of a small trading company, Sunray Ltd. The company's year end is 30 June 2016. On 15 April 2016, Sunray Ltd makes an interest-free loan of £20,000 to Paddy. The company is due to pay its corporation tax for the year on 1 April 2017. Paddy is a higher rate taxpayer.
>
> What are the consequences for Sunray Ltd and Paddy if Paddy repays the loan in full on:
> 1. 15 March 2017?
> 2. 15 April 2017?
>
> *Solution*
> 1. Since the loan is repaid in full before 1 April 2017, Sunray Ltd will not have to pay section 455 tax at 32.5% of the loan. Paddy will be taxed under the benefit in kind rules and charged to income tax on interest on the loan at the official rate from 15 April 2016 to 15 March 2017. Say, 4% × 11/12 months × £20,000 = £733 @ 40% = £293.
> 2. Since the loan has not been repaid by 1 April 2017, Sunray Ltd must pay tax on that date at 32.5% of the loan, i.e. £5,000, and cannot claim repayment of the tax until the payment date for corporation tax for the year ending 30 June 2017, i.e. 1 April 2018.
>
>   Paddy will be taxed under the benefit in kind rules and charged to income tax on interest on the loan at the official rate from 15 April 2016 to 15 April 2017. Say, 4% × £20,000 = £800 @ 40% = £320. The amount will be allocated over the tax years.

Funds can be extracted from companies by writing off loans made to participators. This is not tax efficient for the following reasons:

- the loan write-off is taxed as a distribution on the participator and will therefore be subject to tax at 32.5% for higher rate taxpayers;
- the company will not be able to obtain a corporation tax deduction for the loan write-off;
- the release of the loan is likely to be treated as "earnings" for NIC purposes.

7.2.5 Rent of Company Premises Owned Personally

It may be tax efficient for one or more of a company's shareholders to hold the premises used by the company personally and rent them to the company for a market rent.

The company will obtain a corporation tax deduction for the rent paid and the owner will be subject to income tax on the net rental income.

This is more tax efficient than extracting salary from the company because no NIC is payable by the company or the individual on the rent.

7.2.6 Capital Taxes Consequences

There are no immediate CGT, IHT or stamp duty liabilities on the extraction of cash using any of the above methods. However, renting property to a company can impact on ER on the sale of the property as an associated disposal (see **Section 6.5.3**).

Furthermore, a business property held outside the company will qualify for 50% BPR only if the owner controls the company. Where a large amount of cash is withdrawn from a company whose shares qualify for IHT BPR, the shareholder has decreased the value of the shares and increased the amount of cash held in the estate. If the cash is invested in non-IHT-efficient investments, this could increase the IHT payable on the shareholder's death.

7.3 Company Buy-back of Shares

The acquisition by a company of its own shares is dealt with in detail in **Chapter 20** of the *CA Proficiency 2: Taxation 2 (NI) 2016–2017* textbook. You should also read HMRC *Statement of Practice 2/82* (SP 2/82), which discusses the "trade benefit test" in section 1033(2)(a) CTA 2010 and sets out the format for clearances under sections 1044 and 1045 CTA 2010. It is available as part of a pdf document at www.gov.uk/government/collections/statements-of-practice.

The purchase of own shares by a company will be a distribution for the shareholder and, under basic principles, is taxed as an income distribution under section 100 CTA 2010.

Where the conditions in sections 1033–1048 CTA 2010 are met, the buy-back of shares will be treated as a capital receipt and will be subject to CGT in the hands of the shareholder.

Regardless of the tax treatment, the company must have sufficient distributable reserves to undertake the buy-back. It is not a matter of electing for one treatment or the other. Where the conditions of section 1033 *et seq.* are met, the capital gains treatment is mandatory and automatic.

7.3.1 Income Distribution

Where the taxpayer wishes for the income treatment to apply, at least one of the conditions at section 1033 *et seq.* must be broken.

Prior to 23 June 2010, it was unusual for the income tax treatment on the buy-back of shares to be more tax efficient than the CGT treatment. The income tax treatment would have been preferred where the amount received on the buy-back was small and fell entirely within the basic rate band, meaning that the effective rate of income tax on the distribution was 0%.

However, the increase in the CGT rate to 28% for higher rate taxpayers, with effect from 23 June 2010, meant that more careful consideration had to be given as to whether income tax or CGT treatment was more tax-efficient. The new rates for CGT and dividend income introduced by Finance Act 2016 (and which took effect from 6 April 2016) return us to the pre-23 June 2010 situation, i.e. CGT treatment is likely to be the more tax-efficient. This is even more likely where the capital gain would qualify for entrepreneurs' relief (ER) and thus be taxed at 10%.

Example 7.7

Anna and Bert are equal shareholders in a small, unquoted trading company. The company was founded by Anna and Bert in 2000 when they each subscribed for one £1 ordinary share.

The company has been trading profitably for a number of years and has accumulated reserves of £200,000. Anna wishes to retire from the business and sell all her shares. Bert cannot afford to buy them personally, so their accountant has suggested that the company buy back Anna's 50% shareholding. Anna's shareholding has been valued at £80,000.

The share buy-back will take place in December 2016. Anna is expected to have income of £50,000 in 2016/17 and has already utilised her CGT annual exemption. Anna has previously utilised her full £10 million lifetime limit for ER.

Is income tax or CGT treatment more tax efficient for Anna?

Solution

Income Distribution
Taxable income = £74,999 (i.e. £80,000 less £1 subscribed for shares, less £5,000 dividend allowance)
Income tax payable = £74,999 @ 32.5% = £24,375

Capital Distribution

	£
Proceeds	80,000
Less: cost	(1)
Chargeable gain	79,999
CGT @ 20%	16,000

In these circumstances, the capital treatment will be more tax-efficient for Anna.

7.3.2 Capital Distribution

Provided certain conditions are met, the buy-back will not be treated as an income distribution. Rather, the shareholder will be treated as receiving a capital sum on the disposal of the shares equal to the amount paid.

This treatment applies only to the purchase of own shares by **unquoted trading companies** that are not 51% subsidiaries of a quoted company or unquoted holding companies.

Summary

The repurchase must be made to wholly or mainly benefit the trade carried on by the company or a 75% subsidiary, and must not be part of a scheme the main purpose of which is the avoidance of tax. In addition:

1. The vendor must be resident in the UK at the time of purchase.
2. The vendor must have owned the shares for at least five years (three years if as a result of death). Holding periods of a spouse will count.
3. There must be a substantial reduction in the vendor's shareholding (see below).
4. Following the buy-back, the vendor must not be connected with the company (see below).

The "Trade Benefit Test"

Where the CGT treatment is desired (as will usually be the case), one of the most difficult conditions to meet can be the condition in section 1033(2)(a) that the purchase is being made **wholly or mainly for the purpose of benefitting the company's trade** (or the trade of any of its 75% subsidiaries). This trade benefit test is discussed in SP 2/82.

HMRC states, at paragraph 1 of SP 2/82, that the trade benefit condition is not satisfied where the transaction is designed to serve the personal or wider commercial interests of the vending shareholder.

Paragraph 2 gives examples of circumstances where the buy-back will be regarded as satisfying the trade benefit test. These include removing a dissenting shareholder where a disagreement over the running of the company is having, or is expected to have, an adverse effect on the company's trade, and buying back the shares of an unwilling shareholder who wishes to end their association with the company to ensure that they do not sell their shares to someone who might not be acceptable to the other shareholders.

Paragraph 2 also gives examples of unwilling shareholders.

Substantial Reduction in the Vendor's Shareholding

Section 1037 CTA 2010 requires that the vendor's shareholding be substantially reduced as a result of the buy-back in order to qualify for the CGT treatment.

For this condition to be satisfied, the shareholding of the vendor and the associates must be reduced by a proportion of at least 25% as a result of the purchase of shares by the company. For example, a reduction in shareholding from 20% to 15% represents a 25% reduction in the original shareholding which is sufficient to meet this condition.

"Associate" for these purposes is defined by section 1057 and includes a spouse or civil partner, any trust created by them, and their minor children. **Adult children, siblings and parents are excluded from the definition of "associate" for these purposes.**

However, where a dissenting or unwilling shareholder retains shares in the company, HMRC is unlikely to accept that the trade benefit condition has been met. This is dealt with at paragraph 3 of SP 2/82.

If the company is not buying all the shares owned by the vendor, or the vendor is selling all the shares but retaining another connection with the company (e.g. a directorship, an appointment as a consultant), HMRC states that it is unlikely that the transaction could benefit the company's trade.

HMRC accepts that there are some exceptions. For example, where the company does not currently have the resources to buy out its retiring controlling shareholder completely, but purchases as many of his shares as it can afford with the intention of buying the remainder when possible.

HMRC also accepts that the trade benefit test can be met where a retiring director retains a small shareholding (not exceeding 5% of the issued share capital) for sentimental reasons.

Scheme or Arrangement

In addition to the trade benefit test, section 1033(2)(b) CTA 2010 requires that the redemption, repayment or purchase does not form part of a scheme or arrangement, the main purpose, or one of the main purposes, of which is:

1. to enable the owner of the shares to participate in the profits of the company without receiving a dividend; or
2. the avoidance of tax.

7.3.3 Advance Clearance Procedure

If a shareholder wishes to have the buy-back of shares treated as a capital gain, it is vital to demonstrate that there are commercial reasons for the transaction and that the transaction will benefit the trade.

Given the potential attractiveness of the CGT treatment over the income tax treatment, HMRC will look for sound reasons to satisfy itself that one of the main purposes of the transaction is not the avoidance of tax.

It is recommended that the vendor's tax advisors take advantage of the advance clearance procedure in section 1044 CTA 2010.

This clearance procedure allows the tax advisor to write to HMRC before the transaction, setting out all the circumstances and stating the reasons why the contemplated transaction should meet all the conditions for the CGT treatment. Details on the advance clearance procedure are set out in the Annex to SP 2/82.

Where clearance is also being sought under section 701 Income Tax Act 2007 (ITA 2007) (see below), HMRC requires a single clearance application to be made.

If HMRC agrees that the contemplated transaction qualifies for the CGT treatment, it provides assurance for the vendor. If HMRC does not accept that the conditions are met, there may be scope to change the transaction to meet the conditions or find another method of realising the vendor's gain.

Even where clearance is obtained, it is necessary to notify HMRC of the transaction within 60 days of the payment, explaining why the company believes that the payment is exempt from treatment as a distribution.

7.3.4 Other Considerations

Companies undertaking a buy-back of shares should always take legal advice, as there are a number of requirements for such transactions set out in the Companies Acts/Orders. **Failure to comply with the legal requirements will result in the transaction being void**, and therefore the vendor will not have sold their shares.

Section 66 Finance Act 1986 provides that 0.5% stamp duty is payable on the purchase consideration for the shares paid by the company.

There are no immediate IHT consequences for an individual whose shares are bought back by a company. However, in many cases the individual will have sold shares that qualify for BPR and received cash. This will have the result of increasing the IHT that could be payable on the individual's death. IHT planning should be undertaken to minimise the exposure. This could include investing in IHT-efficient investments or gifting some or all of the proceeds to remove them from the estate.

7.4   Liquidation of a Company

A company may be put into liquidation voluntarily by its shareholders or it may be forced into liquidation by its creditors where it is insolvent. **This section will concentrate on voluntary solvent liquidations, as these can be utilised for tax planning purposes.**

A company's shareholders may decide to voluntarily liquidate the company following a sale of the company's trade and assets or a planned closure of the business. **This is known as a members' voluntary liquidation and can be undertaken where the company is solvent, i.e. able to pay its debts within the next 12 months.** A licensed insolvency practitioner must be appointed as liquidator to hold the company's assets, oversee the discharge of its liabilities and distribute any surplus to the company's members.

As a formal voluntary liquidation can be quite expensive, another option to wind up a solvent company is to use the strike-off procedure in the Companies Order. Prior to 1 March 2012, HMRC accepted that such a dissolution is a "winding up" for tax purposes under Extra-Statutory Concession (ESC) C16.

However, under the Enactment of Extra-Statutory Concessions Order 2012, this favourable treatment will only apply to companies whose total distributions are £25,000 or less, making it a much less useful tax planning tool than it was formerly.

7.4.1   Corporation Tax on Disposal of Assets

Where a company placed in liquidation still holds assets, **corporation tax will arise on the disposal of the assets**. This may be on the sale of assets to a third party or a distribution *in specie* to the company's shareholders.

A trading profit may be realised on the sale of the company's stock or due to a balancing charge on the sale of plant or machinery.

The most significant tax liabilities are likely to arise from the sale or distribution *in specie* of chargeable assets, e.g. land and buildings, held by the company. Where an asset is distributed *in specie*, the company will be deemed to have disposed of it, and the shareholder acquired it, for market value.

The benefit of distributing land or buildings to the members *in specie* is that there is no liability to SDLT on the acquisition by the shareholder, which can result in a saving of 5% of market value.

Under section 28 TCGA 1992, the chargeable event for CGT purposes is the signing of an unconditional contract for the sale of the asset. If the company has significant trading losses in the final period of trading that could shelter a chargeable gain on the disposal of property, it may be possible to enter into an unconditional sale contract for the property before trading ceases. Completion of the contract can take place after the trade has ceased. Entering into an unconditional sale contract while the trade is continuing permits the current period trading losses to be set against the capital gain. This will not work if the contract is signed after the trade has ceased, as unutilised losses are forfeited on cessation of a trade.

7.4.2   Tax on Capital Distributions on a Winding Up

Section 1030 CTA 2010 specifically excludes distributions made in respect of share capital on a winding up from being taxed as income. Instead, a **distribution on a winding up is taxed as a capital gain** under section 122 TCGA 1992.

With the introduction of the 28% rate of CGT for higher rate taxpayers and all trusts on 23 June 2010, there were circumstances where it was more tax-efficient to receive an income distribution taxed at 25%. However, this is less likely to be the case with the new CGT rates and dividend taxation introduced by Finance Act 2016, and which took effect from 6 April 2016.

Example 7.8

Letts Ltd traded as a commercial property investment business. It ceased trading in 2015 and sold all its investment properties. It has cash of £360,000 available to distribute to its two equal shareholders, Lucie and Billie. It is January 2017 and the shareholders have approached their accountants for advice on the most tax-efficient means of extracting the £360,000 from the company. Lucie and Billie have no further use for the company.

Lucie is retired and has no other income. Billie is an entrepreneur and has annual income exceeding £150,000. Both Lucie and Billie have utilised their CGT annual exemptions for 2016/17. The base cost of the shares in Letts Ltd is negligible.

Advise Lucie and Billie.

Solution

1.   A dividend of £180,000 each is paid to Lucie and Billie.

Lucie:

Lucie's personal allowance will be withdrawn as her income exceeds £121,200 and the personal allowance is reduced by £1 for every £2 of income received in excess of £100,000. Therefore, the income tax liability on the taxable dividend income of £175,000 (after deducting the dividend allowance of £5,000) would be:

	£
£32,000 @ 7.5%	2,400
£150,000 − £32,000 = £118,000 @ 32.5%	38,350
£175,000 − £150,000 = £25,000 @ 38.1%	9,525
Income tax on dividend	50,275

Billie:

As Billie's income already exceeds £150,000, the taxable dividend of £175,000 (after the dividend allowance of £5,000) will be subject to income tax at a rate of 38.1%:

£175,000 @ 38.1% = £66,675

2.   The company is placed in liquidation and a capital distribution of £180,000 each is paid to Lucie and Billie.

Lucie:

Lucie's CGT liability on a dividend of £180,000 would be:

	£
£32,000 @ 10%	3,200
£180,000 − £32,000 = £148,000 @ 20%	29,600
CGT on dividend	32,800

Billie:

As Billie's income already exceeds £150,000, the full dividend of £180,000 will be subject to CGT at 20%:

£180,000 @ 20% = £36,000

Billie can save tax of £30,675 and Lucie can save £17,475 by receiving a capital, rather than an income, distribution. Note that entrepreneurs relief will not be available, on the basis that the company carries on a property investment business as opposed to a trade.

A new targeted anti-avoidance rule (TAAR) is introduced by Finance Act 2016 to apply to certain company distributions in respect of share capital in a winding up which, if certain conditions are met, will result in a distribution being treated as being chargeable to income tax. The TAAR will apply to distributions made on or after 6 April 2016. (See **Section 7.5.2.**)

For corporate shareholders, capital gains treatment is likely to be less beneficial than the income treatment. A UK resident company receiving an income distribution from another company should be able to qualify for the dividend exemption and pay no corporation tax on the dividend.

If the dividend exemption is not available, for example where the recipient is a small company and the paying company is not resident in a qualifying territory, the capital gain treatment may be more beneficial if the distribution on liquidation qualifies for the substantial shareholdings exemption (SSE). There are no territorial restrictions on the location of the subsidiary for the SSE, but there are other conditions to be met (see **Section 8.4**).

For CGT purposes, a shareholder is treated as making a disposal when the entitlement to receive the capital distribution from the company arises. The commencement of a liquidation does not trigger any deemed disposal for the shareholder.

7.4.3   Double Charge to Tax on Liquidation

It is important to recognise that there is a **double charge to tax where a company is liquidated while holding chargeable assets**.

Example 7.9

Jewel Investments Ltd is placed in liquidation on 1 May 2016. It was a property investment company and holds an office building, which is let to third parties, when it is placed in members' voluntary liquidation. The office building was acquired in March 2005 for £1 million.

On 28 May 2016, the property is distributed *in specie* to the sole shareholder of Jewel Investments Ltd, Harry Jewel. Harry holds one £1 ordinary share in Jewel Investments Ltd, which he subscribed for in January 2005 at nominal value.

The market value of the office building on 28 May 2016 is £1.6 million.

Calculate the corporation tax payable by the company (assuming that it pays at the full rate of tax) and the CGT payable by Harry (assuming that Harry has utilised his CGT annual exemption for 2016/17 and is a higher rate taxpayer) on the distribution *in specie* of the property.

Solution

Corporation Tax on Chargeable Gain

	£
Proceeds	1,600,000
Less: cost	(1,000,000)
Gain before indexation	600,000
Indexation allowance:	
Say 0.372 × £1 million	(372,000)
Chargeable gain	228,000
Corporation tax @ 20%	45,600

The liquidator must ensure that the company has sufficient funds to pay the corporation tax.

CGT payable by Harry

	£
Value of capital distribution	1,600,000
Less: cost of shares	(1)
Chargeable gain	1,599,999
CGT @ 20%	320,000

As the property is distributed *in specie*, no SDLT will be payable by Harry.

The total tax paid on the distribution is £365,600, which is 22.85% of the market value of the property.

7.4.4 Part Disposals

If a shareholder receives more than one capital distribution on the winding up of a company, all but the last distribution will be treated as a part disposal of his shares.

The part disposal formula set out in section 42 TCGA 1992 is used to apportion the base cost of the shares, as follows.

$$\text{Deductible cost} = \frac{A}{A + B}$$

where: A = the amount of the interim capital distribution; and
         B = the residual share value at the date of the interim distribution.

Example 7.10

Stringer Ltd went into liquidation on 10 November 2016, having ceased trading on 6 October 2016. After the trade ceased, the company leased out its trading premises on a short lease until the property was sold during the liquidation.

Billy formed the company in September 2001, subscribing for all the 30,000 ordinary £1 shares at par.

The liquidator made the following distributions to Billy:
16 January 2017 − £68,000
18 June 2017 − £42,000

Calculate the CGT payable by Billy on each distribution (assuming that he has no entitlement to ER on the gains and has used his annual exemptions for both years). Billy is a higher rate taxpayer.

Solution

16 January 2017

	£
Value of capital distribution	68,000
Less: cost of shares	
£30,000 × £68,000/(£68,000 + £42,000)	(18,545)
Chargeable gain	49,455
CGT @ 20%	9,891

18 June 2016

	£
Value of capital distribution	42,000
Less: cost of shares	
£30,000 − £18,545	(11,455)
Chargeable gain	30,545
CGT @ 20%	6,109

7.4.5 Other Considerations

It should be noted that by placing a company in voluntary liquidation, income profits can be turned into capital profits. As a result, there may be scope for HMRC to seek to apply the anti-avoidance legislation on transactions in securities set out at sections 682–713 ITA 2007, as discussed below.

There are no immediate IHT consequences on the liquidation of a solvent company. Again, where a large amount of value accrues in a taxpayer's estate as a result of a liquidation, IHT planning should be undertaken to minimise IHT payable on death.

There is no stamp duty payable as a result of capital distributions on a winding up.

7.4.6   CGT Reliefs

Where a company becomes **insolvent**, there are certain CGT reliefs that can be claimed by the shareholders.

Negligible Value Claim

A shareholder can make a negligible value claim under section 24(2) TCGA 1992 where the shares have become worthless.

A negligible value claim will result in the shareholder being deemed to dispose of the shares for little or no consideration and will thereby crystallise a capital loss. Any proceeds subsequently received will be fully taxable as the base cost of the shares will have become nil following the claim. Where a negligible value claim is not made, the shareholder's capital loss will be deemed to arise when the liquidation of the company is complete.

Irrecoverable Loan by Shareholder

Generally, a simple debt is outside the scope of CGT and, therefore, if a shareholder makes a loan to a company and it becomes irrecoverable, relief would not be available for the shareholder's loss.

However, section 253 TCGA 1992 can be used by an individual shareholder to obtain a capital loss equal to the principal element of a qualifying loan that has become irrecoverable due to the company's insolvency.

A qualifying loan for these purposes is one used by a UK resident borrower wholly for the purposes of a trade, profession or vocation that is not a debt on security. It is therefore not limited to loans to companies. It can include monies used for the setting up of the trade subsequently carried on by the borrower.

If loss relief has been claimed and a payment is subsequently received in respect of the outstanding loan, a chargeable gain will accrue to claw back the loss relief claimed.

Similar relief is available to a guarantor of a qualifying loan who has been required to make payment under the guarantee.

Offsetting Capital Loss Against Other Income

It may be possible for individuals who are the shareholders of a company in liquidation to utilise the relief in section 131 ITA 2007 to offset the capital loss arising on the shares against other taxable income.

The shares must be shares in an EIS company or a qualifying trading company, which were subscribed for (i.e. not acquired second-hand) by the individual.

The relief can be claimed where the loss on disposal of the shares is by way of an arm's length sale, a distribution on the dissolving or winding up of the company or a deemed disposal as a result of a negligible value claim.

7.5   Anti-avoidance Legislation: Transactions in Securities

Chapter 1 of Part 13 of ITA 2007 allows HMRC to counteract income tax advantages in relation to transactions in securities. This legislation was previously contained in sections 703–709 ICTA 1988.

"Income tax advantage" is defined by section 683 ITA 2007 and includes the avoidance of a possible assessment to income tax.

Section 684(2) sets out five circumstances when the legislation can apply:

- Circumstance A – abnormal dividends used for exemptions or reliefs.
- Circumstance B – deductions from profits obtained following distribution or dealings.
- Circumstance C – receipt of consideration representing a company's assets, future receipts or trading stock.
- Circumstance D – receipt of consideration in connection with relevant company distribution.
- Circumstance E – receipt of assets of relevant company.

The legislation is complex and you are not expected to be fully aware of its implications.

You should be aware that HMRC can seek to apply this legislation where it perceives that sums which should have been subjected to income tax are instead being subjected to CGT. Given the disparity between the top level of income tax (45%) and the rate of CGT (20%, or 28% for residential property and carried interest), HMRC has an incentive to seek to apply this legislation where possible.

7.5.1   Circumstances where the Legislation could Apply

The circumstances where you should be aware of the possible use of this legislation by HMRC include:

- the sale of a company with significant cash balances and distributable reserves, as HMRC can argue that a dividend (which would be subject to income tax in the hands of the shareholders) should have been paid before the sale to reduce the proceeds realised on sale;
- the buy-back of shares from an individual shareholder that can qualify for the CGT treatment, as HMRC can again argue that an income dividend could have been paid to the individual; and
- where a company with retained profits is put into liquidation and its business is sold to another company under the same or substantially the same ownership, as the distribution of the retained profits during the liquidation will be a CGT, rather than an income tax, receipt.

A taxpayer is not required to self-assess under this legislation. Instead, where HMRC believes that the legislation applies, it will issue a counteraction notice.

This notice will specify adjustments to be made to counteract the income tax advantage. For example, the notice could require all or part of a capital distribution received during the winding up of a company to be subjected to income tax at a rate of between 7.5% and 32.5%, rather than CGT at 10%.

The legislation cannot be applied where the person shows that there was no tax avoidance motive. This requires conditions A and B in section 685 ITA 2007 to be met.

Condition A is that the transaction is effected for genuine commercial reasons or in the ordinary course of making and managing investments. Condition B is that enabling income tax advantages to be obtained is not the main object or one of the main objects of the transaction.

7.5.2   Targeted Anti-avoidance Legislation

Finance Act 2016 introduces a targeted anti-avoidance rule (TAAR) within the transactions in securities rules. The TAAR will apply to distributions paid after 5 April 2016 in respect of a winding up where the distribution is part of a tax-driven 'phoenix arrangement', which broadly involves the carrying on of a similar activity by the individual within two years of the distribution.

The following conditions must all be satisfied:

- immediately before the winding up, the individual shareholder has at least a 5% equity and voting interest;
- the distributing company is a close company, or was so at some point in the two years before the winding up;

▥ within two years of the receipt of the liquidation distribution, the shareholder or a connected person is involved with carrying on a similar trade to the distributing company through any business format; and

▥ it is reasonable to assume that the main purpose, or one of the main purposes, of the liquidation or arrangements is the avoidance or reduction of income tax.

7.5.3 Advance Clearance Procedure

The important point to note is that there is an advance clearance procedure under section 701 ITA 2007.

This procedure permits the taxpayer to write to HMRC giving all the details of a contemplated transaction. If HMRC is satisfied that no counteraction notice ought to be issued in respect of the contemplated transaction, it will confirm this in writing. This clearance procedure gives comfort to the taxpayer (and his or her advisors) and should always be used where there is any possibility that this legislation could be applied by HMRC.

Questions

Review Questions

(See Suggested Solutions to Review Questions at the end of this textbook.)

Question 7.1

Harper Ltd has been trading for a number of years as a manufacturer of plastic bottles. It currently rents its factory, but is planning to acquire new premises for £600,000 as part of its expansion plans. Jack is the sole director and shareholder of Harper Ltd. The company operates an SSAS for Jack's benefit and the pension scheme currently holds liquid assets of £1.5 million.

It is February 2017 and Jack has come to you for tax advice on the most tax-efficient means of acquiring the premises to be used by Harper Ltd.

Requirement
Outline the tax considerations of the following potential courses of action:

(a) Harper Ltd acquires the premises and uses them in its trade.
(b) Jack acquires the premises and rents them to Harper Ltd for use in its trade.
(c) The SSAS acquires the premises and rents them to Harper Ltd for use in its trade.

Question 7.2

Dolly Investments Ltd has been operating for a number of years as a property investment company. Richard is the sole shareholder of Dolly Investments Ltd and he acquired his 100 £1 shares in the company for £1,000 in June 2000. At 30 September 2016, the company's only remaining assets are a shopping centre and cash. The shopping centre was acquired in December 2006 for £5 million and has an open market value of £6.8 million at 30 September 2016.

The company's summary balance sheet at 30 September 2016 is:

	£	£	£
Shopping centre at valuation		6,800,000	
Cash at bank		2,550,000	
Gross assets			9,050,000
Less:			
Debt on shopping centre	(2,000,000)		
Other creditors	(150,000)		
Total liabilities			(2,150,000)
Net assets			6,900,000
Share capital			100
Share premium			900
Revaluation reserve			1,500,000
Profit and loss reserves			5,399,000
Total capital and reserves			6,900,000

The company makes significant profits from rental income each year and pays corporation tax at the full rate.

Richard no longer wishes to operate the business through the company and wants to hold the shopping centre in his own name, so that future capital appreciation will be taxed at the individual CGT rates.

He has been advised that he has the following three options:

(a) he can acquire the shopping centre from the company for market value;
(b) the company can distribute the property *in specie* to Richard and then be placed in liquidation; or
(c) the company can be placed in members' voluntary liquidation and the property then distributed *in specie* to Richard.

Requirement
Assume that it is the start of October 2016 and advise Richard and Dolly Investments Ltd on the tax consequences of each of the three options above. Richard has a number of successful businesses and an annual income of around £200,000.

Challenging Questions

(Suggested Solutions to Challenging Questions are available through your lecturer.)

Question 7.1

Aidan Malone is the controlling shareholder of Malone Materials Ltd, a company that makes and supplies art materials. He founded the company in 1991 and owns 600 of the 1,000 issued £1 shares. He acquired his shares for nominal value in 1991.

Aidan's wife, Grainne, owns 100 shares. The remaining shares are split equally between his son, Gerry (age 30), and his daughter, Brigid (age 28).

Aidan, Gerry and Brigid are all directors of the company.

Aidan is 55 years old and wishes to retire from the company. He wants to sell his shares in the company and buy a villa in Italy, where he and Grainne will spend each winter. Grainne does not work in the company and has not decided if she would also like to sell her shares at this time.

Gerry and Brigid both work in the business and Gerry is anxious that the company remain in the control of the family. However, Gerry and Brigid cannot afford to buy out their father personally.

The company has been trading profitably for many years and currently has distributable reserves of £1.5 million.

Aidan's 60% shareholding in the company has been independently valued at £1.2 million. Aidan has never previously claimed ER.

It is December 2016. Aidan and Grainne's only income for 2016/17 is a dividend of £200 per share paid by Malone Materials Ltd in July 2016.

Requirement

Advise on the tax implications of Aidan's shares being bought back by Malone Materials Ltd.

Capital Taxes Planning for Companies

Learning Objectives

In this chapter you will learn to do the following:

■ Demonstrate a detailed working knowledge of the events that trigger the charge to inheritance tax (IHT), capital gains tax (CGT) and stamp duty, with particular focus on the following themes:

● reorganisation of a business;
● retirement planning;
● share-for-share exchanges (CGT);
● demergers (CGT); and
● substantial shareholdings exemption (CGT).

8.1 Transfer/Sale of Assets by a Company

Where the owner of shares in a company wishes to pass value to the next generation, it is likely that this will be effected by the transfer of shares, whether this takes place during the owner's lifetime or on death.

Where there are individual valuable assets in the company, e.g. land or buildings, it may be worthwhile to transfer such assets from the company to family members or a family trust.

8.2 Reorganising a Family Company

The structure that has been used by a family-owned company or group may not be tax efficient when it comes to selling one or more companies or passing shares to the next generation.

A number of tax planning tools that can be used in retirement planning or reorganising a family company have been discussed in other parts of this book and are not repeated here. These include:

■ company buy-back of shares (**Chapter 7**);
■ liquidation of a company (**Chapter 7**); and
■ gift holdover relief (**Chapter 6**).

8.2.1 Objectives of a Reorganisation

There are a number of reasons why shareholders may wish to reorganise a family company.

A common objective is to separate the ownership of different businesses held by a company or a group of companies to split the business risk or to allow the businesses to be run by different owners. This is often the case when family members can no longer agree on 'day-to-day' issues and/or the direction of the business.

Another reason for a reorganisation may be to allow some of the company's/group's assets to be sold and the rest retained.

The tax objectives of a reorganisation are generally to avoid a tax charge for the company and its shareholders, except to the extent that sales proceeds are received from a third party, and to obtain CGT rather than income tax treatment for the shareholders where sales proceeds are received.

8.2.2 CGT Reliefs

There are a number of reliefs in the CGT legislation that can be utilised in a reorganisation, including the following:

1. **Section 171 TCGA 1992** – the transfer of chargeable assets within a capital gains group is at no gain/no loss for CGT purposes (although be aware of the exit charge in section 179 TCGA 1992).
2. **Sections 126 and 127 TCGA 1992** – a reorganisation or reduction of share capital is not a disposal for the shareholder.
3. **Section 127 TCGA 1992** – the original shares and the new shares are treated as the same asset, acquired at the same time and for the same cost as the original shares.

Section 135 TCGA 1992: Share-for-share Exchange

Section 135 TCGA 1992 deals with share-for-share exchanges and is an important relief when considering a reorganisation.

It applies in three circumstances where Company B issues shares to a person in exchange for shares in another company, Company A.

Case 1 Where Company B holds, or as a result of the exchange will hold, more than 25% of the ordinary share capital of Company A.

Case 2 Where Company B issues the shares in exchange for shares as a result of a general offer:

1. made to members of Company A or any class of them; and
2. made in the first instance on a condition such that, if it were satisfied, Company B would have control of Company A.

Case 3 Where Company B holds, or as a result of the exchange will hold, the greater part of the voting power in Company A.

Section 136 TCGA 1992: Scheme of Reconstruction

Section 136 TCGA 1992 deals with a "scheme of reconstruction" involving the issue of shares. A scheme of reconstruction is defined in Schedule 5AA TCGA 1992. In order to be a scheme of reconstruction, the transaction must meet conditions **(a) and (b) below and either (c) or (d)**:

(a) the scheme must involve the issue of ordinary shares in the successor company (Company B) to the holders of ordinary share capital of the original company (Company A); **and**

(b) the shareholders of ordinary shares in the original company (Company A) must be entitled to be issued with ordinary shares by the successor company (Company B) in proportion to their holdings of ordinary shares in the original company; **and**

(c) the effect of the restructuring must be that the business, or substantially the whole of the business, carried on by the original company (Company A) is carried on by the successor company (Company B); **or**

(d) the scheme is carried out in pursuance of a compromise or arrangement under section 425 Companies Act 1985 and no part of the business of the original company is transferred under the scheme to any other person.

Section 136 applies where:

(a) an arrangement between Company A and the persons holding shares (or a class of shares) in Company A is entered into in connection with a "scheme of reconstruction"; and

(b) under the arrangement:

(i) Company B issues shares to those persons in respect of and in proportion to their relevant holdings in Company A; and

(ii) the shares in Company A are retained by those persons or are cancelled.

Operation of Section 135 or Section 136

Where section 135 or section 136 applies, the old shares and the new shares are treated as the same asset (in the same way as a reorganisation of share capital under section 127 TCGA 1992).

Section 137 TCGA 1992 contains an anti-avoidance rule. It states that neither section 135 nor section 136 applies where the shareholder holds more than 5% of the shares in Company A unless the exchange is effected for bona fide commercial reasons and does not form part of a scheme or arrangement for the avoidance of CGT or corporation tax.

There is a clearance procedure in section 138 TCGA 1992, which should be used to obtain advance clearance from HMRC.

Section 139 TCGA 1992

Section 135 and section 136 provide relief to the shareholders (whether individuals or corporate bodies), whereas section 139 TCGA 1992 **provides relief to the transferor company** by treating the transfer as occurring at no gain/no loss.

Section 139 applies where any scheme of reconstruction involves the transfer of the whole, or part, of a company's business from one UK resident company to another and in which the transferor company receives no consideration for the transfer of assets, except the assumption of the liabilities of the business.

Section 139(5) contains a similar anti-avoidance provision to section 137, except that one of the prohibited purposes includes the avoidance of income tax. Section 139(5) also contains an advance clearance procedure.

8.2.3 Example Using Sections 136 and 139 TCGA 1992

These reliefs are difficult to understand in isolation. They will only be fully understood by working through examples.

Example 8.1

Sebastian and Samantha have been equal shareholders in Rags & Riches Ltd since their mother died 10 years ago. The company was established by their mother over 20 years ago and has two separate businesses: running shops selling vintage and nearly-new designer goods (Rags); and making one-off designs for customers (Riches). Sebastian wishes to run the shops, whereas Samantha is a designer and wants to focus on the dress-making business.

You are required to advise Sebastian and Samantha how they could achieve their aims in a tax-efficient manner.

Solution

Directly transferring the retail business (Rags) to Sebastian or the dress-making business (Riches) to Samantha would give rise to tax. The best means of minimising the tax is to carry out a scheme of reconstruction, within the meaning of Schedule 5AA TCGA 1992.

The first step would be to create new classes of ordinary shares in Rags & Riches Ltd. The shares held by Sebastian would be reclassified into 'A' shares and would derive their value from the 'Rags' trade. The shares held by Samantha would be reclassified into 'B' shares and would derive their value from the 'Riches' trade.

The next step would be to transfer the 'Riches' trade to a new company (Sam's Riches Ltd) and in exchange Sam's Riches Ltd would issue shares to Samantha. Samantha would then agree to cancel her 'B' shares in Rags & Riches Ltd, as they have become valueless, leaving Sebastian as the 100% owner of that company.

Under section 136 TCGA 1992, Samantha's shares in Sam's Riches Ltd would be treated as the same asset as her original shares in Rags & Riches Ltd, so no CGT disposal occurs.

Under section 139 TCGA 1992, the disposal of chargeable assets (e.g. property, goodwill) by Rags & Riches Ltd to Sam's Riches Ltd would be treated as being made at no gain/no loss, so no corporation tax would be payable on the disposal.

This is subject to the anti-avoidance provisions and it should be recommended that advance clearance be obtained.

There remains a large tax issue in **Example 8.1** above. Samantha has received a distribution from Rags & Riches Ltd and section 1000 CTA 2010 will therefore impose a charge to income tax on the market value of the 'Riches' trade.

It is for this reason that the statutory and "non-statutory" demerger provisions are often used in such situations.

8.3   Demergers

It should be possible to split or demerge a company or group of companies in a tax-efficient manner by undertaking either a statutory or a "non-statutory" demerger.

A **statutory demerger** involves distributing one or more trading subsidiaries directly to all or some of the shareholders (or one or more trades or trading subsidiaries to new companies owned by some or all of the shareholders) under the statutory provisions in Part 23, Chapter 5 CTA 2010. A statutory demerger avoids the winding up of the company. However, there are a number of restrictions, one of the most important being that there must not be any intention to sell the demerged company.

A **non-statutory demerger** (also known as a section 110 reconstruction) involves winding up the company and distributing the relevant businesses and assets, or subsidiaries, to new companies owned by some or all of the shareholders, using the procedure set out in section 110 Insolvency Act 1986 (or the Northern Ireland equivalent).

8.3.1 Statutory Demerger

There are a number of general conditions that must be satisfied to obtain the statutory demerger relief in sections 1076 and 1077 CTA 2010. In addition, there are further preconditions for each type of statutory demerger. The most important of the **general conditions** are:

1. all companies participating in the demerger transaction must be resident in an EU Member State;
2. the distributing company must be a trading company or a member of a trading group;
3. at the time of its distribution, a demerged 75% subsidiary must be a trading company or a member of a trading group;
4. the distribution must be made wholly or mainly for the benefit of some or all of the trading activities formerly carried on by the company/group; and
5. the distribution must not form part of a scheme or arrangement for:
   (a) the avoidance of tax;
   (b) the making of a chargeable payment (i.e. a payment to the members of the distributing company); or
   (c) the sale of the company/trade or the liquidation of the trade after its distribution.

If the conditions contained in sections 1081–1085 CTA 2010 for an exempt demerger are met, then no distribution will arise under section 1075 CTA 2010.

The statutory demerger rules permit three types of demerger. Each takes the form of a distribution *in specie* of one or more trades, or shares in one or more 75% subsidiaries.

Type I Demerger

A Type I demerger is a direct statutory demerger under section 1076 CTA 2010. **This involves the direct distribution by a company of shares in a 75% subsidiary (or subsidiaries) to all or any of its members.**

The only charge in this type of demerger is a CGT charge on the distributing company, based on the market value of the subsidiary. However, in many cases this gain will be exempt under the substantial shareholdings exemption (see **Section 8.4**).

Example 8.2

Shelby Ltd, a UK resident holding company, holds 100% of the shares in two UK resident trading subsidiaries, Candy Ltd and Choc Ltd. The shares in Shelby Ltd are equally held by Gina and Grace. Gina and Grace wish to go their separate ways. They have agreed that Gina will retain the holding company and Choc Ltd. In exchange, Grace will obtain sole control of Candy Ltd.

You are required to advise Gina and Grace on how their objective could be attained in a tax-efficient manner through a direct statutory demerger.

Solution

Candy Ltd could be separated from the group through a Type I statutory demerger by Shelby Ltd distributing the shares in Candy Ltd to Grace, and Grace's shares in Shelby Ltd being cancelled.

This would result in Grace directly holding 100% of the share capital in Candy Ltd. Gina would then hold all the shares in Shelby Ltd, which would still wholly own Choc Ltd.

If all the conditions for a direct statutory demerger are met, the tax consequences would be as follows:

1. The gain on the disposal of the shares in Candy Ltd by Shelby Ltd is exempt under the Substantial Shareholdings Exemption.
2. Section 127 TCGA 1992 would apply so that Grace's shares in Candy Ltd stand in the shoes of her shares in Shelby Ltd for CGT purposes.
3. Grace is not treated as receiving a distribution equal to the market value of Candy Ltd as the conditions for an exempt demerger in sections 1075 and 1076 CTA 2010 are met.

Figure 8.1: Type I Demerger

Pre-Demerger

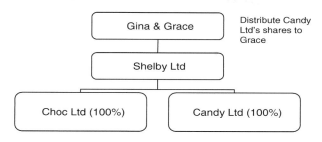

Post-Demerger

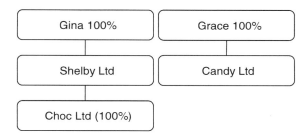

Type II Demerger

A Type II demerger is an indirect statutory demerger under section 1077(1)(a)(i) CTA 2010. **This involves the transfer of a company's trade or trades to one or more transferee companies in consideration for the issue of shares in those companies to all or any of the members of the distributing company.**

Example 8.3

The transaction described above in **Example 8.1** is an indirect demerger. The 'Riches' trade of Rags and Riches Ltd is transferred to Sam's Riches Ltd in exchange for the issue of shares in that company to Samantha.

The reliefs under section 136 TCGA 1992 and section 139 TCGA 1992 will apply, as described in **Example 8.1**.

In addition, where the conditions for a statutory indirect merger are met, Samantha will not be treated as having received a distribution equal to the market value of the 'Riches' trade. Thus, the reorganisation is achieved in a tax-efficient manner.

Figure 8.2: Type II Demerger

Pre-Demerger

Post-Demerger

Type III Demerger

A Type III demerger is an indirect statutory demerger under section 1077(1)(a)(ii) CTA 2010. **This involves the transfer of shares in a 75% subsidiary (or subsidiaries) to one or more transferee companies in consideration for the issue of shares in the companies to all or any of the members of the distributing company.**

A Type III demerger may be used instead of a Type I demerger in a situation where the transfer of shares would not qualify for SSE. Under a Type III demerger, relief should be available under section 139 (which wouldn't be available under a Type I demerger as this involves a direct transfer of the shares to the shareholders).

Example 8.4

The facts are as in **Example 8.2** above. You are required to advise Gina and Grace how they could achieve their objectives through a Type III indirect statutory demerger.

Solution

This could be the preferred route if Grace does not wish to hold the shares in Candy Ltd directly. A new holding company (Newco) could be formed. Shelby Ltd could transfer the shares in Candy Ltd to Newco in exchange for Newco issuing shares to Grace, and Grace's shares in Shelby Ltd could then be cancelled.

If all the conditions for an indirect statutory demerger are met, the tax consequences would be as follows:

1. The shares in Candy Ltd are treated as being disposed of by Shelby Ltd at no gain/no loss under section 139 TCGA 1992. (Note that section 139 overrides the SSE.)
2. Section 136 TCGA 1992 would apply so that Grace's shares in Candy Ltd stand in the shoes of her shares in Shelby Ltd for CGT purposes.
3. Grace is not treated as receiving a distribution equal to the market value of Candy Ltd as the conditions for an exempt demerger in sections 1075 and 1077 CTA 2010 are met.

Figure 8.3: Type III Demerger

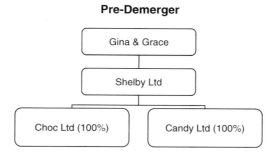

Pre-Demerger

Post-Demerger

Advance Clearance Procedure

HMRC's practice for applying the exempt demerger provisions is set out in *Statement of Practice SP 13/80*. There is an advance clearance procedure in section 1091 CTA 2010, which should be used when a statutory demerger is being contemplated. It is likely that a combined clearance application under this section and section 138 TCGA 1992, section 139(5) TCGA 1992 and section 701 ITA 2007 would be made.

Limitations on Using the Statutory Demerger Provisions

The **two main issues** in meeting the conditions for a statutory demerger are that the companies involved must be **trading companies** and there must be **no intention to sell** the shares **or liquidate** the company following the transaction.

As reorganisations are likely to be undertaken to achieve a more tax-efficient structure before a sale of all or part of a group, this means that the statutory demerger provisions are often unavailable.

Likewise, the statutory demerger provisions cannot be used for non-trading or investment companies. Note that, for these purposes, the "trading company" or "trading group" requirements refer to the "wholly or mainly" trading test, rather than to the more stringent "no substantial non-trading activity" test.

8.3.2 Non-statutory Demergers

Non-statutory demergers are commonly used in the following cases:

- where an investment business (e.g. property rental) is being demerged;
- if there is an intention to dispose of one or more of the demerged businesses; or
- where the company has insufficient distributable reserves to declare a dividend *in specie* equal to the underlying book value of the assets or the subsidiary transferred.

Under a non-statutory demerger, the procedure set out in section 110 Insolvency Act 1986 (or the Northern Ireland equivalent) is used to wind up the company and distribute the relevant businesses and assets, or subsidiaries, to new companies owned by the shareholders.

Example 8.5

The circumstances are as set out in **Example 8.1** above. The solution outlined in **Example 8.1** is not tax efficient as there will be a distribution made to Samantha unless the conditions for a statutory demerger are met. Assume that these conditions are not met, as Sebastian is in negotiations with a third party about acquiring the 'Rags' trade.

You are required to advise Sebastian and Samantha as to how the non-statutory demerger provisions could be used to achieve their aims in a tax-efficient manner.

Solution

The steps to be undertaken to carry out a section 110 reconstruction would be as follows:

1. The first step would be to create new classes of ordinary shares in Rags & Riches Ltd. The shares held by Sebastian would be reclassified into 'A' shares and would derive their value from the 'Rags' trade. The shares held by Samantha would be reclassified into 'B' shares and would derive their value from the 'Riches' trade.
2. Rags & Riches Ltd would then be put into members' voluntary liquidation by Sebastian and Samantha holding an extraordinary general meeting and passing a special resolution at the meeting.
3. A liquidator would be appointed to carry out a transfer of the two businesses under section 110 Insolvency Act 1986.
4. Sebastian will form Seb's Rags Ltd to take over the retail operation, selling vintage and nearly new clothing. Samantha will form Sam's Riches Ltd to take over the design and dressmaking business.
5. A scheme of reconstruction takes place under section 110 Insolvency Act 1986, enabling the liquidator to:

    (a) transfer the 'Rags' business to Seb's Rags Ltd, which in turn issues shares to Sebastian as consideration; and
    (b) transfer the 'Riches' business to Sam's Riches Ltd, which in turn issues shares to Samantha as consideration.

The chargeable assets (e.g. property, goodwill) distributed by Rags & Riches Ltd to Seb's Rags Ltd and Sam's Riches Ltd should be transferred at no gain/no loss under section 139 TCGA 1992.

As Rags & Riches Ltd is being liquidated, the receipt of value by Sebastian and Samantha is not an income distribution taxable under section 1030 CTA 2010. Normally, the value of the shares acquired by Sebastian and Samantha would fall to be treated as a capital distribution. However, section 136 TCGA 1992 should apply so that the new shares are treated as standing in the shoes of the old shares for CGT purposes.

Note that stamp duty at 0.5% will be payable by Sebastian and Samantha on the value of the shares received by each of them, as the conditions for relief in section 75 Finance Act 1986 are not met.

8.3.3 Anti-avoidance

It should be remembered that the types of transaction being described above are likely to fall within the "transactions in securities" anti-avoidance rules in sections 682–713 ITA 2007 (see **Chapter 5**).

Therefore, in addition to the relevant clearances under the demerger and CGT provisions, applying for advance clearance under section 701 ITA 2007 should also be recommended. As previously highlighted (**Section 7.5.2**), Finance Act 2016 introduced a new TAAR within the transactions in securities rules that can impact on liquidations in certain situations. However, HMRC have clarified that the new TAAR is not intended to impact on liquidation demergers.

8.4 Substantial Shareholdings Exemption

With effect from 1 April 2002, the substantial shareholdings exemption (SSE) applies to the disposal of shares by UK companies. Gains arising on qualifying shareholdings on or after this date are tax-free and losses not allowable. **It can never apply to the disposal of shares by an individual.**

SSE applies not only to actual disposals of shares but also to other types of disposal for CGT purposes. These include certain deemed disposals and capital distributions on the liquidation of a subsidiary company.

8.4.1 The Main Exemption

The SSE legislation is set out in Schedule 7AC to the Taxation of Chargeable Gains Act (TCGA) 1992. It contains a main exemption and two secondary exemptions.

The main exemption is contained in Schedule 7AC paragraph 1. It states that a gain accruing to a company (the "holding company") on a disposal of shares in another company (the "subsidiary") is not a taxable gain if the requirements in relation to:

1. the substantial shareholding,
2. the holding company, and
3. the subsidiary,

are met. This is subject to an overriding anti-avoidance provision contained in paragraph 5 of the Schedule.

Substantial Shareholding

The first requirement, in paragraph 1, in relation to the shareholding itself is that the holding company must have held a "substantial shareholding" in the subsidiary throughout a **12-month period** in the two years before the disposal takes place. Paragraph 15A was inserted into Schedule 7AC by Finance Act 2011 and took effect from 19 July 2011 (or 1 April 2011 if elected).

Paragraph 15A extends the period (by up to 12 months) during which a parent company is treated as holding the shares in a subsidiary company by the length of time any trade and assets transferred to the subsidiary company were previously operated by another group company.

In theory, this permits the transfer of trade and assets provided they have operated for at least 12 months, into a newly incorporated subsidiary, the sale of that subsidiary the same day, and the disposal qualifies for SSE.

The meaning of "substantial shareholding" in this context is set out in paragraph 8 and is a holding of shares in the subsidiary company by virtue of which the holding company:

1. holds at least 10% of the company's ordinary share capital;
2. is beneficially entitled to at least 10% of the profits available for distribution to equity holders of the company; and
3. would be beneficially entitled on a winding up to at least 10% of the assets of the company available for distribution to equity holders.

As only a 10% holding of shares is required, it is not technically correct to use the terms "holding company" and "subsidiary". The legislation uses the terms "the investing company" and "the company invested in". For ease of understanding, this chapter will continue to refer to holding companies and subsidiaries, but bear in mind that **only a 10% and not a 50% shareholding is required to qualify for SSE**.

Holding Company

The requirements which the holding company itself must meet are contained in paragraph 18.

In order to qualify, the holding company must:

1. have been a sole trading company or a member of a "trading group" throughout the "qualifying period"; **and**
2. be a sole trading company or a member of a trading group immediately after the time of disposal.

The "qualifying period" referred to in 1. is generally the 12 months prior to the date of disposal.

The terms "trading company" and "trading group" require some consideration. Paragraph 20 states that a **trading company** means a company carrying on trading activities whose activities do not include to a substantial extent non-trading activities. A **trading group**, under paragraph 21, is a group:

1. one or more of whose members carry on trading activities; and
2. the activities of whose members, taken together, do not include to a substantial extent activities other than trading activities.

The SSE will not be available if HMRC can show that there is a substantial element of non-trading activities in a company or group. "Substantial" for these purposes is not defined in the legislation, but it is generally taken to be 20% and this can relate to a percentage of turnover, assets or management time. This is the same test as is used for section 165 TCGA 1992 holdover relief and entrepreneurs' relief.

Trading groups often assume that there will be no difficulty in falling below the 20% test when looking at non-trading activities. The problem is that HMRC's interpretation of "non-trading activities" may differ from that of the group or its advisors. Non-trading activities can include items such as the making of inter-company loans.

It can be difficult to meet the requirement at paragraph 18(1)(b) that the holding company be a trading company or a member of a trading group immediately after the time of the disposal.

Example 8.6

Holdco Ltd owns 100% of the shares in Tradeco Ltd, a qualifying trading company. Holdco Ltd is a holding company with no other investments and has held the shares for five years. Holdco sells the shares in Tradeco Ltd to a third party, realising a gain of £10 million.

Before the disposal, Holdco Ltd is a member of a qualifying trading group that meets the minimum shareholding and minimum holding period conditions. However, Holdco Ltd does not meet the condition at paragraph 18(1)(b), as after the disposal its only asset will be the cash received on the sale.

Holdco Ltd is therefore unable to claim the main exemption in paragraph 1 of the SSE legislation.

In the circumstances of this example, the gain on the disposal will benefit from SSE only if the conditions for one of the secondary exemptions are met.

Subsidiary Company

Paragraph 19 states the requirement for the company being sold. It must:

1. have been a "qualifying company" throughout the 12 months prior to the disposal; and
2. be a qualifying company immediately after the time of the disposal.

A **qualifying company** is a trading company or the holding company of a trading group or subgroup. The same definitions of trading company and trading group discussed above apply.

There is no requirement for the subsidiary company to be UK resident.

8.4.2   Interaction of SSE and other CGT Reliefs

It is important to understand how SSE interacts with other CGT reliefs available to corporate entities. As a result of paragraph 6, the no gain/no loss rule in section 139 TCGA 1992 for the transfer of chargeable assets on a reconstruction takes precedence over any entitlement to SSE.

Similarly, the section 171 TCGA 1992 provisions on transfers within a capital gains group override the SSE rules where shares in trading companies are transferred between group companies.

Under paragraph 10, where a company acquires a subsidiary as a result of a group no gain/no loss transfer, the company's deemed period of ownership is extended to include the period for which the transferor company held the shares.

De-grouping Charge

Paragraph 38 deals with the de-grouping charge in section 179 TCGA 1992.

Where a de-grouping charge arises under section 179 in relation to a holding of shares that, at the time the company leaves the group, would qualify for SSE on an actual disposal of the shares, the SSE rules effectively override section 179.

This is achieved by treating the deemed sale and reacquisition of the shares as taking place immediately before the company leaves the group, for a consideration equal to the market value at that time. FA 2011 introduced new legislation to enable the de-grouping charges to be treated as deemed proceeds on the sale of shares in a company. This means that in situations where SSE applies, the de-grouping charge would effectively be wiped out.

Therefore, provided that the other conditions for SSE are satisfied at the time of the de-grouping event, SSE will apply to exempt the section 179 charge.

FA 2011 did not make any corresponding change to the manner in which corporate intangibles de-grouping profits/losses were dealt with. Consequently, even though SSE might be available to exempt the gain on the sale of the subsidiary, an intangibles de-grouping charge could still arise in the subsidiary company. However, it is possible to reallocate an intangibles de-grouping profit to another 75% group member under section 792 CTA 2009, or it may be rolled over against qualifying reinvestment on goodwill/intangibles by the group under section 791 CTA 2009.

8.4.3   Planning Points

The SSE is an extremely beneficial relief. Planning should therefore should be undertaken to ensure that corporate groups can benefit from it to the maximum extent possible.

The extent of non-trading activities within a group should be kept under review to ensure that SSE is not jeopardised.

Where a group has a mix of trading and investment activities, consideration should be given to undertaking a reorganisation to remove the investment activities so that the group can benefit from SSE. However, these decisions should not be taken in isolation and, where the group is privately owned, the impact of any reorganisation on the individual owners' CGT and IHT positions should also be considered.

Questions

Review Questions

(See Suggested Solutions to Review Questions at the end of this textbook.)

Question 8.1

Tangle Ltd has owned 18% of the shares in Neon Ltd since 2004. Both companies are trading companies.

On 1 March 2016 Tangle Ltd sold a 10% stake in the company at a profit. The directors of Tangle Ltd are now considering selling the remaining 8% shareholding.

Requirement

Briefly advise the directors as to:

(a) the tax consequences of the sale of the shares in March 2016; and

(b) the tax consequences of the sale of the remaining 8% stake in Neon Ltd, considering both the possibility that the sale gives rise to a gain and to a loss.

Question 8.2

Since 1999, Bon Ltd has owned 3,000 25p shares in Good Ltd, a trading company with 20,000 25p shares in issue.

Bon Ltd sold the following shares to Trotter plc:

31 March 2016	1,200
28 February 2017	800

You should assume that the shareholding in Good Ltd initially met the conditions of Schedule 7AC TCGA 1992 in all other respects.

Requirement

Explain, with reasons, which (if any) of the two disposals of shares qualify for SSE.

Challenging Questions

(Suggested Solutions to Challenging Questions are available through your lecturer.)

Question 8.1

Tania owns 60% of the ordinary share capital in Fairy Good Food Ltd. The other 40% of the company is owned by Alex. Fairy Good Food Ltd has two divisions: 'Fairy Cakes', which manufactures and distributes baked goods, and 'Good Food', which offers high-quality catering for small or large functions.

The Fairy Cakes division has been operating since the company was incorporated by Tania and Alex 20 years ago. In recent years, margins have been squeezed by the large supermarket chains and this division has been making a loss. At 31 December 2016, the unutilised trading losses carried forward were £800,000.

The Good Food division started on a small scale eight years ago. It is a highly profitable business and its turnover has increased steadily. It now accounts for 20% of the company's turnover.

Tania and Alex are considering restructuring the company. They have undertaken cost-saving measures and hope that the Fairy Cakes division will return to profitability in the next few years. However, it consumes a lot of the company's capital and the majority of their time for very little reward. Therefore, if they received a good offer, they would consider selling the business.

They think that the two businesses could operate more efficiently if they were held in separate companies. However, Tania and Alex do not wish to form a group of companies. They want to be able to benefit from the personal rate of CGT and possibly claim ER, should the opportunity to sell one of the businesses arise.

Tania and Alex are clients of a small accountancy firm without a tax partner, Compter & Co. They approached their audit partner, Beatrice Compter, for some advice. She suggested that the two divisions could be separated by putting Fairy Good Food Ltd into liquidation and distributing the two businesses to Tania and Alex. However, she cautioned that she was not a tax expert and advised them to seek tax advice before acting.

On Beatrice Compter's recommendation, Tania and Alex have contacted your firm for advice on any tax-efficient means of achieving their aim of separating the two divisions.

Requirement

You are required to prepare notes for the file in advance of a meeting with your tax partner to discuss the matter.

Question 8.2

Steve is the sole shareholder of Steve Holdings Ltd. This is a dormant holding company that holds the shares in two wholly owned trading subsidiaries: Steve Supplies Ltd and Steve Transport Ltd. Steve used to hold the trading subsidiaries personally, but he incorporated the holding company and undertook a reorganisation in 2002 to transfer the shares in the two trading companies to the holding company. His base cost of the shares in the holding company is negligible.

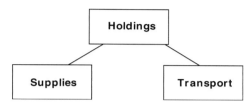

Steve has received an offer from a third party interested in buying Steve Supplies Ltd for £3.5 million. He is 55 years old and is considering accepting the offer. He would be happy to continue to own the transport company, which is a smaller business, estimated to be worth £2 million.

Steve has heard about the SSE and thinks that it is great that he will receive the £3.5 million proceeds for the sale of Steve Supplies Ltd tax-free. He is planning to buy a yacht with the proceeds, as it has always been his dream to sail around the world.

Your partner is Steve's tax advisor and is meeting with him to discuss the tax implications of the potential sale. Your firm has recently undertaken a review of the group's tax position and is satisfied that the group, including both of the subsidiaries individually, meet the trading conditions in the SSE legislation.

Requirement

Your partner has asked you to consider the situation and draft notes of issues to discuss with her in advance of her meeting with Steve, including any suggestions to improve the tax position of Steve Holdings Ltd and Steve personally.

Capital Taxes Planning on Transfer of a Business/Company

Learning Objectives

In this chapter you will learn to do the following:

- Identify and explain the interaction of taxes arising as a consequence of effecting the transfer of a benefit in an efficient manner from a capital taxes perspective, with particular focus on the following themes:
  - retirement planning; and
  - transfer of a business to a family, a third party or on death.

9.1 Transfer/Sale of a Sole Trade

The tax issues discussed in this section relating to the sale or transfer of a sole trade should all be familiar to you from your earlier studies or other parts of this textbook. The aim of this section is to consider the tax implications of a transaction and any possible means of mitigating tax liabilities through planning. This chapter should also enable you to understand the impact one transaction may have across a number of taxes.

Three different types of scenario will be considered:

1. the sale/gift of a business to a family member;
2. the sale of a business to a third party; and
3. the transfer of a business on death.

9.1.1 When a Sole Trade is Being Sold or Gifted to a Family Member

Capital taxes planning issues to consider when a **sole trade is being sold or gifted to a family member** include the following:

Tax Issue	Implications/Solutions
Capital Gains Tax	
▪ If there is a sale, is it to a connected person?	▪ If so, market value imposed by section 18 TCGA 1992.
▪ If not a connected person, unlikely that the sale/ transfer is being made at arm's length?	▪ Therefore, market value imposed by section 17 TCGA 1992.
▪ If a market valuation is required, who will perform it?	▪ Inform client of danger of HMRC challenge to any valuation and strongly recommend valuation be carried out by independent expert valuer.
▪ Can holdover relief under section 165 TCGA 1992 be claimed?	▪ Remember, full holdover relief can only be claimed where the business is being gifted.
▪ Is the vendor eligible to claim ER?	▪ Is it beneficial for some proceeds to be paid so that ER can be utilised?
▪ Is the CGT annual exemption available for that year?	▪ Should some proceeds be paid to utilise the annual exemption?
▪ If transfer is a chargeable lifetime transfer for IHT purposes and section 165 holdover relief is not available, should holdover relief under section 260 TCGA 1992 be claimed?	▪ Remember that section 260 is not available where gifted to settlor-interested trust.
	▪ Consider implications for trustees' future CGT liability.
Inheritance Tax	
▪ What value is being transferred?	▪ Remember that transfer of value for IHT is based on "loss to donor" principle.
▪ If a gift or transfer at undervalue, is it a chargeable lifetime transfer (CLT) or a potentially exempt transfer (PET)?	▪ If a CLT, calculate the amount of chargeable gain to IHT.
▪ Is BPR available?	▪ Consider if conditions are met.
▪ If a CLT and full BPR unavailable, who should pay the tax?	▪ Remember, if donor pays tax, this is also a loss to his estate and grossing-up applies.
▪ Consider impact of transferor's death within seven years.	▪ Will any (additional) IHT be payable?
	▪ Will BPR still be available?
VAT	
▪ Is the business registered for VAT?	▪ If yes, VAT should be charged on the sale of taxable assets, unless TOGC applies.
▪ Is the TOGC treatment available?	▪ Consider conditions for both vendor and buyer.
▪ If TOGC treatment applies, should the VAT number be transferred?	▪ As the business is being transferred within the family, consider transferring the VAT number to minimise interruption to the business.
▪ Has more than £250,000 been spent on land or buildings in the past 10 years?	▪ If so, consider the implications of the Capital Goods Scheme.
▪ Is any property being transferred?	▪ Consider if exempt, zero-rated or standard-rated.
▪ Has property been opted to tax?	▪ If no, should it be opted prior to transfer?
	▪ If yes, are additional conditions re: TOGC met?
Stamp Duty/SDLT	
▪ Is land or property being transferred?	▪ What rate of SDLT is payable?
	▪ Is VAT being charged? If so, SDLT payable on the VAT-inclusive amount.

continued overleaf

▪ What is the value that is subject to SDLT?	▪ Remember, there is no deemed market value rule for SDLT unless purchaser is a company. This means there is generally no SDLT charge when an asset is gifted.
▪ Stamp duty is no longer charged on debtors or goodwill.	▪ Stamp duty should apply only if shares or securities are being transferred.

9.1.2 When a Sole Trade is Being Sold to a Third Party

Capital taxes planning issues to consider when a sole trade is being sold to a third party include the following:

Tax Issue	Implications/Solutions
Capital Gains Tax	
▪ Is the vendor eligible to claim ER?	▪ Is there a disposal of all or part of the business rather than just assets?
▪ Should some or all of the proceeds be reinvested in EIS shares?	▪ This will be more attractive where the vendor is connected with the EIS company.
Inheritance Tax	
▪ As the business is being sold to a third party, there should be no transfer of value.	▪ No immediate IHT on sale of business.
▪ Vendor may have exchanged assets qualifying for BPR for cash.	▪ Consider impact of sale on vendor's taxable estate.
VAT	
▪ Is the business registered for VAT?	▪ If yes, VAT should be charged on the sale of taxable assets, unless TOGC applies.
▪ Is the TOGC treatment available?	▪ Consider conditions for both vendor and buyer.
▪ If TOGC treatment applies, should the VAT number be transferred?	▪ As the business is being sold to a third party, the buyer is unlikely to want to bear the risks of taking over the VAT number.
▪ Has more than £250,000 been spent on land or buildings in the past 10 years?	▪ If so, consider the implications of the Capital Goods Scheme.
▪ Is any property being transferred?	▪ Consider if exempt, zero-rated or standard-rated.
▪ Has property been opted to tax?	▪ If no, should it be opted prior to transfer?
	▪ If yes, are additional conditions re: TOGC met?
Stamp Duty/SDLT	
▪ Is land or property being transferred?	▪ What rate of SDLT is payable?
	▪ What amount of the proceeds is being allocated to land or buildings?
▪ What is the value that is subject to SDLT?	▪ Is VAT being charged? If so, SDLT payable on VAT-inclusive amount.
▪ Stamp duty is no longer charged on debtors or goodwill.	▪ Stamp duty should apply only if shares or securities are being transferred.

9.1.3 When a Sole Trade is Being Transferred on Death

Capital taxes planning issues to consider when a sole trade is being transferred on death include the following:

Tax Issue	Implications/Solutions
Capital Gains Tax	
▣ Uplift to market value of all chargeable assets on death.	▣ Market value for CGT will equate to value for IHT purposes.
Inheritance Tax	
▣ What is the value of the estate?	▣ Valuation of business for IHT purposes should be undertaken by independent expert valuer.
▣ Is BPR available?	▣ Consider if conditions are met.
▣ Are assets on which full BPR is available being transferred to spouse?	▣ Consider use of deed of variation to pass assets on to next generation on which no IHT is payable.
VAT	
▣ Is the business registered for VAT?	▣ If yes, VAT should be charged on the sale of taxable assets, unless TOGC applies.
▣ Is the TOGC treatment available?	▣ Consider conditions for both transferor and transferee.
▣ If TOGC treatment applies, should the VAT number be transferred?	▣ As the business is being transferred within the family, consider transferring the VAT number to minimise interruption to the business.
▣ Has more than £250,000 been spent on land or buildings in the past 10 years?	▣ If so, consider the implications of the Capital Goods Scheme.
▣ Is any property being transferred?	▣ Consider if exempt, zero-rated or standard-rated.
▣ Has property been opted to tax?	▣ If no, should it be opted prior to transfer? ▣ If yes, are additional conditions re: TOGC met?
Stamp Duty/SDLT	
▣ No SDLT payable, even if underlying assets include UK land, provided no consideration.	

9.2   Transfer/Sale of Assets by a Company

Where the owner of shares in a company wishes to pass value to the next generation, it is likely that this will be effected by the transfer of shares, whether this takes place during the owner's lifetime or on death.

Where there are individual valuable assets in the company, e.g. land or buildings, it may be worthwhile to transfer such assets from the company to family members or a family trust.

Two different types of scenario will be considered:

1. the sale/gift of company assets to a shareholder or family member of shareholder; and
2. the sale of company assets to a third party.

9.2.1   Sale or Transfer of Company Assets to a Connected Person

Capital taxes planning issues to consider **when assets are being sold or transferred to a shareholder, or the family member of a shareholder**, include the following:

Tax Issue	Implications/Solutions
Capital Gains Tax	
▪ If there is a sale, is it to a connected person?	▪ If so, market value imposed by section 18 TCGA 1992.
▪ If not a connected person, unlikely that the sale/transfer is being made at arm's length?	▪ Therefore, market value imposed by section 17 TCGA 1992.
▪ If a market valuation is required, who will perform it?	▪ Inform client of danger of HMRC challenge to any valuation and strongly recommend valuation be carried out by independent expert valuer.
▪ Is the company 'close'?	▪ If so, consider impact of section 125 TCGA 1992.
▪ If there are sufficient distributable reserves and the transferee is a shareholder, is a distribution *in specie* more tax efficient?	▪ Company still deemed to dispose of asset at market value.
Inheritance Tax	
▪ Is the company 'close'?	▪ If so, consider impact of sections 94–102 IHTA 1994.
VAT	
▪ Is the business registered for VAT?	▪ If yes, VAT should be charged on the sale of taxable assets, unless TOGC applies.
▪ Is the TOGC treatment available?	▪ Consider conditions for both vendor and buyer, especially 'similar trade'.
▪ Has more than £250,000 been spent on land or buildings in the past 10 years?	▪ If so, consider the implications of the Capital Goods Scheme.
▪ Is any property being transferred?	▪ Consider if exempt, zero-rated or standard-rated.
▪ Has property been opted to tax?	▪ If no, should it be opted prior to transfer?
	▪ If yes, are additional conditions re: TOGC met?
Stamp Duty/SDLT	
▪ Is land or property being transferred?	▪ What rate of SDLT is payable?
▪ What is the value that is subject to SDLT?	▪ Is VAT being charged? If so, SDLT payable on VAT-inclusive amount.
	▪ Remember, there is no deemed market value rule for SDLT unless purchaser is a company.
▪ If there are sufficient distributable reserves and the transferee is a shareholder, is a distribution *in specie* more tax efficient?	▪ No SDLT payable on distribution *in specie*, provided no other consideration.
▪ Stamp duty is no longer charged on debtors or goodwill.	▪ Stamp duty should apply only if shares or securities are being transferred.

9.2.2 Sale or Transfer of Company Assets to a Third Party

Generally speaking, a shareholder will prefer to sell the shares in the company to a third party, rather than sell the trade and assets in the company. Where this is not the case, or **the purchaser insists on acquiring the trade and assets**, the following tax-planning issues should be considered:

Tax Issue	Implications/Solutions
Capital Gains Tax	
▥ Gains on sale of chargeable assets by company subject to corporation tax.	▥ Are there any capital losses brought forward?
	▥ Are there any current year losses to be utilised against the capital gain?
	▥ Can group/consortium relief be claimed?
▥ Consider disposal of goodwill of the business.	▥ Is it 'old' goodwill falling within CGT regime or 'new' goodwill falling within the IFA regime in Schedule 29 FA 2002?
▥ How will proceeds be extracted by shareholders?	▥ Consider liquidation of company post-sale.
Inheritance Tax	
▥ As the business is being sold to a third party, there should be no transfer of value.	▥ No immediate IHT on sale of assets by company.
▥ Company may no longer be qualifying trading company and therefore BPR may not be available.	▥ Consider impact of sale on taxable estates of shareholders.
VAT	
▥ Is the business registered for VAT?	▥ If yes, VAT should be charged on the sale of taxable assets, unless TOGC applies.
▥ Is the TOGC treatment available?	▥ Consider conditions for both vendor and buyer.
▥ If TOGC treatment applies, should the VAT number be transferred?	▥ As the business is being sold to a third party, the buyer is unlikely to want to bear the risks of taking over the VAT number.
▥ Has more than £250,000 been spent on land or buildings in the past 10 years?	▥ If so, consider the implications of the Capital Goods Scheme.
▥ Is any property being transferred?	▥ Consider if exempt, zero-rated or standard-rated.
▥ Has property been opted to tax?	▥ If no, should it be opted prior to transfer?
	▥ If yes, are additional conditions re: TOGC met?
Stamp Duty/SDLT	
▥ Is land or property being transferred?	▥ What rate of SDLT is payable?
▥ What is the value that is subject to SDLT?	▥ What amount of the proceeds is being allocated to land or buildings?
	▥ Is VAT being charged? If so, SDLT payable on VAT-inclusive amount.
▥ Stamp duty is no longer charged on debtors or goodwill.	▥ Stamp duty should apply only if shares or securities are being transferred.

9.3   Transfer/Sale of a Company

As noted above, where the owner of shares in a company wishes to pass value to the next generation, it is likely that this will be effected by the transfer of shares, whether this takes place during the owner's lifetime or on death.

It is important to remember that many of the CGT and IHT reliefs are only available for "trading" companies. You should check the conditions for each of the reliefs carefully, as "trading" is not the same in each instance. **Where the shares being transferred or sold are in an investment company, many of the favourable reliefs will not be available.**

Where there are no IHT, VAT or stamp duty/SDLT implications of a transaction, you should state that this is the case to show that you have considered all the capital taxes and the possible issues.

Three different types of scenario will be considered:

1. The sale/gift of company shares to a family member.
2. The sale of company shares to a third party.
3. The transfer of company shares on death.

9.3.1   When Shares in a Company are Being Sold or Gifted to a Family Member

Capital taxes planning issues to consider when shares in a company are being sold or gifted to a family member include the following:

Tax Issue	Implications/Solutions
Capital Gains Tax	
▪ If there is a sale, is it to a connected person?	▪ If so, market value imposed by section 18 TCGA 1992.
▪ If not a connected person, unlikely that the sale/transfer is being made at arm's length?	▪ Therefore, market value imposed by section 17 TCGA 1992.
▪ If a market valuation is required, who will perform it?	▪ Inform client of danger of HMRC challenge to any valuation and strongly recommend valuation be carried out by independent expert valuer.
▪ Can holdover relief under section 165 TCGA 1992 be claimed?	▪ Look carefully at the qualifying conditions.
	▪ Remember, full holdover relief can be claimed only where the shares are being gifted.
▪ Is the vendor eligible to claim ER on the gift/transfer of the shares?	▪ Look carefully at the qualifying conditions.
	▪ Is it beneficial for some proceeds to be paid so that ER can be utilised?
▪ Is the CGT annual exemption available for that year?	▪ Should some proceeds be paid to utilise the annual exemption?
▪ If transfer is a CLT for IHT purposes and section 165 holdover relief is not available, should holdover relief under section 260 TCGA 1992 be claimed?	▪ Remember that section 260 is not available where gifted to settlor-interested trust.
	▪ Consider implications for trustees' future CGT liability.
▪ If the vendor needs the proceeds from the sale of the shares and the family members cannot raise the funds, is a purchase of own shares by the company appropriate?	▪ Is the income tax or CGT treatment more favourable?
	▪ If the CGT treatment is beneficial, are all the conditions met?
Inheritance Tax	
▪ What value is being transferred?	▪ Remember that transfer of value for IHT is based on the 'loss to donor' principle.
	▪ Look carefully at shareholdings before and after transfer.
	▪ Related property rule to be considered.

▪ If a gift or transfer at undervalue, is it a chargeable lifetime transfer or PET?	▪ If a chargeable lifetime transfer, calculate the amount of chargeable gain to IHT.
▪ Is BPR available?	▪ Consider if conditions are met.
	▪ Consider the impact of any "excluded assets".
▪ If chargeable lifetime transfer and full BPR unavailable, who should pay the tax?	▪ Remember, if the donor pays tax, this is also a loss to his estate and grossing up applies.
▪ Consider impact of transferor's death within seven years.	▪ Will any (additional) IHT be payable?
	▪ Will BPR still be available?
VAT	
▪ No VAT on gift/transfer of shares as exempt transaction.	
Stamp Duty/SDLT	
▪ No SDLT payable, even if underlying assets include UK land when gifted.	▪ Fixed duty of £5 where shares transferred otherwise than on sale.
▪ Stamp duty payable by purchaser.	▪ *Ad valorem* duty of 0.5% on consideration for shares.

9.3.2 When Shares in a Company are Being Sold to a Third Party

Capital taxes planning issues to consider when shares in a company are being sold to a third party include the following:

Tax Issue	Implications/Solutions
Capital Gains Tax	
▪ Is the vendor eligible to claim ER?	▪ Look carefully at the qualifying conditions.
	▪ Are there any "associated disposals"?
▪ Should some or all of the proceeds be reinvested in EIS shares?	▪ This will be more attractive where the vendor is connected with the EIS company.
Inheritance Tax	
▪ As the business is being sold to a third party, there should be no transfer of value.	▪ No immediate IHT on sale of business.
▪ Vendor may have exchanged shares qualifying for BPR for cash.	▪ Consider impact of sale on vendor's taxable estate.
VAT	
▪ No VAT on gift/transfer of shares as exempt transaction.	
Stamp Duty/SDLT	
▪ No SDLT payable, even if underlying assets include UK land.	▪ *Ad valorem* duty of 0.5% on consideration for shares.
▪ Stamp duty payable by purchaser.	

9.3.3 Transfer of Company Shares on Death

Capital taxes planning issues to consider when shares in a company are being transferred on death include the following:

Tax Issue	Implications/Solutions
Capital Gains Tax ▪ Uplift to market value of all chargeable assets on death.	▪ Market value for CGT will equate to value for IHT purposes.
Inheritance Tax ▪ What is the value of the shares?	▪ Valuation of the shares for IHT purposes should be undertaken by independent expert valuer. ▪ Related property rule to be considered.
▪ Is BPR available?	▪ Consider if conditions are met.
▪ Are assets on which full BPR is available being transferred to spouse?	▪ Consider using a deed of variation (on which no IHT is payable) to pass assets on to next generation.
VAT ▪ No VAT on gift/transfer of shares as exempt transaction.	
Stamp Duty/SDLT ▪ No SDLT payable, even if underlying assets include UK land.	

Questions

Review Questions

(See Suggested Solutions to Review Questions at the end of this textbook.)

Question 9.1

Your client, Polly North, is managing director and sole shareholder of Circus Ltd, which owns and operates 10 restaurants in Northern Ireland. She established the company 15 years ago. The majority of the company's revenues are generated from the operation of the restaurants. However, the company also owns a significant portfolio of quoted shares, which generates a steady investment income.

Polly is 65 years old and due to retire shortly. Regarding succession planning, she has identified two options, either of which could be executed on the day of her retirement:

1. Sell the shares in Circus Ltd to her son at their market value. This would have the advantage that Polly would be able to buy a substantial holiday villa and retire to Florida. If desirable, the consideration for the shares could be paid over a number of years.
2. Alternatively, the shares could be transferred to her son for a nominal amount.

Requirement
You are required to prepare a memorandum for the tax partner discussing the CGT and IHT implications for Polly of the above plans. It is April 2016.

Question 9.2

It is March 2016. Glenn Simpson, who is 60 years old, has approached you for advice on tax mitigation in advance of his planned retirement. Glenn's estate is made up of the following assets:

Private residence	£550,000
Business (about to be sold)	£5,215,000
Shares and investments	£70,000
Cash	£5,800
Freehold commercial property	£345,000

Glenn anticipates a CGT bill on the sale of his sole trade business in the region of £125,000 and plans to spend the rest of the proceeds on holiday homes in Co. Kerry and the Algarve. The sale of the business will utilise Glenn's CGT annual exemption for the year and his remaining lifetime allowance for ER.

Glenn is in good health and has one daughter, Freya. He is a higher rate taxpayer.

Glenn has decided that he would like to give Freya the freehold commercial property, on the basis that Freya pays any CGT on the property gift. He acquired the property in March 2001 for £35,000 and it remained unused until he brought it into use in the business when it was established in September 2006. Glenn exercised an option to tax on the property at this point in time.

The purchasers of the business will be taking a lease on the property, which will provide a good rental return, and Glenn is keen that Freya has a steady income as she is trying to earn a living as a writer.

Requirement

Outline the tax implications of the proposed gift of the freehold property to Freya. Your answer should refer to the CGT, VAT, SDLT and IHT implications of the gift and any tax relief that may be available.

Challenging Questions

(Suggested Solutions to Challenging Questions are available through your lecturer.)

Question 9.1

The audit partner of your firm came to see you about a new client, Rory O'Neill, who is the managing director and sole shareholder of Kiddies Ltd. The company's principal activity is running children's day nurseries from four large Victorian houses situated within the local area, the freehold of which it owns.

He explained that the client was looking to slow down and was considering letting the properties and licensing the use of the trading name and businesses under a separate lease and contract, in return for a quarterly rental and a twice-yearly franchise payment, respectively.

Requirement

The audit partner is concerned that the above transactions may have tax implications for either the company or for Rory and would like you to prepare some notes on the subject.

Controlled Foreign Company Legislation

10.1   Introduction

The controlled foreign company (CFC) legislation was introduced in the UK to prevent UK resident companies from establishing companies overseas in order to benefit from a lower rate of corporation tax. Where a CFC exists and it cannot qualify for one of the exemptions, its profits will be attributed to its UK parent and taxed in the UK at the main rate of corporation tax, thereby negating the benefit of a lower rate of tax overseas.

The CFC legislation can be found at Part 9A of the Taxation (International and Other Provisions) Act 2010 (TIOPA 2010). The regime will also apply, to an extent, to permanent establishments (PEs) – see Chapter 3A of Part 2 CTA 2009.

The new regime introduced by FA 2012 has effect for accounting periods beginning on or after 1 January 2013.

Note that the CFC regime applies to **income profits only**. Capital gains are not covered by the regime. Anti-avoidance legislation for CGT with similar aims is found in section 13 TCGA 1992, and is discussed in **Section 4.4.1**.

The purpose of the new rules is to better target the CFC charge so that it is not applied to profits arising from genuine foreign economic activities or where there has been no artificial diversion of UK profits.

10.1.1   Basic Definition of a CFC

The CFC regime applies to companies resident outside the UK that are controlled by UK residents. It also applies by extension to exempt foreign branches (PEs) of UK resident companies. The rules (set out at Chapter 18 of Part 9A TIOPA 2010) define what is meant by UK control, including by reference to accounting standards.

Under section 371AA TIOPA 2010 **any** controlled foreign company is a CFC, but there is an exemption for CFCs that do not pay a low rate of tax. This is in contrast to the previous rules where a lower level of tax was part of the definition of a CFC.

Chapter 2 of Part 9A TIOPA 2010 sets out the steps for determining if a CFC charge arises once it is established that a foreign company is a CFC. There is a CFC charge only if the following apply:

▣ the CFC has "chargeable profits";
▣ none of the CFC exemptions apply; and
▣ there is a UK "interest holder" (see **Section 10.4**) that is not exempt and that (together with connected and associated companies) holds an interest of at least 25%.

These conditions may be applied in any order, so that, for example, if one of the CFC exemptions applies to a CFC it is not necessary to consider whether or not it has any chargeable profits.

If a CFC charge arises, it is charged on each "chargeable company" that holds a relevant interest.

10.2 Exemptions from the CFC Charge

As stated above, there are still "entity level" exemptions which, if they apply, will exempt all the profits of a CFC from the CFC charge. These are as follows:

▣ Exempt period (for foreign companies becoming CFCs for the first time) – details in Chapter 10 of Part 9A TIOPA 2010. The exempt period is 12 months with the possibility of an extension if certain conditions are met.
▣ Excluded territories (for CFCs resident in certain territories, subject to conditions) – details in Chapter 11 of Part 9A TIOPA 2010.
▣ Low profits (for CFCs with low levels of profit) – details in Chapter 12 of Part 9A TIOPA 2010. Generally speaking, this exemption applies if the total accounting or taxable profits of the CFC are less than £50,000, or if total accounting or taxable profits are less than £500,000 and the non-trading income included within those profits is less than £50,000.
▣ Low profit margin (for CFCs whose profit is a small margin above certain defined expenditure) – details in Chapter 13 of Part 9A TIOPA 2010. This exemption applies for a CFC's accounting period if the accounting profits are no more than 10% of the CFC's relevant operating expenditure.
▣ Tax exemption (for CFCs that pay at least 75% of the tax they would have paid in the UK) – details in Chapter 14 of Part 9A TIOPA 2010. See **Examples 10.1** and **10.2** below.

Example 10.1

Carrot Ltd, a UK resident company, owns 100% of Parsnip BV, a company resident in Utopia. Parsnip BV's accounts are prepared in accordance with UK GAAP and its accounting profit before tax in the year ended 31 March 2017 was £2 million. Included in the accounts is depreciation of £200,000.

The tax rate in Utopia is 19% and depreciation is not tax deductible. Parsnip BV is able to take advantage of a special tax regime in Utopia so that it obtains a 100% tax deduction for the costs of tangible fixed assets in the year of acquisition. In the year ended 31 March 2017, Parsnip BV acquired fixed assets costing £500,000.

You have calculated that, under the UK rules, Parsnip BV would be entitled to capital allowances of £150,000 in the year ended 31 March 2017.

Does Parsnip BV qualify for the tax exemption for the year ended 31 March 2017?

continued overleaf

Solution

Tax payable in Utopia:

	£
Profit before tax	2,000,000
Add: depreciation	200,000
Less: 100% allowance	(500,000)
Taxable profits	1,700,000
Tax @ 19%	323,000

Corresponding UK tax:

	£
Profit before tax	2,000,000
Add: depreciation	200,000
Less: capital allowances	(150,000)
Taxable profits	2,050,000
Corresponding UK tax @ 20%	410,000
75% of Corresponding UK tax	307,500

Parsnip BV does qualify for the tax exemption in the year ended 31 March 2017, as the tax payable of £323,000 is more than 75% of the corresponding UK tax.

Example 10.2

Broccoli BV is a subsidiary of a UK resident company and is resident in Country A. There is a total of seven companies in the group.

Broccoli BV has chargeable profits of £1,250,000 in the year ended 31 March 2017. It paid tax of £150,000 in Country A in respect of those profits. In addition, it paid tax of £125,000 in Country B, where it has a permanent establishment (PE). This is its only source of income. The £150,000 tax paid in Country A is net of double tax relief given for tax paid in Country B.

Does Broccoli BV qualify for the tax exemption in the year ended 31 March 2017?

Solution

Corresponding UK tax:

	£	£
Chargeable profits:	1,250,000	
UK tax @ 20%		250,000
Less: double tax relief – lower of:		
(i) £1,250,000 @ 20%	250,000	
(ii) Foreign tax paid	125,000	(125,000)
Corresponding UK tax		125,000
75% of corresponding UK tax		93,750

Broccoli BV does qualify for the tax exemption in the year ended 31 March 2017, as the tax paid of £150,000 is more than 75% of the corresponding UK tax.

10.3   Determining Chargeable Profits: The "CFC Charge Gateway"

An important change from earlier legislation is that, even if the above exemptions do not apply, the CFC charge will apply **only** to those profits that are identified by the legislation as being "chargeable profits" within the scope of the CFC charge.

A CFC's chargeable profits are the part of its profits that pass through the "CFC charge gateway". The gateway is set out in Chapters 3–8 of Part 9A TIOPA 2010 and is a series of definitions of profits that may fall within the CFC regime.

The gateway begins by providing a number of tests by which companies can check whether any of the chapters that define the amounts of chargeable profits apply. These tests are contained in Chapter 3 of Part 9A TIOPA 2010, the purpose of which is to provide a simple and accessible means for the identification of companies for which there can be no CFC charge because there are no chargeable profits.

The different chapters of Part 9A TIOPA 2010 deal with different types of profit:

- Chapter 3 is the "initial" gateway that determines whether any of Chapters 4–8 need to be considered. If none of Chapters 4–8 is engaged by Chapter 3, then there are no chargeable profits.
- Chapter 4 deals with any profit other than non-trading finance profits and profits arising from a property business. It therefore deals with trading profits.
- Chapter 5 deals with non-trading finance profits. (**Note:** Chapter 9 can stand in place of Chapter 5 if the chargeable company so elects – it gives partial or full exemption for certain intragroup non-trade finance profits.)
- Chapter 6 deals with trading finance profits.
- Chapter 7 deals with captive insurance business.
- Chapter 8 deals with certain subsidiaries of banks.

Chapters 3–8 are subject to the application of Chapter 9 (exemptions for profits from qualifying loan relationships) and Chapter 10 (the exempt period exemption).

For most CFCs, there will be no need to consider the CFC legislation beyond Chapter 3. Where appropriate, HMRC will give CFC clearances by reference to Chapter 3, considering the later gateway chapters only where the Chapter 3 rules make it necessary to do so.

10.3.1   The "Initial" Gateway and Trading Profits

The trading profits to which the CFC charge will apply are determined by reference to Chapter 4. As stated above, Chapter 3 (section 371, Part 9A TIOPA 2010) provides an "initial" gateway through which profits must pass before further chapters need to be considered.

Profits will not pass through the initial gateway, and so not be subject to Chapter 4, if one or more of conditions A, B, C or D are met. This means that if any of the conditions are met, Chapter 4 does not apply and no CFC charge will be applied to the profits under that chapter.

The four conditions are:

Condition A – a two-part test of the purpose of the arrangements by which a CFC holds assets or bears risk. This condition is met if, broadly, the CFC does not hold assets or risks under an arrangement that results in it benefitting from a reduction of tax in any territory, where the arrangement would not have been made but for the tax benefit. In addition, for condition A to apply, the main purpose (or one of the main purposes) of the arrangement must not be a reduction of UK tax, the consequence being that the CFC is more profitable (other than negligibly so) than it would otherwise have been.

Condition B – asks whether the CFC has any assets or risks for which key management activities are in the UK.

Condition C – applies if Condition B is not met, and asks whether the CFC has the capability, on a stand-alone basis or with third-party support, to ensure that its business would be commercially effective if the assets or risks were to stop being managed/controlled in the UK.

Condition D – excludes companies that have only property business profits and/or non-trade finance profits. This means that Chapter 4 does not apply if the CFC has no trading profits.

In analysing the above conditions, it is evident that one of the main aims of the legislation is to counteract the avoidance of tax through the diversion of profits from the UK.

10.3.2 Trading Profits

If none of the "initial" gateway conditions set out in Chapter 3 are met, it will be necessary to undertake the steps in Chapter 4. The steps involve identifying the CFC's assets and risks that have created its "assumed total profits". Any assets or risks that have only a negligible impact on profits can be ignored. Next, the "significant people functions" (SPFs) of the CFC need to be determined, and then allocated either as UK SPFs or non-UK SPFs. If none of the SPFs is a UK SPF, then it is not necessary to look any further. If some of the SPFs are UK SPFs, then the profits of the CFC need to attributed to the UK on the assumption that the UK SPFs are carried out by a permanent establishment in the UK.

General Exclusions

Note that even if UK SPFs are identified in Chapter 4, and accordingly an amount of UK profits has been calculated, there are a number of general exclusions that can prevent a CFC charge from arising. For example, the profits of a CFC are excluded if **all** of the following five conditions are met (section 371DF):

1. *Business premises condition* If the CFC has premises in the CFC's territory that are occupied (or are intended to be occupied) with a reasonable degree of permanence.
2. *Income condition* If no more than 20% of the CFC's trading income derives from the UK.
3. *Management expenditure condition* If UK management expenditure is no more than 20% of total related management expenditure.
4. *IP condition* If the CFC does not exploit intellectual property transferred to it by a connected person/company in the UK within the previous six years.
5. *Export of goods condition* If no more than 20% of the CFC's trading income arises from goods exported from the UK, excluding exports from the UK to the CFC's territory of residence.

Where, in relation to a CFC, it is necessary to consider the more detailed gateway rules in one or more of Chapters 4–8, only those profits (if any) that pass through the gateway may be included within its "assumed total profits". These are what its profits would be if it were a standalone UK tax resident company (i.e. not a member of a UK group) but before deduction of amounts that are relieved against a company's total profits, being mainly management expenses (amounts relieved under Step 2 of section 4 CTA 2010).

10.4 Applying the CFC Charge

If the CFC has an amount of assumed total profits, the next step is to determine its "assumed total taxable profits". In determining those profits, relief may be given by way of a deduction from the assumed total profits of the related expenses and charges to the extent that it is just and reasonable to do so.

Unless there is some reason to use a different figure, such as the application of other legislation that disallows a particular deduction, the proportion of deductions for which relief will be granted will correspond to the proportion of assumed total profits passing through the gateway. This means that if half of total profits pass through the gateway, then relief will be allowed so that half of the taxable profit will so pass. For example, if a quarter of the CFC's assumed total profits would pass through the CFC charge gateway, only a quarter of the amounts that would otherwise be relievable against the assumed total profits are to be deducted in arriving at the CFC's assumed taxable total profits (and, thus, its chargeable profits). Management expenses are the most common type of deduction against total profits.

Note that most types of loss relief available to a CFC are set against a particular category of profits rather than being set against total profits; in particular, losses arising from a trade carried on wholly outside the UK may not be set against total profits.

In practice, it will probably be necessary to determine chargeable profits before it is possible to determine the proportion of deductions available against total profits that it is just and reasonable to deduct from the chargeable profits.

Once the taxable profits on which a charge is due have been determined, the charge will be apportioned to each chargeable company holding a relevant interest.

The general rule is that a relevant interest holder is a chargeable company if its interest, together with interests of connected or associated companies, is at least 25%. In that case, a CFC charge is made of an amount equivalent to the proportion determined under the rules in Chapter 17 of Part 9A TIOPA 2010.

10.5   Impact of the CFC Rules

Overall, taking account of the gateway and the rest of the CFC legislation, the impact of the regime may be summarised as follows.

Non-trading finance profits derived from lending (or arrangements equivalent to lending) may be brought within the CFC charge by Chapter 5 of Part 9A TIOPA 2010 if:

- the profits are derived from activity (such as lending decisions) undertaken in the UK;
- the lending is derived from UK capital investment or some other UK capital contribution; or
- the loans are made to UK residents.

This is subject to an exception for lending that is incidental to an exempt trade or property business, or to a business of holding shares in subsidiary companies.

Profits derived from loans may qualify for full or partial exemption under Chapter 9 of Part 9A TIOPA 2010 if the loan is made to another CFC under common control with the lender (referred to as a qualifying loan relationship). Chapter 9 replaces Chapter 5 in the event of a claim made by the chargeable company. A claim will bring all the CFC's qualifying loan relationships into the Chapter 9 provisions, but profits from other loan relationships continue to be dealt with under Chapter 5.

Where the CFC charge results from capital investment or other capital contributed to the CFC, as much profit as reflects the value of work undertaken by the CFC is excluded from the Chapter 5 charge.

If the financial profits arise from a trading activity, then Chapters 4 and 6 of Part 9A TIOPA 2010 may be relevant.

10.6   Interaction of CFC Legislation and Double Tax Relief

The profits of the CFC to be apportioned are calculated together with any creditable tax claimable. Creditable tax is the sum of:

1.   double tax relief on foreign tax paid under the normal rules (foreign tax is the tax paid in the territory of residence of the CFC and any other countries, excluding the UK);
2.   UK income tax deducted at source or charged on the CFC's income (e.g. on UK rental income, bank interest); and
3.   UK corporation tax paid on the CFC's income as a result of the CFC having a permanent establishment in the UK.

Where the chargeable profits of the CFC contain income in respect of a payment that has been reduced for tax purposes by the application of the worldwide debt cap rules, then the apportioned profits may be reduced (subject to HMRC approval). The related tax credit will also be reduced.

The concepts of apportioning the profits of a CFC and its creditable tax are illustrated in **Example 10.3**.

Example 10.3
Cauliflower Ltd, a UK resident company, has taxable profits of £80,000 in the year ended 31 March 2017. It has one wholly owned subsidiary, Champignon SAS, which does not qualify for any of the CFC exemptions in the accounting period.

Champignon SAS is resident in Jersey. In the year ended 31 March 2017, it had interest income of £75,000 from the RoI and paid tax at source of £2,000 on this income. It also paid tax of £7,500 on this income in Jersey and was unable to obtain any credit for the tax paid in the RoI.

1.   Advise whether Champignon SAS is subject to a lower level of taxation in Jersey in the year ended 31 March 2017.

2.   Calculate the UK corporation tax liability of Cauliflower Ltd for the year ended 31 March 2017.

Solution

Tax payable in Jersey = £7,500
Corresponding UK tax:

		£
Chargeable profits:	£75,000	
UK tax @ 20%		15,000
Less: double tax relief – lower of:		
1. £75,000 @ 20%	£15,000	
2. Foreign tax paid	£2,000	(2,000)
Corresponding UK tax		13,000
75% of corresponding UK tax		9,750

The tax paid in Jersey of £7,500 is less than 75% of the corresponding UK tax, therefore Champignon SAS is subject to a lower level of taxation in the year ended 31 March 2017.

continued overleaf

	£	£
Total taxable profits	80,000	
UK tax @ 20%		16,000
Add: CFC apportionment		
£75,000 @ 20%	15,000	
Less: creditable tax	(9,500)	
UK tax on CFC apportionment		5,500
UK corporation tax liability		21,500

Questions

Review Questions

(See Suggested Solutions to Review Questions at the end of this textbook.)

Question 10.1

Broccoli BV is a subsidiary of a UK resident company and is resident in Country A. There is a total of seven companies in the group.

Broccoli BV has chargeable profits of £750,000 in the year ended 31 March 2017. It paid tax of £35,000 in Country A in respect of those profits. In addition, it paid tax of £25,000 in Country B, where it has a PE. The £35,000 tax paid in Country A is net of double tax relief given for tax paid in Country B.

Included in its chargeable profits is income of £45,000 from a PE in the UK.

Requirement
Compute if Broccoli BV meets the tax exemption criteria for CFCs in the year ended 31 March 2017.

Challenging Questions

(Suggested Solutions to Challenging Questions are available through your lecturer.)

Question 10.1

Your firm is undertaking a due diligence for a client who has made an offer to purchase the Apricot group of companies, whose parent company is resident in the UK. In the course of the tax element of the due diligence exercise, you have noted the existence of certain non-UK entities within the Apricot group, none of which has ever paid a dividend to the UK parent. These include the following:

1. Apricot Insurance Ltd, a captive insurance company incorporated in Guernsey where, following the making of an appropriate election, it has been agreed that it will pay income tax at 21.5% of its accounting profit.
2. Apricot Traders (China) Ltd, a company incorporated in China in 2007, which acquires goods manufactured by Taiwanese third parties and, after sorting, packaging and labelling them, sells them to third-party distributors for sale to customers. About 75% of these sales are to UK-based distributors.

The corporate tax rate in China is 25%, but the company is based in a special economic zone entitling it to a 10-year exemption from tax on its profits.

3. Apricot Engineers Pte Ltd, a company incorporated in Hong Kong, where it carries on the business of providing engineering design services throughout the Asia Pacific region. Most of this business is carried on as a sub-contractor to other companies in the Apricot group, divided equally between Apricot companies in the UK and Apricot companies outside the UK. The rate of corporate tax in Hong Kong is 16.5%.

4. Apricot Developments Pte Ltd, a company incorporated in Hong Kong, which has acquired intellectual property relating to various developments carried out by group companies over the years and licenses this intellectual property to third-party customers around the world.

Requirement

Draft a memo to the tax partner explaining the UK CFC issues that arise in relation to these non-UK subsidiary companies.

Trusts and Estates

11.1 Introduction to Trusts

A trust or settlement arises where there is an obligation binding a person or persons (the trustee(s)) to hold or deal with property in a particular way for the benefit of another person or class of persons (the beneficiaries) whose interests are protected by the equitable jurisdiction of the courts.

A trust may be established either on a death, usually under the terms of a will, or during the lifetime of the settlor (*inter vivos*).

A trust can be created without written documentation. However, there are certain legal requirements that must be met to ensure the validity of a trust, including the "three certainties":

1. **Certainty of Words and Intention** – a trust deed should clearly state the intention of the trust.
2. **Certainty of Subject Matter** – the trust property and the interests in that property of each of the beneficiaries or class of beneficiaries should be clearly identified.
3. **Certainty of Beneficiaries** – the persons who are to be regarded as beneficiaries should be clearly identifiable by the trustees.

11.1.1 Definitions

Trust
There is no legal definition of the term 'trust' in UK legislation. Trusts are part of equity law in the UK, a branch of law that emerged from common law; common law being unwritten and evolving from custom

and precedent over time. It is the part of UK law derived from judicial decisions. The concept of a trust is recognised in other countries where the legal system is based on common law (e.g. USA, Australia). Jurisdictions (such as France) that operate a civil law system, in which all laws are codified in the legislation, may not recognise the concept of a trust in their domestic legislation.

A definition that works from a legal perspective is that a trust is a disposition of property to a person (trustee) or persons jointly (trustees) in whom the legal title then vests, in the confidence that the benefits will be applied to the advantage of one or more other persons (beneficiaries) or some other object permitted by law.

So, generally speaking, the legal ownership of the property is separated from the beneficial ownership of the property, but the legal owners (trustees) are under a duty to apply the property for the benefit of the beneficial owners (beneficiaries).

Settlor

The settlor of a trust is the person who settles the property on (i.e. transfers property into) the trust. This transfer can be by way of a settlement between the living (*inter vivos*) or in a will. A settlor in a will is usually referred to as the 'testator'.

The settlor can appoint themselves as a trustee, but they cannot do what they like with the property. As a trustee, they hold the assets in a fiduciary capacity. This means that they must exercise their rights and powers in good faith and for the benefit of beneficiaries. Trust property does not pass to the settlor's personal representatives when they die.

Under anti-avoidance provisions at section 620 Income Tax (Trading and Other Income) Act 2005 (ITTOIA 2005), a person is treated as having made a settlement, and so being the settlor, if they:

■ have made or entered into the settlement directly or indirectly;
■ have provided funds directly or indirectly for the purpose of the settlement;
■ have undertaken to provide funds directly or indirectly for the purpose of the settlement; or
■ have made a reciprocal arrangement with another person for the other person to make or enter into the settlement.

Trusts set up by a will are not caught by this section.

Trustee

A trustee holds property on trust for another and is entrusted with the administration of the trust.

There is no agreed definition of a trustee. One generally accepted definition of a trustee's duties (taken from *Law of Trusts and Trustees* by Sir Arthur Underhill) is that the trustee has an equitable obligation binding them to deal with property over which they have control (the trust property) for the benefit of persons (of whom they may themselves be one), any one of whom may enforce the obligations.

Beneficiary

A beneficiary is the person for whose benefit property is held. The person holding the property can be an administrator, an executor or a trustee.

There are various interests that a beneficiary may have in the property held by the trust, for example:

Absolute Interest – a full and complete interest in both the income and capital held by the trust. It can refer to the present or to the future when the interest vests.

Interest in Possession – the immediate entitlement (subject to any prior claims by the trustees for expenses, etc.) to any income produced immediately, as it arises. No immediate right to the capital.

Life Interest – the beneficiary (life tenant) has an interest in the income arising for a period of time. This often ends with the life tenant's death, but it can be for some other period.

Limited Interest – less than a full or absolute interest. For example, a life interest is limited. It confers only a right to income (normally, but not always, for the period of the beneficiary's lifetime) and no right to capital.

Discretionary Interest – the beneficiary's right to income is at the discretion of the trustees. The trustees must exercise their power fairly. No beneficiary has a right to the income arising, i.e. none has an interest in possession.

Reversionary Interest – a future or deferred right to property.

Determinable Interest – applies to a life interest that ends following an action by the beneficiary. The beneficiary may, for example, assign his interest.

Contingent Interest – an interest that is dependent on an event that is not certain to occur. For example, this could be the beneficiary reaching the age of thirty.

Vested Interest – a right that exists at present. It is not necessarily in possession, but it will become so in the future.

Immediate Post-death Interest – Finance Act 2006 defined an immediate post-death interest (IPDI) as one where a person has an interest in possession in settled property and the settlement was effected by will or under an intestacy, and the beneficiary became beneficially entitled to the interest in possession on the death of the testator or intestate.

Transitional Serial Interest – where an interest in possession trust arose before 6 April 2008 but on or after 22 March 2006, it will be regarded as a transitional serial interest (TSI), provided that it followed a previous interest in possession in effect immediately before that date. An interest in possession trust may also be regarded as a TSI if it arises on the death of the holder of the previous interest on or after 6 April 2008 and if either the new holder is the spouse or civil partner of the previous holder or the settled property consists of a contract of life insurance.

11.1.2 Reasons to Create a Trust

There are various scenarios in which the use of a trust or settlement may be considered:

1. Gifting to Young Beneficiaries

Trusts are often used to gift assets to beneficiaries who are regarded as being too young to manage and control the property immediately. By gifting the assets via a trust, the settlor can make a gift in life whilst still retaining some degree of control over the level of income or capital received by the beneficiary.

2. Succession of Assets

Trusts are often used to ensure that assets are succeeded to as the settlor intended, e.g. a settlor could create a trust for his wife for her life with the provision that, on her death, all the assets held by the trust pass to his children, thereby guaranteeing that the assets remain in his family in the event that the wife remarries and/or has other children.

3. Concealing Beneficial Ownership

Trusts can be used to disguise the true beneficial ownership of an asset or assets. This is most commonly achieved through use of a nominee arrangement.

4. Tax Planning

A trust can be a useful tax planning tool, although the tax advantages of holding assets through a trust have been dramatically reduced in recent years. Care should be taken when using trusts as a tax planning tool not to trigger the anti-avoidance legislation. Also, as tax legislation is in an almost constant state of flux, what saves tax this year may not be effective in the future.

11.2 Types of Trust

11.2.1 Bare Trust

A bare, or simple, trust is one in which each beneficiary has an immediate and absolute title to both capital and income. The beneficiaries of a bare trust have the right to take actual possession of trust property. In effect, the trustees hold the property as 'nominee'. The beneficiaries of a bare trust are treated for tax purposes as personally receiving the income and gains as they arise. The trustees are not required to make a tax return.

Example 11.1

Dorothy gifts shares in Cadbury plc to her nephew, Tim, age 12. Tim's parents hold the shares as nominees until Tim reaches age 18.

Tim is entitled to the dividend income and any proceeds on sale of the shares. He will be subject to income tax/CGT and must return any income or gains on his tax return.

He has a right to both income and capital and, therefore, has beneficial ownership. His parents hold the legal title to the shares as trustees/nominees because he is a minor.

This is an example of a bare trust.

11.2.2 Interest in Possession Trusts

The main authority for the definition of an interest in possession is the House of Lords case *Pearson and others v. IRC* ((1980) STC 318). A person has an interest in possession when they have "a present right of present enjoyment" or an immediate right to the income or enjoyment of property (irrespective of whether the property produces income).

If the trustees have the power to withhold income from the beneficiaries, then there is no interest in possession (IIP).

The rights of a beneficiary, or life tenant, under an IIP trust can be brought to an end, for example on the beneficiary reaching a certain age or on the occasion of their marriage or death, but the trust will remain an IIP until then.

An IIP trust may be used where the settlor wishes to give a beneficiary an immediate entitlement to the income, but intends to gift the capital to someone else. It could also be used to give a child or young person an income stream with the entitlement to the capital deferred until they are mature enough to manage it responsibly.

Example 11.2

Dorothy gifts shares in Cadbury plc to an IIP trust. The beneficiary of the trust is her nephew, Tim, age 12, and the trustees are his parents. Tim will become entitled to the capital in the trust on reaching age 21.

Until he reaches 21, Tim is entitled to the income arising from the shares only. In simple terms, Tim is liable to income tax on the dividend income.

Until he reaches 21, Tim does not have control over the shares themselves and cannot make any decisions on selling or retaining them. If the trustees sell the shares, the trust will be subject to CGT at 28%. Tim would not be entitled to the proceeds of any sale until he is 21.

11.2.3 Discretionary Trusts

A discretionary trust is a trust where no individual has a right to an interest in possession. As the name suggests, the distribution of the income and capital of the trust is at the discretion of the trustees. The trustees can decide to accumulate income within the trust for future use or reinvestment; they are not under an obligation to distribute the income to the beneficiaries as it arises, as none of the beneficiaries has a present right to present enjoyment of the income and/or capital.

> **Example 11.3**
>
> Dorothy gifts shares in Cadbury plc to a discretionary trust. The beneficiary of the trust is her nephew, Tim, age 12, and the trustees are his parents.
>
> Tim is not entitled to receive the dividend income. The dividend income is received by the trustees and subject to income tax in their hands. Tim's parents can decide whether to accumulate some or all of the dividend income or distribute it to him. In simple terms, Tim is liable to income tax only on distributions made by the trustees to him, and he will be given a tax credit relating to tax paid by the trust.
>
> Tim is not entitled to the shares themselves or to the proceeds of any sale. If the trustees sell the shares, the trust will be subject to CGT at 20%. Tim's parents have discretion to distribute some or all of the shares, or proceeds on the sale of shares, to Tim, but are not required to do so.

Given the amount of discretion trustees of a discretionary trust have over the application of the income and capital of the trust, it is vital for the settlor to choose the trustees wisely. Where the trust is established during the settlor's lifetime, the settlor may choose to be a trustee.

The settlor should consider giving the trustees a 'letter of wishes'. This letter sets out the settlor's present and future intentions for the trust property. It may provide suggestions to the trustees on how their discretion might be exercised in the light of potential future circumstances, but it cannot instruct the trustees or fetter their discretion.

Accumulation and Maintenance Trusts

Up to 22 March 2006, an accumulation and maintenance (A&M) trust was a discretionary trust where the property in the trust was held for the maintenance, education or benefit of the beneficiaries, or accumulated until the beneficiaries reached the age of 25. The property in these trusts was not subject to exit/proportionate charges or 10-yearly charges (see **Section 11.6** below) and gifts/transfers into them were treated as potentially exempt transfers for IHT purposes.

From 22 March 2006, if the trustees changed the terms of the trust before 6 April 2008 to ensure that the beneficiary became absolutely entitled to the property in the trust on or before their 18th birthday, the trust will have continued to be an A&M trust. If the trustees changed the terms before 6 April 2008 to ensure that the beneficiary became absolutely entitled to the property in the trust between their 18th and 25th birthdays, the trust will have become an "age 18 to 25 trust" and so will be subject to an age 18 to 25 exit charge whenever property leaves the trust and when the beneficiary becomes absolutely entitled to the property in the trust between their 18th and 25th birthdays.

If nothing was done to change the terms of an existing A&M trust before 6 April 2008, it will have become a relevant property trust and, as such, will be subject to exit/proportionate and 10-yearly charges.

Age 18 to 25 Trusts

From 22 March 2006, an age 18 to 25 trust is a discretionary trust set up under the will or intestacy of a deceased parent or step-parent, where the property is held on trust for the benefit of someone aged over 18 and under 25 years old. The property in an 18 to 25 trust is subject to age 18 to 25 exit charges when property leaves the trust on or before the beneficiary's 25th birthday.

11.2.4 Trusts for Vulnerable Beneficiaries

Some trusts for disabled people and children get special tax treatment which means they may pay less tax. These trusts are known as trusts for "vulnerable beneficiaries". A vulnerable beneficiary is either:

- a person who is mentally or physically disabled; or
- someone under 18 – called a "relevant minor" – who has lost a parent through death.

Qualifying Trusts for a Disabled Person
The assets in these trusts can be used only to benefit a disabled person. The disabled person must be entitled to all of the income or, if they are not, none of the income can be applied for the benefit of anyone else.

Qualifying Trusts for a Relevant Minor
These trusts are commonly set up by the will of a parent who has died. The assets and income must be used only for the relevant minor and, when they reach 18 years of age, they must get all of the trust's assets.

11.2.5 Parental Trusts for Minors

Some trusts are set up to give benefits to a minor, unmarried child of the person who put the assets into the trust – the 'settlor'. These types of trust are known as "parental trusts for minors". The income from the trust is taxed as the income of the settlor. A parental trust for minors is one where a "relevant child" (a child under 18 who has never been married or in a civil partnership) of the settlor can benefit from a trust. In this case, the settlor must be one of the child's parents.

Parental trusts for minors aren't a type of trust in their own right; they will be one of the following types of trust:

- bare trusts – where the child is absolutely entitled to the income and the capital of the trust;
- interest in possession trusts – where the child may be entitled to all the income after expenses;
- accumulation trusts – where trustees can retain and add income to capital on behalf of the child; or
- discretionary trusts – where trustees can make payments at their discretion to the child.

With parental trusts for minors, the child's income from the trust is deemed to be the income of the settlor for tax purposes. This rule only applies to trusts where a relevant child can benefit, and the settlor and his/her spouse or civil partner are excluded. If the settlor (and spouse or civil partner) isn't excluded, then the rules for settlor-interested trusts apply instead.

Reciprocal Arrangements
A person will be regarded as a settlor if they have made a reciprocal arrangement with any other person for that person to make or enter into a settlement.

Particular attention is paid by HMRC to settlements where minor beneficiaries are involved and which have not been made by the parents.

Example 11.4
David, who is 12 years old, owns shares in his parents' company that cost £15,000. The investment is said to be a gift from his uncle, Alex. Alex's daughter, Lesley, who is nine years old, has £15,000 invested in a savings account. The source of the deposit is said to be a gift from her aunt, Anne, who is David's mother. Under such a reciprocal arrangement, Alex would be the settlor in respect of the settlement to his daughter, Lesley, and Anne would be the settlor in respect of the settlement to her son, David. HMRC will "look through" such arrangements to ascertain their true nature.

11.2.6 Settlor-interested Trusts

If the settlor or their spouse or civil partner may benefit from income or gains from assets held in a trust, it is regarded as a "settlor-interested trust".

Settlor-interested trusts aren't a type of trust in their own right; they will be one of the following types of trust:

- interest in possession (IIP) trusts – where the settlor or the settlor's spouse or civil partner may be entitled to all the income;

- accumulation trusts – where trustees can retain and add income to capital on behalf of the settlor or the settlor's spouse or civil partner; or
- discretionary trusts – where trustees can make payments to the settlor or the settlor's spouse or civil partner.

Example 11.5

John has an illness and can no longer work. He decides to set up a discretionary trust to ensure he has money in the future. He places some of his money in the trust. This makes him the settlor, but he may also benefit from the trust, so he "retains an interest". This is because the trustees can make payments to him. This is therefore a settlor-interested trust and will be taxed accordingly.

11.2.7 Relevant Property Trusts

The term "relevant property" is an IHT term and refers to property in which no qualifying interest in possession exists. Section 59 Inheritance Tax Act 1984 (IHTA 1984) provides a definition of those "qualifying interests". Where a person becomes beneficially entitled to an interest in possession on or after 22 March 2006, this will only be a qualifying interest in possession if it is an:

- immediate post-death interest;
- disabled person's interest; or
- transitional serial interest.

All property settled on discretionary trusts is relevant property unless it is held in one of the "special trusts" (e.g. a trust for a bereaved minor or an age 18 to 25 trust), or was excluded property (e.g. non-UK property with a non-domiciled beneficiary or a reversionary interest).

11.3 Taxation of Trusts

This section will look at the taxation of trusts from an IHT and CGT perspective. You are not required to deal with the income tax treatment of trusts; however, it is worthwhile to note that discretionary trusts are penalised from an income tax perspective. For example, the additional rate of income tax applies to all income over £1,000, with dividend income over this amount taxed at 38.1%.

It is useful to split the life of a trust into stages to examine the tax treatment for IHT and CGT purposes:

1. the taxation on the creation of a trust through the transfer of property;
2. the taxation during the existence of the trust while it holds the property; and
3. the taxation on the termination of a trust or when property leaves the trust.

11.3.1 Creation of a Trust: Inheritance Tax Treatment

On the creation of a trust, the settlor shall transfer assets to the trustees. This transfer may have both IHT and CGT consequences.

From an IHT perspective, the consequences will depend on whether the transfer is a chargeable lifetime transfer (CLT) or a potentially exempt transfer (PET).

Chargeable Lifetime Transfers
Further informations on CLTs can be found in **Chapter 23** of *CA Proficiency 2: Taxation 2 (NI) 2016–2017*.

Lifetime IHT on CLTs
Since 22 March 2006, the rule is that lifetime transfers of value to relevant property trusts (see **Section 11.2.7**) are CLTs. This means that the transfer of value is immediately chargeable to IHT at the lifetime IHT rate, i.e. half of the death rate (the rate at time of death). The current rate of IHT is 40%, so the lifetime rate is 20%.

In determining how much of the nil rate band is available to set against the transfer of value, it is necessary to take into consideration CLTs made in the seven years prior to the current CLT.

Due to the requirement to look back over a number of years when calculating the available nil rate band, it is important to appreciate the rules on lifetime transfers prior to 22 March 2006. Prior to that date, lifetime transfers to IIP trusts and A&M trusts were PETs (see **Section 11.3.2**) on which an IHT charge could be avoided if the donor survived seven years from the date of the transfer. PETs utilise the annual exemption(s), but are not treated as diminishing the nil rate band when calculating the IHT payable during lifetime on a CLT.

Transfers of value to a company are, and were before 22 March 2006, CLTs.

The liability to lifetime IHT on a CLT lies with the donee, i.e. the trustees. However, the donor may decide to pay the IHT liability. Where this is the case, the donor is treated as making a chargeable transfer of the value of the asset **plus** the amount of IHT payable on the transfer. The IHT payable on the transfer is therefore grossed-up by 20% ÷ (100% − 20%), i.e. 20/80. In this way, the donor pays tax on the total transfer of value, i.e. the value of the asset and the IHT payable.

As discussed in **Chapter 6**, gift holdover relief may be available for CGT purposes where a transfer of value is immediately chargeable to IHT. It should be noted that this relief is not always available in respect of settlor-interested trusts.

The principles set out above are demonstrated in **Example 11.6**. You should be aware of the level of the nil rate bands in previous years, which can be found at www.gov.uk/government/publications/rates-and-allowances-inheritance-tax-thresholds.

Example 11.6

Ken makes a gift of £415,000 to an interest in possession trust on 30 June 2013. He elects to pay any IHT due on the lifetime transfer.

Ken has previously made the following gifts:

▪ 5 August 2008 – gift of £100,000 to his son, Matthew, on the occasion of his marriage; and

▪ 9 September 2009 – gift of £250,000 to his daughter, Sarah, on her 30th birthday.

Compute the IHT payable on the gift to the IIP trust and the amount of Ken's gross chargeable transfer.

The gifts made in the seven years before the CLT are PETs and therefore do not utilise the nil rate band to be set against the lifetime transfer.

	£	£
Cumulative chargeable transfers within previous seven years		-
Gift to interest in possession trust		415,000
Less: annual exemption 2013/14	(3,000)	
Less: annual exemption 2012/13	(3,000)	
		(6,000)
Less: nil rate band for 2013/14		(325,000)
Net chargeable transfer		84,000
IHT @ 20% on net chargeable transfer, i.e. £84,000 × 20%		16,800
IHT grossed up as donor paying tax:		
£16,800 × 20/80		4,200
Total lifetime IHT payable by Ken		**21,000**
IHT paid by Ken		21,000
Gross chargeable transfer (i.e. gift plus IHT less annual exemptions)		430,000

Additional IHT on CLTs on Death

Additional IHT on CLTs will become payable where the donor dies within seven years of making the transfer. When calculating the IHT due on death, lifetime gifts are included at the value they held at the date of the transfer. However, the rate of tax payable and nil rate band are those that apply at the date of death. Where there has been a fall in the value of the gift, a claim for relief may be made under section 131 IHTA 1984.

Taper relief is available to reduce the IHT payable on death where the CLT was made at least three years prior to the death. Credit is given for any lifetime IHT paid after taper relief has been deducted. The credit cannot result in a repayment of IHT.

The taper relief rates are:

Years between gift and death	% reduction in tax payable
0 to 3 years	0%
3 to 4 years	20%
4 to 5 years	40%
5 to 6 years	60%
6 to 7 years	80%

These principles are best illustrated by continuing **Example 11.6** above and considering the impact of the death of the donor, Ken.

Example 11.7

Ken dies on 21 October 2016 having made no further gifts and leaving his estate, valued at £150,000, to his wife, Grace, who is domiciled in the UK.

Compute the IHT payable on Ken's death.

The PETs made by Ken are exempt from IHT, as they were made more than seven years before his death.

There will be no IHT due on Ken's estate at death, as he has made an exempt transfer to his wife.

The only IHT payable on death will be on the CLT made within seven years of death:

	£
June 2013 transfer	
Cumulative chargeable transfers within previous seven years	-
Gift to IIP trust	430,000
Less: nil rate band for 2016/17	(325,000)
Net chargeable transfer	105,000
IHT @ 40%	42,000
Less: taper relief @ 20%	(8,400)
IHT after taper relief	33,600
Less: lifetime IHT paid	(21,000)
IHT payable on death	12,600

It is important to appreciate that it may be necessary to look back up to 14 years prior to the date of death when calculating the IHT payable on CLTs. This can be illustrated by reworking **Examples 11.6** and **11.7** above, with a slight amendment to the facts.

Example 11.8

As **Examples 11.6** and **11.7** above, except that the gift of £250,000 made by Ken on 9 September 2009 was to a discretionary trust, so that it was a CLT. The trustees of the discretionary trust paid any IHT due.

You are required to:

1. Calculate the IHT payable by Ken on the lifetime gift to the discretionary trust on 9 September 2009.
2. Calculate the IHT payable by Ken on the lifetime gift to the interest in possession trust on 30 June 2013.
3. Calculate the IHT payable on Ken's death on 21 October 2016.

	£	£
September 2009 transfer		
Cumulative chargeable transfers within previous seven years		-
Gift to discretionary trust		250,000
Less: annual exemption 2009/10 (Note)		(3,000)
Less: nil rate band for 2009/10		(325,000)
Net chargeable transfer		Nil
IHT @ 20% on net chargeable transfer		Nil
Gross chargeable transfer		247,000
June 2013 transfer		
Cumulative chargeable transfers within previous seven years		247,000
Gift to IIP trust		415,000
Less: annual exemption 2013/14	(3,000)	
Less: annual exemption 2012/13	(3,000)	(6,000)
Less: nil rate band for 2013/14		(325,000)
Net chargeable transfer		331,000
IHT @ 20% on net chargeable transfer		66,200
IHT grossed up as donor paying tax:		
£66,200 × 20/80		16,550
Total lifetime IHT payable by Ken		**82,750**
IHT paid by Ken		82,750
Gross chargeable transfer (£415,000 − £6,000 + £82,750)		491,750
Accumulated gross chargeable transfers		738,750
Death tax		
Cumulative chargeable transfers within previous seven years		491,750
Less: nil rate band for 2016/17		(325,000)
Net chargeable transfer		166,750
IHT @ 40%		66,700
Less: taper relief @ 20%		(13,340)
IHT after taper relief		53,360
Less: lifetime IHT paid		(82,750)
IHT payable on death		Nil

Note: the annual exemption for 2008/09 is not available as it is used against the August 2008 PET.

When you compare the total IHT payable in the circumstances set out in **Examples 11.6** and **11.7** with that payable on the slightly altered circumstances set out in **Example 11.8** it demonstrates that, although the gift on 9 September 2009 does not come into charge on Ken's death more than seven years later, it does increase the overall liability and has an impact of the available nil rate band at death where it is a CLT. It is generally more efficient from an IHT perspective to make PETs rather than CLTs. From a practical perspective, however, making absolute gifts to children or young adults is unlikely to be attractive.

Potentially Exempt Transfers

You should be completely familiar with the detailed rules and tax implications of PETs (see **Chapter 23**, **Sections 23.1** and **23.5** of *CA Proficiency 2: Taxation 2 (NI) 2016–2017*).

From 22 March 2006, only the following transfers will be treated as PETs:

▪ gifts to an individual;
▪ gifts into a disabled trust;
▪ gifts into a bereaved minor's trust;
▪ on the coming to an end of an immediate post-death interest; and
▪ on the creation of a transitional serial interest.

IIP trusts created on or after 22 March 2006, other than those included in the above list, will be taxed under the relevant property regime in the same way as discretionary trusts.

As discussed above, it is important to remember that, prior to 22 March 2006, gifts to IIP trusts and A&M trusts were PETs.

A PET is a lifetime gift that is not subject to an immediate IHT charge at the date of transfer. The gift will escape IHT altogether if the donor survives for at least seven years after the date of the transfer. This is subject to certain anti-avoidance legislation, e.g. the gifts with reservation of benefit rules discussed at **Section 11.5**.

IHT when Death Occurs within Seven Years of a PET

If the donor dies within seven years of making the gift, an IHT charge is triggered. Taper relief is available to reduce the IHT payable where death occurs more than three years from the date of the transfer. The rates are the same as those set out above. The IHT liability that arises on the donor's death will normally be borne by the donee.

As a PET has the effect of 'freezing' the value of the gifted asset for IHT purposes at the date of the transfer, it can be useful where the value of an asset is expected to appreciate significantly. Where the value of the PET has fallen by the date of death, a claim may be made under section 131 IHTA 1984 to use the reduced value in the calculation of the IHT liability.

It should be noted that there is no 'freezing' of the value for CGT purposes. This means that the donee could receive an asset with a much lower base cost for CGT purposes than might have been the case if the transfer was made at a later stage, on the death of the donor. This has the effect of increasing the potential CGT liability of the donee in the event of a future disposal.

Example 11.9 illustrates the calculation of IHT on a PET becoming chargeable on death.

Example 11.9

Melody dies on 27 February 2017, leaving her estate, valued at £100,000, to her son, Ed.

She had made the following lifetime gifts:

▪ 16 March 2009 – gift of £50,000 to her niece, Charlotte;
▪ 24 March 2010 – gift of £150,000 to her son, Ed, on the occasion of his marriage; and
▪ 20 January 2012 – gift of £225,000 to a bereaved minor's trust for one of her grandchildren.

Compute the IHT payable on Melody's death.

	£	£
PET on 16 March 2008		
Gift to Charlotte		50,000
Less: annual exemption 2008/09	(3,000)	
Less: annual exemption 2007/08	(3,000)	(6,000)
Exempt transfer (as made more than seven years prior to death)		44,000

continued overleaf

PET on 24 March 2010		
Cumulative chargeable transfers within previous seven years		Nil
Gift to Ed		150,000
Less: gift on marriage	(5,000)	
Less: annual exemption 2009/10	(3,000)	(8,000)
(**Note**: 2008/09 AE set against PET of 16 March 2009)		
Taxable transfer		142,000
Less: nil rate band for 2016/17		(142,000)
Net chargeable transfer		Nil
PET on 20 January 2012		
Cumulative chargeable transfers within previous seven years		142,000
Gift to bereaved minor's trust		225,000
Less: annual exemption 2011/12	(3,000)	
Less: annual exemption 2010/11	(3,000)	(6,000)
Less: nil rate band for 2016/17		(325,000)
Net chargeable transfer		36,000
IHT @ 40% on net chargeable transfer		14,400
Less: taper relief @ 60%		(8,640)
IHT after taper relief		5,760
IHT on Death Estate		
Value of estate at death	100,000	
IHT @ 40%		40,000
Total IHT payable on death		**45,760**

As a PET is not immediately chargeable to IHT, holdover relief for CGT will only be available under section 165 Taxation of Chargeable Gains Act 1992 (TCGA 1992), i.e. where the asset being transferred is a qualifying business asset.

11.3.2 Creation of a Trust: Capital Gains Tax Treatment

Under section 70 TCGA 1992, a transfer of property into a settlement is a disposal of the entire property by the settlor for CGT purposes. This applies even if the settlor is a beneficiary and/or trustee of the settlement. This means that, regardless of the type of trust, the settlor is treated as making a disposal of the property at deemed market value. The trustees' base cost of the asset will be the market value at the date of the transfer into the settlement.

As mentioned above, where the property is a qualifying business asset and/or the transfer is to a relevant property trust and so immediately chargeable to IHT, holdover relief may be claimed by the settlor under section 165 TCGA 1992 or section 260 TCGA 1992. If both sections are available, section 260 takes priority. If the settlor claims holdover relief, the trustees acquire the asset at the settlor's base cost rather than at the market value at the date of the transfer.

Holdover relief cannot be claimed where the trust is a settlor-interested trust (see **Section 11.2.6**), except for transfers to trusts that benefit disabled persons.

Where the transfer to a trust gives rise to an allowable loss for CGT purposes, the loss relief available to the settlor will be restricted, as the settlor and the trustees will be connected persons. This means that the losses will only be available to set against future gains on a disposal to the same trust.

11.3.3 Existence of a Trust

By transferring property to a trust, a settlor removes the value of that property from the estate for IHT purposes. In order to prevent trusts being utilised to avoid IHT on the appreciation of assets, certain IHT charges are applied to trust property. These are the principal charge (also known as the 10-year charge) and the exit charge (also known as the proportionate charge).

Principal Charge

On every 10-year anniversary of the creation of a trust, HMRC levies a principal charge on the trustees of a relevant property trust. This charge is calculated as a percentage of the value of the trust property at each 10-year interval. To avoid a principal charge, trustees need to distribute all assets before the first 10-year anniversary, unless other reliefs are available to alleviate the charges, such as APR/BPR.

Exit Charge

Exit charges are applied when a property ceases to be "relevant property", such that the value of the property in the trust is reduced; for example, when the trustees of a discretionary trust distribute cash and/or assets to a beneficiary. The exit charge is calculated as a percentage of the value of the property exiting the trust at the date of the distribution.

If two trusts are set up on the same day, they are related trusts. This is important as it impacts on the calculation of the principal and exit charges. From a tax planning perspective, this is unlikely to occur during the settlor's lifetime. However, it could arise on the death of an individual where their will creates more than one settlement for different beneficiaries.

Exceptions from the Charges

Exceptions from these IHT charges can apply where the asset is:

- put into an IIP trust before 22 March 2006;
- put into an IIP trust by the terms of a will or the rules of intestacy;
- set aside for a disabled person;
- set aside for a bereaved minor; or
- put into an age 18 to 25 trust.

Where property leaves a trust within three months of the creation of the trust or a 10-year anniversary, its value will not be charged to IHT.

Calculating the Principal Charge

On the 10th anniversary of the creation of the trust, and on every subsequent 10-year anniversary while the trust remains in existence, IHT is payable on the value of the property in the trust at a rate equal to 30% of the "effective rate" of IHT, up to a maximum of 6%. The effective rate is determined by carrying out an IHT calculation on a deemed transfer of value. The amount on which IHT is charged can be reduced by the nil rate band and reliefs such as APR/BPR.

The 10-year charge is calculated as follows:

1. Calculate the Cumulative Total

This is used to determine how much, if any, of the nil rate band is available. It is found by adding together:

▪ the cumulative total of chargeable transfers of value made by the settlor of the trust in the seven years prior to the creation of the trust, excluding transfers made on the day the trust commenced; and

▪ any distributions made out of the trust in the 10 years before the date of the current 10-year anniversary.

2. Calculate the Deemed Transfer of Value
This is the current value of the relevant property immediately before the 10-year anniversary, *plus* the initial value of any non-relevant property in the trust, *plus* the initial value of any property in a related settlement.

The initial value is the value of the property at the date of the creation of the trust(s) less any IHT paid on the transfer by the trustees.

3. Calculate the Effective Rate
IHT on the deemed transfer is calculated at the lifetime rate in the normal way and the effective rate is determined by the following formula:

$$\frac{\text{Deemed IHT charge}}{\text{Deemed transfer of value}} \times 100 = \text{Effective rate}$$

4. Calculate the IHT Liability
The IHT payable by the trustees is 30% of the effective rate (as calculated at step 3.), applied to the value of the relevant property immediately before the 10-year anniversary. This is best illustrated by way of an example.

Example 11.10

On 1 May 2016, Liam gifted the assets listed below to a discretionary trust, thereby creating the trust. He had already used his annual exemption for each year. The trustees paid any IHT due on the transfer.

In the seven years prior to 1 May 2016, Liam had made cumulative gross chargeable transfers of £250,000.

Asset gifted:	Value at 1 May 2016	Value at 1 May 2026
	£	£
Shares in unquoted trading company	100,000	200,000
Shares in unquoted investment company	175,000	300,000

The shares in the unquoted trading company qualified for BPR on 1 May 2016 and 1 May 2026. Assume that the nil rate band in 2026/27 is £400,000. There is no other relevant property in the trust at 1 May 2026.

Calculate the principal charge payable by the trustees.

		£	£
1.	Cumulative total		
	Liam's cumulative total in seven years prior to 1 May 2016	250,000	
	Amounts distributed in 10 years prior to 1 May 2026	-	250,000
2.	Deemed transfer of value		
	Value of relevant property immediately prior to 1 May 2026	500,000	
	Less: value of property qualifying for BPR	(200,000)	
			300,000
	Less: nil rate band 2026/27		(400,000)
			150,000

continued overleaf

---

3. Calculate effective rate:
   £150,000 @ 20% = £30,000
   £30,000/£300,000 × 100 = 10%
4. IHT payable at 30% of effective rate:
   10% @ 30% = 3%
   IHT payable: £300,000 @ 3%   9,000

As part of the nil rate band is available, IHT is payable at 3% rather than the maximum rate of 6%.

11.3.4 Termination of a Trust or Property Leaving the Trust

When capital is distributed to the beneficiaries of a relevant property trust by the trustees, there is a potential charge to both CGT and IHT.

Section 71 TCGA 1992 deems a disposal to take place at market value when chargeable assets are distributed to a beneficiary. As this is a chargeable transfer for IHT purposes, the capital gain may be held over under section 260 TCGA 1992. This relief cannot be claimed on assets distributed within the first three months of a trust's life or within the three months following a 10-year anniversary/principal charge. However, where the asset transferred is a qualifying business asset, holdover relief may be claimed under section 165 TCGA 1992.

It should be noted that section 261 TCGA 1992 does not permit holdover relief to be claimed under section 260 TCGA 1992 where the transferee is neither resident nor ordinarily resident in the UK.

Calculating the Exit Charge

The calculation of the IHT exit charge depends on whether the property leaves the trust before or after the first 10-year anniversary.

An exit charge arising before the first 10-year anniversary is calculated as follows:

1. Calculate the Cumulative Total

The cumulative total of chargeable transfers of value made by the settlor of the trust in the seven years prior to the creation of the trust, excluding transfers made on the day the trust commenced.

2. Calculate the Deemed Transfer of Value

This is the initial value of the relevant property on the commencement of the trust, *plus* the value of any added property at the date it was added, *plus* the initial value of any property in a related settlement.

3. Calculate the Effective Rate

IHT on the deemed transfer is calculated at the lifetime rate in the normal way, and the effective rate is determined by the following formula:

$$\frac{\text{Deemed IHT charge}}{\text{Deemed transfer of value}} \times 100 = \text{Effective rate}$$

4. Calculate the IHT Liability

The IHT payable by the trustees is 30% of the effective rate (as calculated at step 3.), reduced by a fraction representing the number of complete quarters that have elapsed since the creation of the trust over the total number of quarters in a 10-year period, i.e. 40, applied to the value of the property that ceases to be relevant property:

$$\text{Effective rate} \times 30\% \times \frac{\text{No. of complete quarters since commencement of trust}}{40} = \text{Actual rate}$$

This is illustrated in **Example 11.11**.

Example 11.11

The facts are as in **Example 11.10**, except that half of the shares in the unquoted investment company are appointed to a beneficiary on 19 May 2023, when the nil rate band is £375,000. The value of the shares in the unquoted investment company before the appointment was £250,000 and is £100,000 after the appointment.

Calculate the exit charge payable by the trustees.

		£	£
1.	Cumulative total		
	Liam's cumulative total in seven years prior to 1 May 2016	250,000	
			250,000
2.	Deemed transfer of value		
	Value of relevant property at 1 May 2016	275,000	
			275,000
	Less: nil rate band 2023/24		(375,000)
	Total to determine rate		150,000
3.	Calculate effective rate:		
	£150,000 @ 20% = £30,000		
	£30,000/£275,000 × 100 = 10.909%		
4.	Calculate the IHT liability:		
	No. of complete quarters 01/05/16 − 19/5/23 = 28		
	10.909% × 30% × 28/40 = 2.29%		
	Chargeable amount:		
	Value of relevant property before appointment	250,000	
	Value of relevant property after appointment	(100,000)	
		150,000	
	IHT payable: £150,000 @ 2.29%		**3,435**

Where no lifetime IHT arises on the transfer of assets to a trust because the transfer of value was fully relieved by the nil rate band, then no IHT will arise on a subsequent appointment to a beneficiary within the first 10 years of the trust's existence.

Calculating the Exit Charge after a 10-year Anniversary

In a simple scenario, the rate used to calculate the exit charge on property distributed by the trustees between 10-year anniversaries is the rate calculated for the last principal charge, reduced by the number of quarters that have passed since the date of the charge. Note that if there has been an increase in the IHT nil rate threshold, the actual rate at the 10-year anniversary will have to be recalculated.

> **Example 11.12**
> The facts are as in **Example 11.10** above. Half of the shares in the unquoted investment company are appointed to a beneficiary on 19 May 2029. The value of the shares in the unquoted investment company before the appointment was £350,000 and is £200,000 after the appointment.
>
> Calculate the exit charge payable by the trustees.
>
> | | £ | £ |
> |---|---:|---:|
> | Rate charged at 10-year anniversary on 1 May 2026 = 3% | | |
> | No. of complete quarters since last principal charge 01/05/26 – 19/05/29 = 12 | | |
> | 3% × 12/40 = 0.9% | | |
> | Chargeable amount: | | |
> | Value of relevant property before appointment | 250,000 | |
> | Value of relevant property after appointment | (100,000) | |
> | | 150,000 | |
> | **IHT payable: £150,000 @ 0.9%** | | **1,350** |

11.3.5 IHT Treatment of an IIP Trust

The IHT regime for IIP trusts that existed before 22 March 2006 continues to apply to IIP trusts established before that date where the present life interest continues. When the present life interest ends, the trust will move into the relevant property trust regime outlined above.

Under the pre-existing rules, the life tenant of such a trust is treated as owning the underlying capital of the trust for IHT purposes, even though he may never be entitled to receive it. This means that where the life tenant dies, his share of the trust fund is included in his death estate and charged to IHT.

For CGT purposes, the underlying assets of a pre-22 March 2006 IIP trust are rebased where an interest ends on the life tenant's death and the trust assets pass to individuals who become absolutely entitled to the trust property. Where the trust assets have been the subject of a holdover claim, the held-over gain will crystallise on the death of the life tenant. However, if the assets continue to qualify for holdover relief under section 165 TCGA 1992, the held-over gain can be subject to a further holdover claim.

11.4 Inheritance Tax Reliefs and Exemptions

Under section 1 IHTA 1984, IHT is charged on the value transferred by a chargeable transfer. A chargeable transfer is defined by section 2(1) IHTA 1984 as any transfer of value by an individual, other than an exempt transfer. An "exempt transfer" is a transfer that is exempted from tax by a specific provision of the legislation.

The following is an overview of the exemptions provided through the legislation.

Exempt Lifetime Transfers

- Transfers by a transferor in any tax year not exceeding £3,000 (referred to as the "annual exemption") – section 19 IHTA 1984.
- Gifts by a transferor to a particular transferee in any tax year not exceeding £250 – section 20 IHTA 1984.
- Gifts forming part of the transferor's normal expenditure out of income – section 21 IHTA 1984.
- Gifts in consideration of marriage/civil partnership (section 22 IHTA 1984) not exceeding:

- £5,000, where the transferor is a parent of a party to the marriage/civil partnership;
- £2,500, where the transferor is a grandparent or remoter issue of a party to the marriage/civil partnership; and
- £1,000 in all other cases.

Exempt Lifetime and Death Transfers

- Transfers between spouses/civil partners (unlimited where recipient is domiciled in the UK, otherwise limited to the prevailing nil rate band (but see **Section 4.8**)) – section 18 IHTA 1984.
- Gifts to charities – section 23 IHTA 1984.
- Gifts to political parties – section 24 IHTA 1984.
- Gifts to housing associations – section 24A IHTA 1984.
- Gifts for national purposes to one of the bodies specified in Schedule 3 IHTA 1984 – section 25 IHTA 1984.
- Transfers of property subsequently held for national purposes – section 26A IHTA 1984.
- Transfers to maintenance funds for historic buildings – section 27 IHTA 1984.
- Transfers to employee trusts – section 28 IHTA 1984.

Exempt Death Transfer

- The estate of a person who has died on active service – section 154 IHTA 1984.

Gifts to Charities

A new IHT relief was introduced by Finance Act 2012. For deaths on or after 6 April 2012, the IHT rate is reduced to 36% where at least 10% of the net estate is left to a charity or registered community club (Schedule 1A IHTA 1984).

The other main inheritance tax reliefs, such as business property relief (BPR) and agricultural property relief (APR), are discussed in **Chapter 6**. You should also review **Chapter 24**, **Sections 24.1** and **24.2** of *CA Proficiency 2: Taxation 2 (NI) 2016–2017*.

11.5 Capital Gains Tax Reliefs and Exemptions for Trustees

11.5.1 Annual Exemption

The annual exemption for most trustees is one half of the annual exemption that applies for individuals, so in 2016/17 this is £5,550. Where the beneficiary is mentally disabled or receiving the middle or higher rate of attendance allowance or disability living allowance, the trust gets the same annual exemption as individuals, i.e. £11,100 in 2016/17.

If a settlor has set up more than one settlement, the annual exemption is divided equally between each individual trust, with a minimum annual exemption available to each of 1/10th of the annual exemption for individuals, i.e. £1,110 in 2016/17.

11.5.2 Entrepreneurs' Relief

The rate of capital gains tax payable by trustees is 20%, except for disposals of investment property where it is 28%. It may be possible to reduce these rates if the trustees qualify for entrepreneurs' relief (ER).

Trustees can claim ER when a trust sells or transfers assets in relation to which there is a qualifying beneficiary who satisfies the relevant conditions. Examples include:

- shares in a beneficiary's personal company where the beneficiary is an officer or employee of the company; and

▓ assets used in the beneficiary's business where the business is no longer operating and the asset was used for at least one year out of the last three before the business stopped operating.

The trustees have no entitlement to the relief in their own right and so must make a joint claim with the qualifying beneficiary for the relief to apply. Each beneficiary qualifies for the lifetime limit, currently £10 million and, where a claim is made, they effectively transfer part or all of that allowance to the trustees, thereby reducing the lifetime limit available to claim on the sale or transfer of their own assets.

Where there is more than one beneficiary and one or more qualifies for ER, then the relief is applied to the relevant proportion of the gain, i.e. the proportion of the gain that represents the entitlement to the trust income of the qualifying beneficiaries. That proportion will be charged to CGT at 10%, with the excess charged to CGT at the trust rate of CGT, currently 20% (or 28% on disposals of residential property).

11.5.3 *Principal Private Residence Relief*

If a residential property held by a trust is occupied by a beneficiary as their main residence, then the trustees may be able to claim principal private residence relief (PPR) on its disposal, provided the normal conditions for the relief are met.

PPR is not available to the trustees if a section 260 holdover claim was made on the original transfer of the property into the trust. However, if the trustees revoke the holdover claim, then they may be able to claim PPR.

11.6 Anti-avoidance Provisions

11.6.1 *Gifts with Reservation of Benefits*

Section 102 FA 1986 contains anti-avoidance legislation that applies to gifts made where the donor gives an asset away but continues to use or enjoy the asset, commonly known as gifts with reservation of benefits (GROB). These rules prevent effective transfers being made for IHT purposes where the donor is still able to enjoy any benefit from the gifted property after the transfer.

If the donor dies while retaining some benefit in the gifted asset, it will be treated as forming part of their chargeable estate on death. If the donor ceases to benefit from the gifted asset during their lifetime, then they will be treated as having made a PET of the asset at that time. It is important, therefore, to ensure that the GROB rules do not apply, as they will negate the donor's IHT planning.

It should be noted that, although a GROB is ineffective for IHT purposes, it is a successful transfer for CGT purposes. This means that, although the asset may remain in the donor's estate for IHT purposes, there is no uplift to market value on the death of the donor for CGT purposes.

Example 11.13

Leon gifted a holiday home in Malta to his son, Pete, in July 2004, on the condition that he could continue to use it rent-free for six weeks each year. The property had a market value of £100,000 at the date of the gift. Leon dies in August 2016, when the holiday home is worth £160,000, having retained the right to use it rent-free.

Leon has made a GROB. As he continued to enjoy rent-free use of the property until the date of his death, the holiday home's value of £160,000 at death will be included in his death estate for IHT purposes.

For CGT purposes, Pete is treated as having owned the property since July 2004, and his base cost is £100,000.

Where the gift of an asset is a PET and the donor dies within seven years of the gift, having retained some benefit in the asset up until the date of death, then a double charge will arise. Relief under the Double Charges Regulations may be available. It will be necessary to prepare two calculations – one for the PET becoming chargeable, and one treating the asset as part of the deceased's estate under the GROB rules. The charge on the calculation that produces the higher amount of IHT payable is the one that will be applied.

11.6.2 Pre-owned Assets

Under the pre-owned assets regime, where a potential IHT liability does not arise under the GROB rules, an income tax charge may be applied to individuals who continue to receive benefits from certain types of asset that they once owned but have since disposed of.

The legislation setting out how and when the pre-owned assets (POA) charge should be applied is at Schedule 15 FA 2004. It applies to individuals who continue to receive benefits from certain types of asset that they once owned after 17 March 1986 but have since disposed of.

The POA charge applies to three types of asset: land, chattels (i.e. household and personal goods) and intangible property (e.g. cash, stocks and shares).

The conditions required for the charge to apply are virtually the same for land or chattels, but they are slightly different for intangible property.

If the individual has either disposed of any such assets by making a gift or, in some circumstances, by selling them, or has contributed towards the purchase of the asset in question and they continue to receive some benefit from it, they are potentially liable to the charge.

The scope of the POA charge is very wide and, to limit this, certain transactions or property are excluded or exempt. If the POA charge does apply, there are provisions that set out how the taxable benefit is to be calculated. This is covered in **Section 25.3.2** of *CA Proficiency 2: Taxation 2 (NI) 2016–2017*.

11.6.3 Other Anti-avoidance Provisions

When dealing with trusts, care should be taken not to fall foul of the settlements legislation. This legislation is intended to prevent an individual from gaining a tax advantage by making arrangements that divert their income to another person who is liable to tax at a lower rate or who is not liable to income tax. It applies only where the settlor has retained an interest in the settled property or income. The legislation is set out at Part 5 of Chapter 5 of ITTOIA 2005.

Where the settlor (or their spouse/civil partner) can benefit from the trust, there is a "look-through" provision for CGT so that any capital gains arising in the trust are treated as being realised by the settlor. As previously discussed, holdover relief under section 165 TCGA 1992 and section 260 TCGA 1992 is not available for gifts to settlor-interested trusts.

Since 22 March 2006, the transfer of property to an IIP trust has been a chargeable transfer for IHT. This applies even where the settlor is entitled to the interest in possession, so, in such a scenario, the settlor makes a transfer of value on which IHT is potentially due. In addition, as the settlor continues to benefit from the assets transferred into the trust, this could fall within the GROB rules. The result is that IHT may not only be payable on the CLT but could also be due on the trust assets on the settlor's death, on the basis that the assets did not effectively pass out of the estate.

11.7 Deeds of Variation

It is worthwhile to briefly consider the use of deeds of variation as a capital taxes planning tool. Deeds of variation can be used to vary the provisions of a deceased's will where it is considered that assets could have been distributed in a more tax-efficient manner.

Deeds of variation are particularly useful where the deceased dies intestate (i.e. without having made a valid will). Where this is the case, the intestacy rules in the Administration of Estates (NI) Act 1955 apply in Northern Ireland to determine the distribution of the deceased's estate. The distribution of the estate depends on the identity of the surviving relatives of the deceased at the time of the death. There can be some surprising outcomes, as illustrated in the example below.

Example 11.14

Marion dies suddenly without having made a valid will. She is survived by her husband, Harry, and her mother, Rosemary (age 86). Marion was an only child and had no children. In addition to her personal chattels, her estate at death was worth £1 million.

The intestacy rules apply on Marion's death.

As her husband, Harry is entitled to her personal chattels plus, in these circumstances, a statutory legacy of £200,000.

The remaining £800,000 (the residue) is split equally between Harry and Marion's mother, Rosemary.

It is very inefficient from an IHT perspective for assets to pass from a child to an elderly parent and, therefore, a deed of variation could be made by Rosemary to direct that her half of the residue is distributed to someone else, possibly Harry.

In the past, deeds of variation were commonly used where the deceased had left their entire estate to their spouse or civil partner, thereby wasting their nil rate band. The deceased's will could be varied so that assets up to the value of the unutilised nil rate band are transferred to other family members. This is less common now that it is possible for a surviving spouse/civil partner to utilise the nil rate band unused by their deceased spouse/civil partner (see **Section 6.8.2** for further discussion of this).

In general terms, a deed of variation is a formal written instruction from a beneficiary under a will or intestacy to the personal representatives of the deceased to redirect property due to pass from them to another.

Section 142 IHTA 1984 provides that, where a beneficiary redirects assets under a deed of variation, the gift of the assets is treated as being made by the deceased for the purposes of IHT. This favourable IHT treatment is only available where the deed of variation is made within two years of the date of death, is made for no consideration and contains an irrevocable statement by the parties whose interests are varied (i.e. the original beneficiaries) that they intend the variation to have that effect (i.e. that they accept that their inheritance will be changed as a result of the variation).

Section 62 TCGA 1992 provides similar beneficial treatment for CGT purposes.

It should be noted that, where property is transferred into a trust as the result of a deed of variation (or the intestacy provisions), the deceased will be the settlor if the property is redirected from an existing trust, or a trust created on the death of the deceased, into another trust. However, the legatee will be the settlor if he was beneficially entitled to the property before the variation, or would have been so entitled but for the variation. This is an important point as it will affect the tax treatment of the trust going forward.

11.8 Territoriality Provisions

Please refer to **Chapter 4** for a discussion of the concepts of residence, domicile and the situs of assets under UK tax law. The rules for determining the residence of a trust are discussed in that chapter.

In the past, offshore trusts were a useful vehicle for tax planning purposes due to the tax advantages they enjoyed. These advantages have now been largely negated by UK anti-avoidance legislation.

Anti-avoidance legislation contained in sections 86 and 87 TCGA 1992, which applies to settlors and beneficiaries of non-UK resident trusts, is discussed in **Section 4.4.**

Questions

Review Questions

(See Suggested Solutions to Review Questions at the end of this textbook.)

Question 11.1

Olivia died on 28 September 2016. She had made a gift to a discretionary trust in June 2009, which gave rise to a chargeable transfer of £160,000. In March 2014 she gave her apartment in Castlerock to her grandson when it was worth £236,000. Due to the fall in the property market, the apartment was only worth £185,000 by September 2016.

These were the only lifetime gifts made by Olivia and she had no chargeable estate at her death.

Requirement
Calculate the IHT payable on the death of Olivia.

Question 11.2

Seamus settled a sum of £350,000 in a discretionary trust on 10 June 2012. Seamus had gross chargeable transfers in the preceding seven years totalling £180,000. On 10 June 2016 the trustees made a distribution of £40,000 to a beneficiary, subject to payment of tax out of that amount.

Requirement
Compute the exit charge payable on the distribution on 10 June 2016.

Challenging Questions

(Suggested Solutions to Challenging Questions are available through your lecturer.)

Question 11.1

Timothy died on 1 July 2006 and by his will, on a tax-paid basis, he left his small minority shareholding in an unquoted family investment company, Swan Investments Ltd, in trust. The residue of his estate was left to his widow. He made cash gifts in the seven years prior to his death, after allowing for annual exemptions, of £100,000.

Timothy is not the settlor of any other trusts.

The trust terms allowed the trustees to pay such income or capital as they wished in their absolute discretion to Walter (Timothy's only child), Kathleen (Walter's wife) and their children and subsequent issue. Walter and Kathleen have three children: Robbie (born 6 January 1985), Katie (born 21 March 1987) and Becky (born 20 July 1989). Timothy also left a letter of wishes in which he stated a desire for his three grandchildren to be treated equally by the trustees and for the shares in Swan Investments Ltd to be retained in the family and not to be sold at any time.

Timothy held 9,000 shares in Swan Investments Ltd out of a total issued share capital of 100,000 shares. The agreed share value on 1 July 2006 was £50 per share. Swan Investments Ltd did not pay any dividends between 1 July 2006 and 31 May 2016.

None of the grandchildren are married, although all are in long-term relationships. None of them has any children. Becky went to live and work in Australia in September 2011.

The value of the holding in Swan Investments Ltd has increased substantially to £200 per share. The longer-term outlook is for a continuing increase in the value of the shares.

Requirement

(a) Compute the IHT that would be payable on a distribution of the entire trust fund to the beneficiaries on 31 May 2016.

(b) Compute the IHT that would be payable on the tenth anniversary on 1 July 2016, if no capital distribution is made.

(c) Comment on the CGT position should the trust be broken; how any liability can be mitigated; and the implications for longer-term IHT planning if the trust were broken now.

VAT on Transactions

Learning Objectives

In this chapter you will learn to do the following:

■ Demonstrate a detailed working knowledge of transactions or events that trigger a charge to value-added tax (VAT), with particular focus on the reorganisation or transfer of a business (including sale of shareholding).

12.1 General Principles

You should review the basic principles of VAT.

12.1.1 Introduction

Value-added tax (VAT) is an indirect tax, whereas income/corporation tax, CGT and IHT are direct taxes.

VAT is charged on the consumption of goods and services. The charge to VAT does not arise solely on the sale of goods and services to end users, but occurs at each stage in the supply chain.

VAT is effectively charged on the "value added" to the supply during each stage.

There is a common system of VAT throughout the EU, and VAT law comes from EU law in the form of directives and regulations. Although VAT is an EU tax, the detailed rules differ in each of the Member States.

The main VAT legislation in the UK is contained in the Value Added Tax Act 1994 (VATA 1994) and the Value Added Tax Regulations 1995 (S.I. 1995/2518).

At present, the standard rate of VAT in the UK is 20%.

12.1.2 Taxable Persons

UK VAT is chargeable on taxable supplies of goods and services made in the UK by taxable persons (often referred to as "traders") in the course of a business. There are rules to determine the place of supply for goods and services.

A taxable person is any person (individual, partnership, company, etc.) who is registered for VAT, or is required to be registered for VAT. When a person making taxable supplies exceeds the registration thresholds, they must register for VAT. If a person making taxable supplies has not reached the thresholds, they may choose to register for VAT.

12.1.3 Input and Output VAT

The terms "input" and "output" VAT are used on the VAT return. In very simple terms, a trader will charge output VAT on goods or services supplied to a customer. Input VAT is the VAT suffered by the trader on goods and services acquired for use in the business.

The amounts of output and input VAT are declared on the VAT return for a period. If, as will normally be the case, a trader has charged more VAT than he has suffered (i.e. outputs exceed inputs), the difference is paid to HMRC. If input VAT exceeds output VAT, a refund will be due from HMRC.

12.1.4 Supply

"Supply" for VAT purposes generally means providing goods or services in return for consideration. The supply of goods or services will fall into one of the following categories:

1. taxable supplies;
2. exempt supplies; or
3. supplies outside the scope of VAT.

Taxable Supplies

Supplies of goods and services are taxable unless they are specifically excluded from the charge to VAT by legislation. There are three rates of VAT on taxable supplies:

1. the standard rate of 20%;
2. the zero rate; and
3. the reduced rate, which is 5% of the net value.

Supplies that qualify for the zero or reduced rates of VAT are specifically listed in the legislation. Schedule 8 VATA 1994 contains the list of goods and services that qualify for zero rating. These include food items, books, children's clothing and footwear. Schedule 7A VATA 1994 lists items which qualify for the reduced rate of 5%, including fuel, power and children's car seats.

The default position is that supplies are taxable at the standard rate.

Exempt Supplies

Exempt supplies, on which no VAT is charged, are listed in Schedule 9 VATA 1994. Exempt supplies include the following types of supplies:

- admission charges to museums, art galleries and zoos;
- betting, gaming and lotteries;
- buildings, land and construction (see **Chapter 13**);
- burial and cremation;
- education and training;
- financial services;
- insurance; and
- shares and securities.

A business that makes only exempt or zero-rated supplies will not have to charge output VAT. However, it is vital to correctly identify whether a supply is exempt or zero-rated. Although no VAT will be charged on either to the customer, there are implications for VAT registration and the recovery of input tax.

A business that makes only exempt supplies cannot register for VAT and will not be able to recover any input VAT. For such businesses, VAT becomes a real cost, rather than just a cash flow issue.

Section 12.2 deals with partial exemption, where a business makes a mixture of taxable and exempt supplies.

Supplies Outside the Scope of VAT

The third category of supplies relates to those that are outside the scope of UK VAT. This can be divided into two sub-categories:

1. where the rules on place of supply of goods or services treat the place of supply as being outside the UK; and
2. sundry transactions that are not subject to VAT, including transactions between companies within the same VAT group (see **Section 12.3** below).

12.2 Partial Exemption

Input tax is the input VAT incurred by a VAT-registered business in respect of supplies that it uses, or intends to use, for the purposes of its business. Any VAT incurred on purchases for non-business purposes or by a non-registered business is generally not recoverable, and is not input tax. Input tax that relates to exempt supplies cannot be recovered. **Where a business is making a mixture of taxable and exempt supplies, it can only recover input tax on expenditure that is attributable to taxable supplies.**

A business making a combination of taxable and exempt supplies is "partially exempt" and a special calculation is required to determine the proportion of input tax recoverable by the business.

The legislation on partial exemption is contained in section 26 VATA 1994 and Part XIV of the VAT Regulations 1995 (S.I. 1995/2518). This section provides a high-level overview of the concept of partial exemption.

12.2.1 Types of Business

Partially exempt businesses will be those that provide goods and services falling within Schedule 9 VATA 1994, as well as taxable supplies. The types of business where partial exemption is likely to be an issue include:

■ banks, financial institutions, building societies and finance brokers;
■ insurance companies and insurance brokers;
■ betting shops, bingo halls and casinos;
■ nursing homes and care homes;
■ opticians; and
■ property investment companies (unless they have "opted to tax" all rental income – see **Chapter 13**).

12.2.2 Calculating Recoverable Input Tax

A partially exempt trader must go through the two stages described below to calculate the recoverable input tax. The basic idea is to split the input tax suffered between taxable supplies and exempt supplies. It is not only directly attributable expenditure that has to be allocated; VAT on overheads must also be apportioned between taxable and exempt supplies. Attributing more input tax to taxable supplies will increase the rate of recovery of VAT. The **two stages** in the process of allocating input VAT are as follows:

1. Directly attribute the input tax, as far as possible, to either taxable or exempt supplies based on the actual or intended use of the goods or services when they are received. Direct attribution can only occur where there is a direct and immediate link between the input tax suffered and the supply to the customer.
2. Apportion any input VAT that is not directly attributable (the residual input tax) using the standard method of apportionment based on outputs, or a special method agreed in advance with HMRC.

The standard method of apportionment involves applying the fraction below to the total residual input tax to determine the proportion attributable to taxable supplies and, therefore, recoverable:

$$\frac{\text{VAT-exclusive value of taxable supplies in period}}{\text{VAT-exclusive value of all supplies in period}} \times 100$$

Certain types of supplies are excluded from the totals used in the above formula. Some of the types of supplies that are excluded from the calculation are:

- supplies of capital goods;
- incidental financial, land or property transactions; and
- the value of any goods and services that are neither taxable nor exempt supplies (e.g. a transfer of a going concern).

The calculation is undertaken for each VAT return period. However, the result is provisional until a review is carried out at the end of a VAT year, when the calculation is undertaken on an annual basis. This is known as the annual adjustment.

12.2.3 *De Minimis* Limits

A business will only be partially exempt if its exempt input tax exceeds both the *de minimis* limits. Where the amount of exempt input tax is below the limits, the business will be treated as fully taxable and will thus be able to recover all input tax. The limits for the amount of exempt input tax are currently:

- £625 per month on average (£1,875 per quarter or £7,500 per year); **and**
- less than 50% of the total input tax for the period.

Where a business exceeds the *de minimis* limits, part of its input tax will not be recoverable and VAT will become a real cost to the business.

12.3 Group Registration

Section 43 VATA 1994 provides that "bodies corporate" under common control may apply to form a VAT group. Bodies corporate include limited companies and limited liability partnerships (LLPs), but not ordinary partnerships. The entities in the VAT group will be treated as a single taxable person for VAT purposes.

12.3.1 *Eligibility Criteria*

Section 43A VATA 1994 sets out the eligibility criteria. It states that two or more bodies corporate are eligible to be treated as members of a group if:

1. each is established or has a **fixed establishment in the UK; and**
2. they are **under common control**, that is:

    (a) one of them controls each of the others,
    (b) one person (whether a body corporate or an individual) controls all of them, **or**
    (c) two or more individuals carrying on a business in partnership control all of them.

Note that, although the terms "VAT group" and "group registration" are used, the companies being grouped need not form a 'group' in the usual sense of the word for accounting and tax purposes. **It is sufficient if two companies are under the control of the same individual.**

A company is established in the UK if the central management and control of the company, or its head office, is in the UK. There is no statutory definition of a **"fixed establishment"**. HMRC's view is that this requires a real and permanent trading presence, not simply a registered office address or a UK subsidiary.

12.3.2 Representative Member

Once the VAT group has been established, one company will act as the "representative member" of the group. The VAT registration will be in the representative member's name, and it is responsible for both accounting for and paying VAT on behalf of the VAT group.

The effect of group registration is that all inputs and outputs are treated as being those of the representative member. Transactions between companies in the same VAT group are ignored for VAT purposes. However, each member of the VAT group is jointly and severally liable for any VAT liability.

12.3.3 Group Members

A corporate group can decide which eligible companies are to be included in the VAT group registration.

The members of a VAT group can later be changed, but this is subject to strict anti-avoidance legislation.

Care should be taken when considering the companies to be included if any of them make exempt supplies, as the group could become partially exempt and, therefore, have the recovery of its input tax restricted.

12.3.4 Advantages of Group Registration

The main advantage of group registration, however, is that it avoids the creation of output tax on transactions between connected companies, e.g. management fees, where the recipient company cannot fully recover input tax due to it being partially exempt.

Where there are large amounts of intragroup transactions, such as management charges, it may be beneficial to include companies making exempt supplies in the group to prevent any VAT leakage.

Another advantage of group registration is that only one VAT return is required. This can potentially reduce the administrative costs for the companies.

12.3.5 Disadvantages of Group Registration

Some of the disadvantages of VAT grouping are as follows:

1. In order to be able to submit the VAT return to HMRC on time, each group member must present its figures to the representative member earlier than if they sent them directly to HMRC, thereby potentially creating an administrative disadvantage.

2. As each member of the VAT group is responsible for the entire VAT debt of the group, minority shareholders in one of the companies could become disadvantaged since, if one or more members of the VAT group became insolvent, the rest of the group would have to pay the VAT liability.
3. The partial exemption *de minimis* limits apply to the group as a whole, so it is possible that otherwise recoverable exempt input tax may be lost.

12.3.6 Procedure

If two or more companies wish to form a VAT group, they must apply to HMRC using the appropriate forms and nominate a representative member. HMRC has the power to refuse an application. If the application is accepted, there will be a new VAT registration in the name of the representative member and a new VAT number will be issued. It is not possible to reallocate a previous VAT registration number.

12.3.7 Anti-avoidance

Section 43(9) VATA 1994 applies Schedule 9A, which makes provisions to ensure that VAT grouping is not used for tax-avoidance purposes.

As well as having the power to refuse an application for VAT grouping, HMRC can exercise the following powers, amongst others:

- remove a company from a group registration;
- order that a supply between group members be treated as a taxable supply;
- require a company to become a member of a VAT group where VAT is being avoided; and
- identify the company that must become the representative member.

Note: whether or not the benefits of group registration will outweigh the disadvantages will depend on the circumstances of the companies involved.

12.4 Reorganisation or Transfer of a Business, Including Transfer of Going Concern

It is important to distinguish between the sale or transfer of a business by a company, sole trader or partnership, and the sale or transfer of shares in a limited company. This section deals with the sale of a business (a "trade and asset" sale). **Section 12.5** below deals with the VAT implications of the sale of a shareholding.

If a business sells its assets, then, under general principles, VAT is chargeable. It makes no difference that the supply is of the assets making up the business, rather than the goods or services supplied by the business. VAT is even due on goodwill, as it represents the right to carry on the business.

12.4.1 Transfer of Going Concern

The sale or transfer of all or part of a business is a taxable supply unless it meets the conditions to be treated as a transfer of going concern (TOGC). The sale or transfer of part of a business can only be treated as a TOGC where the part is capable of being operated separately as a business.

The legislation on TOGC is contained in section 49 VATA 1994, Regulation 6 of the VAT Regulations 1995 (S.I. 1995/2518) and Article 5 of the VAT (Special Provisions) Order 1995. Detailed guidance on TOGC can be found in HMRC's *Transfer of a Going Concern Manual* (VTOGC 3500).

Note: if the sale or transfer qualifies for the TOGC treatment, it will be outside the scope of VAT, meaning that no VAT need be charged.

12.4.2 Conditions for TOGC

A 'transfer' includes a sale at full value, a sale at undervalue, an exchange and a gift. Although the terms "vendor" and "buyer" are used below, the technically correct terms are "transferor" and "transferee". The transferor and transferee may actually be a donor and donee. A TOGC can be to a third party with no previous interest in the business or it can be a change of legal entity, e.g. the incorporation of a sole trade. There are a number of conditions that must be satisfied for a transfer to be treated as a TOGC. These conditions can be subdivided into three categories:

1. VAT registration;
2. business activities; and
3. assets.

1. VAT Registration

    (a) If the vendor is registered for VAT, the buyer must:

        (i) be registered for VAT;
        (ii) be required to compulsorily register for VAT; **or**
        (iii) be accepted for voluntary registration.

    (b) If the vendor is not registered for VAT, there is no requirement for the buyer to be registered.

2. Business Activities

    (a) At the time of the transfer, the business must be a going concern;
    (b) the buyer must acquire something that is capable of being operated as a business, not just a group of capital assets;
    (c) there must be no significant break in trading either before or after the transfer; **and**
    (d) the buyer must actually operate the business; therefore, consecutive transfers do not qualify for TOGC treatment.

3. Assets

The assets transferred must be intended for use by the buyer in a similar business to that carried on by the vendor.

HMRC's *Transfer of a Going Concern Manual* (VTOGC 3500) contains its view of the factors to be taken into consideration in determining whether there has been a transfer of a business or just a sale of assets. The substance of the transaction as a whole must be considered and each case must be considered on its own facts.

HMRC's list of factors includes the following:

- the transfer of a business name strongly implies that the business has been transferred as a going concern;
- the transfer of goodwill is a good indication of a TOGC;
- if the buyer takes over contracts with suppliers and customers from the vendor, and buys work in progress, this is a strong indication that he is taking over the business of the vendor;
- the transfer of premises will imply that a business is being transferred where the premises:

- are vital to the operation of the business, or
- have a significant impact on the goodwill of the business; and

■ if the new business operates using the same staff as the previous business, this implies a TOGC.

There are special rules applying to the sale of land and property. These are covered in **Section 13.4**.

Note: if the conditions for TOGC are met, the treatment is compulsory. There is no requirement for a claim, election or application.

12.4.3 *Transferring the VAT Registration*

Regulation 6 of the VAT Regulations 1995 (S.I. 1995/2518) allows the buyer to take over the vendor's VAT registration number. This creates a potential problem because, by doing so, the buyer takes on all the VAT liabilities of the existing registration and could therefore become liable for VAT on errors made by the vendor.

This should only be recommended where the vendor or buyer are closely connected, for example, on a reorganisation.

12.5   Sale of a Shareholding

A sale of shares is an exempt transaction (Item 6 of Group 5, Schedule 9 VATA 1994), unless the buyer belongs outside the EU. Item 6 exempts the "issue, transfer or receipt of, or any dealing with, any security or secondary security".

This includes stocks, shares, bonds and debentures. **This means that no VAT is charged on the sale of shares in a company.**

If a business holds shares purely as investments, a sale of the shares may be a non-business transaction, rather than an exempt supply. Where the business is one of buying and selling shares, the transactions are business supplies and the sales are exempt.

12.5.1 *Holding Companies*

Where a holding company owns shares in subsidiary companies but has no other business activities, it will not be able to register for VAT in its own right, as it is not making taxable supplies. However, such a holding company may be included in a VAT group.

Where it has other business activities, for example the provision of management services to other group companies, it will be required to register for VAT.

If a holding company, which is registered for VAT, sells shares in a subsidiary, this will impact on its ability to fully recover input tax. As the sale of shares is an exempt supply, a partial exemption calculation will be required. Where the *de minimis* thresholds are exceeded, there will be a restriction on input tax recovery.

No input tax can be recovered on expenditure directly linked to the sale, e.g. lawyers' fees for advising on and drafting the sale agreement. There will also be a restriction on recovery of residual input tax, i.e. input tax not directly attributable to either taxable or exempt supplies.

You should note that the issue of shares or securities in a company to raise finance for a business is not a supply, and is therefore outside the scope of VAT.

Questions

Review Questions

(See Suggested Solutions to Review Questions at the end of this textbook.)

Question 12.1

Parsley Ltd has a number of different business activities and has been VAT-registered since 2003. It is about to sell its cake manufacturing business to Thyme Ltd, an unconnected third party. This part of the business has a steady turnover of £15,000 per month. Thyme Ltd is not registered for VAT, having been told by its VAT adviser that it will not be obliged to register until it reaches the VAT turnover limit.

Requirement
Determine whether the sale of the cake manufacturing business to Thyme Ltd qualifies as a TOGC.

Question 12.2

You have received an e-mail from Johnny, the company accountant at Coriander Ltd. The shares in Coriander Ltd are 100% owned by Mr Spice. Mr Spice also owns 100% of Lemongrass Ltd. Both companies are established in the UK and registered for UK VAT.

Requirement
Johnny has asked you to e-mail him back with the eligibility criteria for VAT grouping in the UK and to state whether Coriander Ltd and Lemongrass Ltd would meet the criteria.

Question 12.3

Gary is acquiring a sole trade business from Julian and all the conditions for TOGC are met. Julian has suggested that Gary take over the VAT number of the business.

Requirement
Briefly explain the consequences for Gary of Julian's VAT number being transferred to him.

Challenging Questions

(Suggested Solutions to Challenging Questions are available through your lecturer.)

Question 12.1

Your firm has recently been appointed as VAT advisor to the Literary Plc group of companies.

1. Literary Plc is the group holding company with its offices in London. It incurs costs and expenses of the type typically incurred by holding companies. It covers these expenses with dividends paid by group companies. It is not VAT registered.
2. Gaskell Ltd is the main trading company operating from factories in Scotland. It is 100% owned by Literary Plc. The company supplies building materials to the UK market. It is fully taxable and pays VAT on returns made for calendar quarters.

3. Austen Ltd, Dickens Ltd and Thackeray Ltd purchase products from Gaskell Ltd for distribution in their local markets. Austen Ltd and Dickens Ltd are wholly owned by Gaskell Ltd. Thackeray Ltd was acquired recently and is 75% owned by Literary Plc, with a third party (the previous owner) holding the other 25%. They are all separately registered and also pay VAT on returns on calendar quarters. The companies are treated as fully taxable, although both Austen Ltd and Dickens Ltd receive exempt rental income from surplus premises and benefit from the partial exemption *de minimis* rules.

4. There is also a French company, Moliere SAS, in which Literary plc has a 70% shareholding. Moliere SAS manufactures and supplies specialist wooden building materials. It has an office in Birmingham with two directors and 25 staff. This office markets the company's products in the UK and provides after-sales support to UK customers. It makes no charges to the customers and its costs are met from the head office in France. It is not registered for VAT.

At a meeting with the client last week, the VAT partner suggested that a VAT group registration may be advantageous. The finance director already has some knowledge of the basic principles of group registration and the application process. He would therefore like advice on the application of it to the specific circumstances of the group.

Requirement
Draft a letter, for review by the VAT partner, providing specific advice on the establishment of a VAT group to the finance director of Literary Plc.

VAT on Property

13.1 General Principles

The VAT aspects of property transactions are complex. There are specific rules governing the place of supply, when a supply is recognised and the VAT rate that applies. This chapter provides a high-level outline of the rules and also highlights the areas that will be worthy of detailed consideration when undertaking a transaction involving property.

13.1.1 Main Headings

The VAT provisions on property can be grouped into six main headings.

1. Zero-rating in Groups 5 and 6, Schedule 8 VATA 1994 for:
   (a) the construction and sale/long lease of dwellings;
   (b) the conversion of non-residential buildings into dwellings; and
   (c) alterations of listed dwellings.

2. The reduced rate of 5% in Groups 6 and 7, Schedule 7A VATA 1994 for certain conversions and renovations.
3. The exemption for sales and leases of existing commercial property in Group 1, Schedule 9 VATA 1994.
4. The exception in Group 1, Schedule 9 VATA 1994, which standard rates "new" commercial buildings, i.e. those up to three years old.
5. The election to waive exemption ("option to tax") for sales/leases of land and commercial property in paragraphs 2 and 3 Schedule 10 VATA 1994.
6. The Do-It-Yourself and charity self-build rules in section 35 VATA 1994.

This chapter will concentrate on points 3., 4. and 5. above. Also included in this chapter, at **Section 13.2**, is an outline of the Capital Goods Scheme.

13.1.2 *New Commercial Buildings*

As stated in point 4. above, Item 1(a) of Group 1, Schedule 9 excepts certain types of property transaction from being exempt from VAT, including the sale of a freehold in a new commercial building. In other words, **the sale of a freehold in a new commercial building is standard rated**, not exempt.

Note 4 to Group 1 defines a building as "new" if it was completed less than three years before the transaction.

Note 2 to Group 1 states that a building shall be taken to be completed at the earlier of an architect issuing a certificate of practical completion or the building being fully occupied. It does not matter how many sales of the building there have been in the first three years of completion – each of the sales will be standard rated.

The exception applies only to the "grant of a fee simple", i.e. the sale of the freehold interest in the building. It would not apply to the assignment of a lease of the building for a premium. This is a statutory exception to the exempt status of transactions in property. Sales of "new" commercial buildings must be standard-rated. It is important not to confuse this exception with the "option to tax" a commercial building discussed in **Section 13.3** below.

13.2 Capital Goods Scheme

The Capital Goods Scheme (CGS) applies if a business reclaims VAT on the acquisition of a single piece of computer equipment costing more than £50,000 (excluding VAT) or on expenditure of more than £250,000 (excluding VAT) on land, or buying, improving or refurbishing a property.

With effect from 1 January 2011, the CGS also applies to ships and aircraft where the cost exceeds £50,000 (excluding VAT). The legislation is contained in Part XV of the VAT Regulations (S.I. 1995/2518).

The aim of the CGS is to ensure that the input tax recoverable on such ships, aircraft, computers, land and property is recoverable in proportion to an asset's use over time. It is generally partially exempt traders who are impacted by the scheme. However, **the impact of the CGS also needs to be considered when an otherwise fully taxable trader is making an exempt sale of land or property that has been used in the trade**.

The application of the CGS to ships, aircraft and computer equipment is rarely encountered in practice. This section will focus on the implications of the CGS for land and property transactions.

13.2.1 *Property Transactions*

Only property where VAT has been charged is relevant. Therefore, zero-rated and exempt acquisitions are ignored.

The following types of property transaction are also excluded:

■ property acquired for resale, or which is sold before it is used for any other purpose; and
■ land acquired for a property developer's land bank.

Regulation 113 of the VAT Regulations (S.I. 1995/2518) lists the items to which the CGS applies. These include:

1. acquisition of land and buildings valued at more than £250,000;
2. building constructed by the owner where the taxable goods and services received are valued at £250,000 or more;

3. alteration, extension or annexe to a building carried out by the owner where taxable goods and services received are valued at £250,000 or more; and

4. refurbishment or fitting out of a building where the taxable goods and services received are valued at £250,000 or more.

13.2.2 Operation of the Capital Goods Scheme

HMRC *VAT Notice 706/2* explains how the CGS works, and the items that are covered by the scheme. It can be downloaded from www.gov.uk.

The notice sets out the types of professional fees that are to be included as part of the value. The following fees are to be included:

- architect;
- site manager;
- surveyor;
- civil engineering contractor;
- security;
- demolition and clearing the site;
- equipment hire;
- haulage; and
- landscaping.

13.2.3 Adjustment Period

The purpose of the CGS is to adjust the recovery of input tax over the expected life of the asset. The "adjustment period" is set out in Regulation 114 of the VAT Regulations (S.I. 1995/2518).

For land and buildings, the adjustment period is approximately 10 years, or five years if the leasehold interest acquired is less than 10 years. The adjustment period for ships, aircraft and computer equipment is five years.

The adjustment periods are not necessarily a full five or 10 years. The adjustment is for "intervals". Interval generally means the VAT year of the trader. The first interval runs from the date of acquisition to the end of the current partial exemption tax year, which will be 31 March, 30 April or 31 May, depending on the VAT stagger. However, the effect of the CGS does not start until the second interval.

13.2.4 Adjustments

The amount of input tax that may be claimed on acquisition is dependent upon the expected level of taxable use for the first interval. The level of taxable use is expressed as a percentage. An asset used exclusively in the making of taxable supplies has 100% taxable use; whereas an asset used exclusively in the making of exempt supplies has 0% taxable use.

The level of taxable use for assets related to both taxable and exempt supplies is calculated in accordance with the partial exemption rules, and usually expressed to two decimal places. No adjustments under the CGS will be required where the use of the asset does not change during the five- or 10-year period. An adjustment will be required where the asset is used for both taxable and exempt supplies at the same time, or the use of the asset changes. The method of adjustment is laid down in Regulation 115 of the VAT Regulations (S.I. 1995/2518). At the end of the second interval, and subsequent intervals, the adjustment percentage must be calculated. This is the difference between the level of taxable use for the first interval and the level of taxable use for the interval under consideration.

The adjustment is calculated using the following formula:

$$\frac{\text{total input tax on item}}{\text{number of intervals in review period (i.e. five or 10)}} \times \text{adjustment percentage}$$

Where the level of taxable use has increased, the business may claim additional input tax equal to the amount calculated. Where the level of taxable use has decreased, the business must repay VAT to HMRC.

Example 13.1

Jamison and Joules is a partnership operating as financial advisors and insurance brokers. The partnership provides both taxable and exempt services. On 1 June 2012, the partnership signed an eight-year lease for office premises, paying a premium of £300,000 plus VAT at 20%. In the VAT year to 31 March 2013, the office had 80% taxable use.

The level of taxable use for the year ended 31 March 2014 was 90%. The taxable use then dropped to 60% for the years to 31 March 2015, 2016 and 2017.

You are required to:
(a) calculate the input VAT recoverable in the first interval; and
(b) calculate any adjustments required under the Capital Goods Scheme over the remaining five-year period and the final input tax recovery.

Solution

1. Initial input VAT recovery
    Total input VAT: £300,000 @ 20% = £60,000
    Input VAT recoverable = £60,000 × 80% = £48,000

2. The CGS adjustments are:

Interval	Calculation	Adjustment £	Overall Position £
1	–	–	48,000
2	£60,000/5 × (90 – 80)%	1,200	1,200
			49,200
3	£60,000/5 × (60 – 80)%	(2,400)	(2,400)
			46,800
4	£60,000/5 × (60 – 80)%	(2,400)	(2,400)
			44,400
5	£60,000/5 × (60 – 80)%	(2,400)	(2,400)
	Final input tax recovery		**42,000**

13.2.5 Sale of a Capital Goods Scheme Asset

Where an asset is sold during the review period, two adjustments are required:

1. the normal adjustment for the interval in which the sale occurs; and
2. an additional adjustment to take into account the remaining intervals after sale.

The additional adjustment depends on whether the sale is taxable, in which case the level of taxable use is deemed to be 100%, or exempt when the level of taxable use is deemed to be 0%.

Example 13.2

Forest Ltd, a partially exempt business, bought the freehold interest in a brand new office on 1 July 2014 for £1 million plus VAT at 20%. The taxable use in the VAT year to 30 April 2015 was 75%. In the second interval, the taxable use increased to 80%.

In the third interval, the taxable use decreased to 65%. The building was sold on 28 February 2017.

You are required to compute the input tax recoverable by Forest Ltd.

Solution

As the building was new (i.e. less than three years old) when sold by Forest Ltd, the sale will be standard-rated and the deemed use for the remaining intervals by Forest Ltd will be 100%.

Interval	Calculation	Additional Adjustment £	Normal Adjustment £	Overall Position £
1	£200,000 × 75%			150,000
2	£200,000/10 × (80 − 75)%		1,000	1,000
				151,000
3	£200,000/10 × (65 − 75)%		(2,000)	(2,000)
				149,000
4	£200,000/10 × (100 − 75)%	5,000		5,000
				154,000
5	£200,000/10 × (100 − 75)%	5,000		5,000
				159,000
6	£200,000/10 × (100 − 75)%	5,000		5,000
				164,000
7	£200,000/10 × (100 − 75)%	5,000		5,000
				169,000
8	£200,000/10 × (100 − 75)%	5,000		5,000
				174,000
9	£200,000/10 × (100 − 75)%	5,000		5,000
				179,000
10	£200,000/10 × (100 − 75)%	5,000		5,000
Final input tax recovery				**184,000**

As Forest Ltd is deemed to have fully taxable use of the building in years 4–10, due to the taxable sale in year 3, it can recover £184,000 of input tax, out of a potential amount of £200,000.

The impact of the sale of a property by an otherwise fully taxable business can be demonstrated by changing the facts of **Example 13.2** above.

Example 13.3

Forest Ltd, a fully taxable business, bought the freehold interest in a brand new office on 1 July 2014 for £1 million plus VAT at 20%.

The building was sold on 28 February 2018, without Forest Ltd having made the "option to tax".

You are required to compute the input tax recoverable by Forest Ltd.

Solution

As the building is more than three years old when sold by Forest Ltd and no option to tax had been made by Forest Ltd, the sale will be exempt and the deemed use for the remaining intervals by Forest Ltd will be 0%.

continued overleaf

Interval	Calculation	Additional Adjustment £	Normal Adjustment £	Overall Position £
1	£200,000 × 100%			200,000
2	£200,000/10 × (100 − 100)%		-	-
				200,000
3	£200,000/10 × (100 − 100)%		-	-
				200,000
4	£200,000/10 × (100 − 100)%		-	-
				200,000
5	£200,000/10 × (0 − 100)%	(20,000)		(20,000)
				180,000
6	£200,000/10 × (0 − 100)%	(20,000)		(20,000)
				160,000
7	£200,000/10 × (0 − 100)%	(20,000)		(20,000)
				140,000
8	£200,000/10 × (0 − 100)%	(20,000)		(20,000)
				120,000
9	£200,000/10 × (0 − 100)%	(20,000)		(20,000)
				100,000
10	£200,000/10 × (0 − 100)%	(20,000)		(20,000)
	Final input tax recovery			**80,000**

Although Forest Ltd is generally a fully taxable business, the exempt sale of the building in year 4 means that it is deemed to have fully exempt use of the building in years 5–10. The exempt sale results in the company having to repay £120,000 of the input tax originally recovered to HMRC. This could have been avoided by 'opting to tax' the property prior to sale, as discussed in **Section 13.3**.

13.2.6 Other Considerations

Where there is a TOCG and an asset falling within the CGS is transferred as part of the transaction, the buyer of the business must continue the annual adjustments for the balance of the adjustment period. This means that the buyer must ensure that the records transferred include all the necessary details, including the date of acquisition, the input tax incurred at that time and the percentage of the input tax recovered by the vendor. The buyer may be able to reclaim, or have to pay, some of that input tax with a resulting decrease or increase in his effective cost of the asset.

Adjustments required by the CGS affect capital allowances, R&D expenditure and CGT computations.

Where a CGS adjustment requires VAT to be paid to HMRC, the cost of the asset is increased for the purposes of capital allowances and R&D expenditure, where applicable. Similarly, where a CGS adjustment results in VAT being repaid by HMRC, this decreases the cost of the asset.

However, where CGT rollover relief has been claimed, HMRC will not require the claim to be adjusted as the result of a change in the cost of a new asset due to a CGS adjustment.

13.3 Option to Tax

Most supplies relating to land and existing commercial buildings are exempt, including the grant of an interest or right over land and the grant of a licence to occupy land.

The legislation on the election to waive exemption ("option to tax") is found in paragraphs 2 and 3 Schedule 10 VATA 1994.

The option to tax converts an exempt sale or rental of property into a standard-rated supply.

The advantage is that the related input tax becomes recoverable. Given that this may include input tax incurred on the purchase, construction or renovation of a building, large sums of VAT may be involved. The potential impact of not making an option to tax is demonstrated in **Example 13.3** above.

13.3.1   Effect of the Option to Tax

The effect of a trader exercising the option to tax a property is that all future supplies of that interest in the property made by him will be standard-rated for the next 20 years.

Before a trader opts to tax a property, he should consider the VAT recovery position of any potential tenants or purchasers to ensure that charging VAT on any supplies of the property does not make it uncompetitive. For example, an exempt or partially exempt business, e.g. a bank, will be unwilling to rent a building on which the option to tax has been made as the VAT charged will be a real cost to the business.

The option to tax is personal to the trader who makes it. For example, if a landlord opts to tax a commercial property and lets it to a tenant, the landlord will charge VAT to the tenant on the rent. If the tenant then sub-lets part of the property, any rental income received by the tenant is not subject to VAT, unless the tenant has also opted to tax the property.

HMRC *VAT Notice 742A* explains the effect of an option to tax and helps a trader to decide whether to exercise the option.

13.3.2   Making the Election

There are two steps to exercising the option: making an election and notifying HMRC. The election to waive exemption in respect of an interest in a particular piece of land or a building is made and signed by an authorised person. Form VAT 1614A can be used to give written notification to HMRC, which must be done within 30 days of the election being made. The option will be effective from the date it is made, or any later date specified in the election. An option to tax can be revoked under certain limited circumstances (see **Section 13.3.3**).

If, prior to opting to tax a property, a business has already made an exempt supply of it (e.g. rent), it cannot exercise the option without permission from HMRC, unless one of the following conditions for automatic approval is met:

1. the exempt supplies have been incidental to the main use of the building, e.g. renting of space for an advertising hoarding, radio mast or electricity substation;
2. it is a mixed-use development (i.e. residential and commercial) and the only exempt supplies made have been in relation to the dwellings;
3. the trader does not wish to recover any input tax on goods or services received before the option has effect and:

    (a)   the consideration for the exempt supplies has been solely by way of rent, **and**
    (b)   the only input tax the trader wishes to recover is on normal overheads;

4. the trader does wish to recover input tax incurred before the option takes effect but:

    (a)   this input tax relates solely to tax charged by tenants upon lease surrenders,
    (b)   the building or relevant part of the building has since been unoccupied, **and**
    (c)   there will be no further exempt supplies of the property.

13.3.3 Revocation of the Option to Tax

As stated above, an option to tax, once made, can only be revoked in limited circumstances. Circumstances in which revocation may be considered include where the VAT status of the tenants or potential purchasers of the property has changed since the option was made, or where the administration costs and risks of applying the option outweigh any tax benefits.

'Cooling Off' Period
There is a 'cooling off' period of six months during which an option can be revoked. If the conditions are met, the option will be treated as never having been in place.

The conditions for revoking an option without prior consent from HMRC are as follows:

1. less than six months has passed since the day on which the option had effect;
2. no tax has become chargeable on a supply of land as a result of the option being in place;
3. no TOGC has occurred since the date the option came into effect; **and**
4. HMRC has been notified of the revocation.

All four of the above conditions, plus one of the three additional conditions below, must be met for an option to be revoked without prior consent:

1. neither the person who exercised the option ("the opter") nor any of his relevant associates has recovered extra property input tax (i.e. input tax attributable to supplies which, if made at a time the option has effect, would be taxable supplies by virtue of the option);
2. by virtue of the revocation, the opter and all of his relevant associates would be liable to account to HMRC (under regulation 107 or 108 of the VAT Regulations 1995) for all of the extra property input tax that they have recovered; **or**
3. extra property input tax has been recovered entirely on one capital item and amounts to less than 20% of the total input tax incurred on that item.

If all of the first four conditions, but none of the three additional conditions, are met, a revocation within the six months immediately following the exercise of an option may still be possible – but only with the consent of HMRC.

When considering whether to grant permission, HMRC will give particular consideration to whether the opter or a third party has received a VAT benefit as a result of their actions.

Automatic Revocation
Except in very limited circumstances, an option to tax will be revoked where the opter has not held an interest in the opted building or land for a continuous period of six years commencing at any time after the option to tax has effect. The revocation is automatic and no notification is required.

Revocation After 20 Years
An option to tax may be revoked where more than 20 years have elapsed since the option first had effect, provided condition 1. below, or all of conditions 2.–5. below are met. If the required conditions are met, the option may be revoked without HMRC consent, but HMRC must be notified.

1. **The relevant interest condition** – neither the taxpayer nor any relevant associates have a relevant interest in the building or land at the time when the option is revoked and, if the taxpayer or one of the relevant associates has disposed of such an interest, no supply for the purpose of the charge to VAT in respect of the disposal is yet to take place, or would be yet to take place if one or more conditions (such as the happening of an event or the doing of an act) were to be met.

2. **The 20-year condition** – the taxpayer or any relevant associates held a relevant interest in the building or land after the time from which the option had effect and more than 20 years before the option is revoked.
3. **The capital item condition** – any land or building that is subject to the option at the time when it is revoked does not fall, in relation to the taxpayer or any relevant associates, for a potential input tax adjustment of more than £10,000 under the CGS.
4. **The valuation condition** – neither the taxpayer nor any relevant associates have made a supply of a relevant interest in the building or land subject to the option in the 10 years immediately before revocation of the option that was for a consideration that was less than the open market value of that supply or arose from a relevant grant.
5. **The prepayment condition** – no part of a supply of goods or services made for consideration to the taxpayer or a relevant associate connected with the taxpayer before the option is revoked will be attributable to a supply or other use of the land or buildings by the taxpayer more than 12 months after the option is revoked.

If the conditions are met, the revocation will take effect from the date on which HMRC is notified.

If all of the conditions have not been met, then it may be possible to obtain permission from HMRC to revoke the option, but only if condition 2. above is met.

This type of revocation has only been available since 1 August 2009, being 20 years since the option to tax was introduced.

If an option is successfully revoked, it will still be possible to make another election to opt to tax the building, which will then be subject to a further 20-year period.

13.4 Property and TOGC

Anti-avoidance legislation contained in Article 5(2) of the VAT Special Provisions Order (S.I. 1995/1268) applies if the assets being transferred as a TOGC include property that is:

- a "new" building (i.e. less than three years old); or
- land or buildings on which the option to tax has been exercised.

Article 5(2) takes the value of such property out of the TOGC provisions, making it standard-rated unless:

1. the buyer of the business opts to tax the property from the date of the transfer;
2. by the date of the transfer, the buyer gives HMRC written notice of the election; **and**
3. the buyer notifies the vendor that the buyer's option will not be disapplied under the anti-avoidance legislation.

The requirement to make this notification prevents any attempt to avoid a non-recoverable VAT charge on a property by acquiring it as part of a TOGC. The vendor is responsible for applying the correct VAT treatment. The vendor must be satisfied that the buyer's option to tax is in place by the date of the transfer. In addition to the buyer's written confirmation, the vendor should obtain external evidence. If possible, the vendor should obtain a copy of HMRC's notification to the buyer. Where this has not been issued by HMRC by the transfer date, the vendor should obtain a copy of the buyer's notification to HMRC of his option to tax the property.

The following table, from *VAT Notice 742A*, will help to determine whether the conditions for a TOGC have been met:

Type of commercial building	Has the vendor opted to tax?	Has the purchaser opted to tax?	Will the purchaser's option to tax be disapplied?	TOGC?
Over three years old, usually exempt	Yes	Yes	Yes	No
	Yes	Yes	No	Yes
	Yes	No	N/A	No
	No	No	N/A	Yes
	No	Yes	Yes	Yes
	No	Yes	No	Yes
New building under three years old, usually standard-rated	Yes	Yes	No	Yes
	Yes	Yes	Yes	No
	Yes	No	N/A	No
	No	No	N/A	No
	No	Yes	Yes	No
	No	Yes	No	Yes

HMRC *VAT Notice 700/9* gives examples of when the transfer of a property rental business will be considered to be a TOGC. HMRC accepts that the sale of a single building let as an investment property can constitute a business so that the sale of an investment property to another investor may be a TOGC, if it meets all the conditions set out in **Section 12.4**.

One situation that cannot be regarded as a TOGC is the sale of property used by a trader as his own premises to a property investor. This is because the buyer will not be carrying on a similar business to that carried on by the vendor.

Example 13.4

Atlantic Ltd has traded for many years as a manufacturer of swimwear. Anita, the sole shareholder of Atlantic Ltd, decides to acquire a factory from the company at market value of £2 million. She wishes to hold the property personally so that any future capital growth accumulates in her hands. She will rent the factory at a market rent to Atlantic Ltd. Atlantic Ltd has opted to tax the factory.

Can this be considered a TOGC? What are the VAT and SDLT implications for Atlantic Ltd and Anita?

Solution

This is not a TOGC as the factory was used by Atlantic Ltd (the vendor) in its manufacturing trade. Anita (the buyer) intends to use the property in a property rental business. Therefore, the buyer is not intending to carry on a similar business to the vendor.

As Atlantic Ltd has opted to tax the factory, it is required to standard rate the sale of the property. At a standard VAT rate of 20%, VAT of £400,000 will be charged to Anita.

Anita should also opt to tax the property so that she can fully recover the £400,000. She will then be obliged to charge VAT at the standard rate on the rent charged to Atlantic Ltd. On the basis that Atlantic Ltd is a fully taxable business, this may have cashflow implications but will not be a real cost to the business.

Anita's acquisition cost for SDLT purposes is £2 million plus VAT, i.e. £2.4 million. Anita will be required to pay SDLT at 2%/5% on this amount, i.e. £109,500. The additional SDLT payable as a result of VAT being charged on the sale is a real cost to Anita.

Questions

Review Questions

(See Suggested Solutions to Review Questions at the end of this textbook.)

Question 13.1

Your client incurred significant amounts of input tax on refurbishing a building two years ago. At that time, your client had not opted to tax because the tenant at the time was not able to recover any input tax it incurred on rent. Your client now has a new tenant who is able to recover VAT on rent and who has taken a 25-year lease on the building. As a result, your client has decided to opt to tax.

Your client has been told that they require permission from HMRC in order to opt to tax and that, before such permission will be given, your client must submit proposals as to how much of the input tax previously incurred they now want to recover.

Requirement
Briefly summarise the advice you would give to your client with regard to the recovery of input tax proposal.

Question 13.2

Grape Ltd, a fully taxable, VAT-registered business, is about to move premises. Their new landlord, instead of fitting out the inside of their new premises, has offered Grape a six-month rent-free period if Grape Ltd agrees to undertake refurbishment of the interior of the premises to a specification to be agreed by both parties. The landlord has opted to tax the premises.

Requirement
Draft a short explanation for Grape Ltd on the VAT issues arising and the best way to deal with them.

Question 13.3

One of your clients, Gilbert Ingles, a VAT-registered sole trader making standard-rated and zero-rated supplies, is in the process of acquiring the trade and assets of another business from Berry Ltd. The business to be acquired makes a mixture of standard-rated and exempt supplies. Gilbert has asked for your advice on the VAT implications of the acquisition.

The projected turnover of the combined business for the next 12 months is as follows:

	£
Standard-rated supplies	750,000
Zero-rated supplies	185,000
Exempt supplies	125,000

Once he has completed the acquisition, Gilbert will consider relocating to new premises currently being constructed that are likely to cost in the region of £500,000. All of the merged trading activities currently undertaken in premises he owns and in Berry Ltd's premises will then be relocated to the new premises.

Requirement
Write a letter to Gilbert explaining the VAT implications of the acquisition and the proposed relocation.

Challenging Questions

(Suggested Solutions to Challenging Questions are available through your lecturer.)

Question 13.1

Your firm has recently been appointed as tax advisors to Pumpkin Entertainment, a UK group that has for many years consisted of several companies active in the manufacture of televisions and other entertainment equipment. The group has recently diversified into investment in commercial property.

Nuala, the finance director, has asked your firm to look at the VAT position. She has two particular concerns:

1. All companies in the group are separately registered for VAT. She wishes to know if it is possible to avoid having each company register separately and, if so, what are the advantages and disadvantages of such a course of action and what procedures would need to be followed.
2. She understands that it may be advantageous to opt to tax property transactions that would otherwise be exempt. She wishes to know what are the advantages and disadvantages of options to tax and what procedures would need to be followed.

Requirement
Write an e-mail to Nuala in response to her questions.

Question 13.2

Eamonn Doyle is the majority shareholder of Doyle Services Ltd, a company that provides IT consultancy services.

The company acquired the freehold of a newly constructed office building for £950,000 plus VAT on 1 April 2015.

On 1 April 2016, the company began to provide insurance broking services in addition to its other services.

Eamonn has contacted you for VAT advice. The company's VAT year ends on 31 March and it submits returns on a quarterly basis.

Requirement
Write a letter to Eamonn Doyle explaining the VAT consequences of the company commencing to provide insurance broking services and any impact on VAT recovery on the acquisition of the office building in April 2015.

Suggested Solutions to Review Questions

Chapter 1

Question 1.1

(a) Freedoms that could apply to the French dividend

Article 45

Article 45 provides for the freedom of movement of workers, so is not applicable to the situation of a shareholder resident in one Member State owning shares in a company established in another Member State.

Article 49

Article 49 on the right of establishment applies to the setting-up of agencies, branches or subsidiaries and includes the right to take up and pursue activities as a self-employed person, and to set up and manage undertakings. In this case, as Mrs Jones owns only 10% of the French company, it is unlikely that she is managing the company.

The ECJ has held that the freedom of establishment applies to shareholders where their holding in the capital of the company gives them definite influence on the company's decisions and allows them to determine its activities, as set out in paragraph 31 of the *Cadbury Schweppes* decision. As Mrs Jones holds only 10% of the share capital in the French company, she would not have this influence, so the freedom of establishment in Article 49 would not apply to Mrs Jones.

Note: the freedom of establishment could apply to other UK residents holding shares in companies based in other Member States, as the UK legislation in issue is applied regardless of the level of shareholding.

Article 56

Article 56 deals with restrictions on the freedom to provide services and so would not apply in this situation.

Article 63

Article 63 prohibits all restrictions on the movement of capital between Member States. Mrs Jones has invested capital in a French company and, as a result, received a dividend; therefore, she has exercised her right to the free movement of capital. Article 63 can apply to ensure that she faces no restriction on this right.

(b) UK legislation at issue

As established at (a) above, only the freedom of movement of capital is at issue in this scenario. It is necessary to consider whether the UK legislation granting a notional tax credit to a UK individual receiving a dividend from a UK company, but granting no such credit where an individual receives a dividend from a company in another Member State, restricts the free movement of capital within the meaning of Article 63(1).

This tax legislation has the effect of deterring UK resident taxpayers from investing their capital in companies established in another Member State. It also has a restrictive effect in relation to companies established in other Member States, as it may constitute an obstacle to their raising capital in the UK. Therefore, the legislation is a restriction on the free movement of capital, which is, in principle, prohibited by Article 63(1).

However, Article 63(1)(a) permits Member States to apply the relevant provisions of their tax law that distinguish between taxpayers who are not in the same situation with regard to their place of residence, or with regard to the place where their capital is invested. This derogation is itself limited by Article 63(3), which states that the provisions shall not constitute a means of arbitrary discrimination or a disguised restriction on the free movement of capital.

The ECJ has held (see *Lenz*, Case C–315/02, paragraph 27) that a distinction must be made between unequal treatment permitted under Article 65(1)(a) and arbitrary discrimination prohibited by Article 65(3). In order to be compatible with the free movement of capital, the difference in treatment must concern situations that are not objectively comparable. The notional tax credit is designed to alleviate the effects of economic double taxation, i.e. where a shareholder is subject to income tax on a dividend which is paid out of the after-tax profits of a company.

The situation of a shareholder receiving dividends from a UK company and a French company are comparable, as the shareholder is subject to UK income tax on both dividends and both companies have paid the dividends from after-tax profits.

Therefore, it is proposed that the derogation in Article 65(1)(a) does not apply and that the UK legislation imposes a restriction on the free movement of capital prohibited by Article 63.

(c) Canadian dividend

The only freedom that could possibly apply to the Canadian dividend is the free movement of capital as, unlike the other freedoms, it can apply between Member States and third countries. In addition to the considerations set out at (a) and (b) above, it would be necessary to consider the derogation in Article 63 that permits restrictive provisions relating to third countries in existence on 31 December 1993.

The notional tax credit in its present form did not exist on that date, but its predecessor, actual tax credits, did exist. As stated in *Holböck*, whether the legislation is covered by the derogation would be a matter to be decided by the UK courts.

Chapter 2

Question 2.1

Permanent Establishment

Your answer should include consideration of the following points:

- It is assumed that the view of the RoI Revenue Commissioners is correct and that Highways Ltd has a PE in the RoI under the RoI domestic legislation.
- The next step is to look at Article 5 of the UK/Ireland DTT to determine if this limits the application of the RoI domestic legislation.

- ▣ Under Article 5(2)(h) of the DTT, a PE includes a building site or construction or installation project lasting more than six months. As the work on the road is scheduled to take 10 months, it would appear to cause Highways Ltd to have a PE in the RoI.
- ▣ In response to Gerry's query about how there can be a fixed place of business when the work will move along the road, this is specifically addressed in the OECD Commentary. This states that the very nature of a construction or installation project may be such that the contractor's activity has to be relocated continuously, or at least from time to time, as the project progresses and gives the example of roads being constructed. It further states that the activities performed at each particular spot are part of a single project, and that project must be regarded as a PE if, as a whole, it lasts more than six months.
- ▣ As Highways Ltd has a PE in the RoI, it will have to submit a corporation tax return in the RoI in respect of the profits of the PE and pay corporation tax in the RoI.
- ▣ Credit for tax paid in the RoI will be given against the UK tax on the profits of the PE. As the corporation tax rate is higher in the UK, it is likely that additional tax will be due in the UK.

Question 2.2

Capital Gains Tax

(a) The disposals will be subject to tax in the following jurisdictions:

(i) The car is a UK situs asset and its disposal by John can only be subject to UK CGT. However, motor vehicles are excluded from CGT.

(ii) The shares in Times plc are UK situs assets and their disposal by John can only be subject to CGT in the UK.

(iii) The holiday home in Donegal is a RoI situs asset. Under RoI domestic legislation, the taxable gain of £10,000 will be subject to 33% CGT in the RoI. Article 14(1) of the UK/RoI DTT permits the RoI to tax this gain, as the asset is immovable property situated in the RoI. As John is UK resident, the UK will also subject the gain to CGT.

(iv) The shares in Skye Ltd are an RoI situs asset. Under RoI domestic legislation, the taxable gain of £5,000 would be subject to 33% CGT in the RoI. However, as the shares do not fall within Article 14(1)–(4) of the UK/Ireland DTT, the RoI is prevented from taxing the gain by Article 14(5). Only the UK, as the state where John is resident, can subject the gain to CGT.

(b) The disposal at (iii) above will be subject to tax in both jurisdictions, with the UK granting double tax relief as follows:

	£
UK CGT @ 28% (as it is a residential property)	2,800
Less: Tax suffered in RoI:	(2,800)
Lower of:	
RoI tax – £3,300	
UK tax – £2,800	
UK tax liability	Nil

The higher RoI rate of CGT of 33% is ultimately paid by John.

Question 2.3

Residence

(a) The tests in Article 4(2) of the UK/Ireland DTT are used to determine the residence of an individual where both the UK and RoI consider him to be resident under their domestic legislation.

The first consideration is whether Pierre has a permanent home in one or both states. As Pierre's family home is in Kinsale, he has a permanent home in the RoI. He rents an apartment in Belfast, so therefore also has a permanent home in the UK.

As he has a permanent home in both states, he will be considered to be Treaty resident in the state with which his personal and economic relations are closest. This is referred to as his centre of vital interests.

Pierre's wife and family remain in the family home in Kinsale and his children attend school in Cork. It therefore appears, at first glance, that his centre of vital interests is the RoI. If this is the case, he will be treated as resident in the RoI for the purposes of the DTT.

If Pierre's centre of vital interests cannot be determined, he will be treated as resident in the state where he has a habitual abode. This is likely to be the state where he stays more frequently.

If he has a habitual abode in both the UK and RoI, the test at Article 4(2)(c) will not be of assistance in determining Pierre's residence, as he is a national of neither state. His residence would then be determined by agreement between the competent authorities of the UK and the RoI.

From the facts given, it appears that Pierre's centre of vital interests is the RoI. This is where his family resides and he travels to the UK for the sole purpose of undertaking the duties of his employment with the Northern Irish subsidiary of Pineapple Inc. He would consequently be resident in the RoI under the UK/Ireland DTT.

(b) Article 15 of the UK/Ireland DTT deals with income from an employment. Under Article 15(3), the Article applies equally to company directors.

As an RoI resident, Pierre's employment income is taxable only in the RoI, unless the employment is exercised in the UK. If the employment is exercised in the UK, remuneration derived from the UK employment may be taxed in the UK.

Under Article 15(1), Pierre's remuneration from his employment with the RoI subsidiary of Pineapple Inc will be taxable only in the RoI. His remuneration from his employment with the Northern Irish subsidiary may be taxed in both the UK and the RoI.

The treatment of the UK remuneration is subject to the exception in Article 15(2). If the conditions in Article 15(2) are met, the remuneration from the employment exercised in the UK will be taxable only in the RoI.

The first condition is that Pierre is not present in the UK for periods exceeding 183 days in a tax year. There is not sufficient information to determine if this condition is met.

The second condition is that the remuneration is paid by an employer who is not a UK resident. This condition will not be met as the employer is a UK resident company.

Therefore, the UK can subject Pierre's UK remuneration to tax. As the state of residence, the RoI will have to give double tax relief for the tax suffered in the UK.

Question 2.4

Double Tax Relief

	UK – Trading £'000	RoI – Trading £'000	UK – LR £'000	IOM – LR £'000	Total £'000
Taxable Income	3,450	750	40	20	4,260
UK Tax @ 20%	690	150	8	4	852
Less: DTR	-	(100)	-	(4)	(104)
UK Tax Liability	690	50	8	-	748

Chapter 3

Question 3.1

Paragraph references below are to Schedule 36 FA 2008.

(a) VAT invoices can be requested by HMRC under paragraph 1, as they are reasonably required to check the position taken on the VAT return.

(b) Under paragraph 21, documents cannot be requested by HMRC in respect of a corporation tax return filed by a taxpayer unless an enquiry has been opened. The exception is where an HMRC officer has reason to suspect that there has been a loss of tax.

(c) Auditors' working papers are protected by paragraph 24. The only exception, provided by paragraph 26, is where they relate to explanatory material given to a client by the auditor in respect of a document already given to HMRC.

(d) HMRC has the power to request these documents under paragraph 1. It is irrelevant that the documents relate to the current tax year.

(e) The answer differs depending on who holds the document requested:

(i) correspondence between a tax advisor and a client about the client's tax affairs, held by the tax advisor, is protected by paragraph 25. This is subject to the exception in paragraph 26. Therefore, HMRC may not have the power to require Add-up & Co to produce a copy of the letter;

(ii) such correspondence is not protected in the hands of the taxpayer. Therefore, HMRC can require Valerie to produce a copy of the letter.

Question 3.2

Disclosure

(a) Whether Sean's disclosure is prompted or unprompted depends on the nature, extent and timing of the disclosure:

(i) as Sean makes full disclosure immediately on discovering the mistake, and at a time when no VAT inspection is in progress, HMRC should regard his disclosure as unprompted.

(ii) Sean does not make any disclosure of the error until a VAT inspection has been notified. HMRC will regard this as prompted disclosure.

(b) Despite the fact that there is a VAT compliance check ongoing when the disclosure is made, HMRC should treat the disclosure of the error in the corporation tax return as unprompted. This is because the ongoing compliance check does not relate to corporation tax.

Chapter 4

Question 4.1

The following amounts of duty are payable by the purchasers:

(a) The office building is in the UK, so Ash Ltd must pay UK SDLT. The amount payable is:

£150,000 @ 0%	0
£100,000 @ 2%	2,000
£2,150,000 @ 5%	107,500
	109,500

(b) The office building is not in the UK, so no SDLT is payable.

(c) Although the completion has not yet occurred, there has been substantial completion and SDLT is payable on the full consideration, i.e.:

£150,000 @ 0%	0
£100,000 @ 2%	2,000
£4,750,000 @ 5%	237,500
	239,500

(d) No stamp duty is payable as consideration is less than £1,000.

(e) Stamp duty at 0.5% × £10,000 = £50 is payable by Fiona. Although the shares are not UK shares, the instrument has been executed in the UK, so UK stamp duty is payable.

(f) No UK stamp duty is payable by Harry as the shares are non-UK and the instrument was executed outside the UK.

(g) Stamp duty at 0.5% × £5 million = £25,000 is payable by Jet Ltd. There is no charge to SDLT, as it is the shares in Klaxon Ltd that have been acquired, rather than the land held by Klaxon Ltd.

Question 4.2

The chargeability to IHT depends on the domicile (or deemed domicile) of the donor, the situs of the asset and whether the transfer is exempt.

Situs of assets:

- an apartment in Northern Ireland – UK situs;
- a holiday home in France – non-UK situs;
- Euro bank account held at an Ulster Bank branch in Dublin – non-UK situs.

1. Laurence is domiciled in the UK, so all the assets are within the charge to UK IHT.
2. Mary is domiciled in the UK, so all the assets are potentially within the charge to IHT. However, Mary has left her entire estate to her husband, which is an exempt transfer.
3. Nuala is not domiciled in the UK – only the apartment is within the charge to UK IHT (subject to the UK/RoI Inheritance Tax Treaty).
4. Owen is not domiciled in the UK – only the apartment is within the charge to UK IHT.
5. Paula is domiciled in the UK, so all the assets are potentially within the charge to IHT. Paula has left her entire estate to her civil partner, but only the first £325,000 will be an exempt transfer as she is not domiciled in the UK.
6. Quincy will be deemed to be domiciled in the UK, so all the assets are within the charge to UK IHT.

Chapter 5

Question 5.1

As Jack and Jill are siblings, this will be a bargain made otherwise than at arm's length. The deemed CGT consideration will be based on the value of the asset that has been disposed of and will be as follows:

Jack

Value of 50% shareholding in Pail Ltd = £120,000.

Jill

Value of 50% shareholding in Hill Ltd + £10,000 paid by Jack = £150,000 + £10,000 = £160,000.

Jill has received the less valuable asset, but has larger consideration for CGT purposes.

The charge to stamp duty is based on the value in money's worth paid by the purchaser and would be as follows:

Jack

Jack has given shares in Pail Ltd worth £120,000, plus £10,000 in cash, in exchange for shares in Hill Ltd, so stamp duty = £130,000 @ 0.5% = £650.

Jill

Jill has given shares in Hill Ltd worth £150,000 in exchange for shares in Pail Ltd, so stamp duty = £150,000 @ 0.5% = £750.

The calculation of the stamp duty liabilities would **not** be different if Jack and Jill were unconnected.

Question 5.2

The deferred gain is:

	£
Consideration = market value of 15% shareholding	150,000
Less: cost	(1,500)
Gain	148,500
Less: section 165 relief	(148,500)
Taxable gain	Nil

Joe's base cost:	
Market value	150,000
Less: held-over gain	(148,500)
Base cost for CGT	1,500

The amount of the potentially exempt transfer for IHT is:

	£
Value of shares before gift: 7,000 @ £500 (Note)	3,500,000
Value of shares after gift: 5,500 @ £300	1,650,000
Value transferred out of estate	1,850,000

Note: the valuation applied to the shares gifted by Mary is based on the value of her shareholding, combined with her husband's shareholding under the related party rules.

Chapter 6

Question 6.1

The value of David's chargeable estate is:

		£	£
1.	Family home		900,000
2.	Personal chattels and cash		40,000
3.	Shares in Sharp Suits plc	2,000,000	

	Less: BPR @ 50%	(1,000,000)	
			1,000,000
4.	Shares in Sharp Retail Ltd	1,500,000	
	Less: excepted assets	(300,000)	300,000
	Value qualifying for BPR	1,200,000	
	Less: BPR @ 100%	(1,200,000)	
			0
5.	Warehouse	750,000	
	Less: BPR @ 50%	(375,000)	
			375,000
	Subtotal		2,615,000
	Less: David's nil band		(325,000)
	Less: % of nil rate band unutilised by Isobel		(162,500)
	Chargeable estate		**2,127,500**

Question 6.2

A letter to Paul should include the points covered in the sample letter below.

Tax Advisor
2 South St
Belfast
1 November 2016

Paul Costello
Director
Massive Bargains Ltd
10 Bargain Lane
Belfast

Dear Paul,

Gift of Shares in Massive Bargains Ltd

Further to our telephone call discussing your gift of 100 ordinary £0.01 shares in Massive Bargains Ltd to your daughter Jo, I set out below the tax issues arising from the transfer of shares.

Capital Gains Tax

Your understanding in respect of capital gains tax (CGT) is correct. You and Jo can jointly make a holdover claim. This has the effect of transferring your latent gain in the shares to Jo and it will increase the CGT payable by Jo when she disposes of the shares. I have calculated the impact of making the election below.

	£
Proceeds = market value	100,000
Less: cost	0
Gain	100,000
Less: section 165 relief	(100,000)
Taxable gain	Nil

Jo's base cost:

Market value	100,000
Less: held-over gain	(100,000)
Base cost for CGT	0

Note: as the shares only cost 1p each, I have assumed a base cost of £nil for these purposes.
Therefore, you have no immediate CGT liability and Jo takes over your low base cost of the shares.

You could choose not to make the holdover election and instead crystallise a capital gain. ER should apply to reduce the rate of tax on the gain to 10% and the amount payable would be further reduced by your annual exemption.

If no claim for holdover relief were made, the CGT payable would be:

	£
Taxable gain	100,000
Less: annual exemption	(11,100)
Chargeable gain	88,900
CGT @ 10%	8,890

You could choose to pay this tax liability, which would be due on 31 January 2018. This would result in Jo's base cost being £100,000 and would minimise the amount of CGT she would pay on a future disposal.

You should note that there is a lifetime limit of £10 million for ER and that by claiming the relief on this gift, you would have £9.9 million to utilise against future disposals of your shares in the company.

Income Tax

As Jo is an employee and has received shares in the company without paying full market value consideration, she could potentially be liable to income tax on the value of the shares.

Jo is already a higher rate taxpayer in the tax year, so income tax would be payable at 40% and 45% (£75,000 at 40% and £25,000 at 45%) of £100,000, i.e. £41,250. On the basis that there is no market for the shares, they should not be "readily convertible assets", meaning that the value will not be subject to PAYE or National Insurance Contributions (NICs). Instead, Jo would pay the income tax through the self-assessment system.

If it can be demonstrated that Jo received the shares by virtue of her familial relationship with you, rather than by reason of her employment in the company, this income tax may not be payable. You have stated that you gifted the shares to her to reward and motivate her for her good work as sales director. However, no other employees have received shares and it may be that these shares would not have been gifted to her if she was not your daughter, especially as the gift caused you and your wife to lose your controlling shareholding in the company.

Inheritance Tax

The transfer of the shares to Jo will be a transfer of value for inheritance tax (IHT) purposes. The transfer is not immediately chargeable to IHT, but is a potentially exempt transfer (PET). This means that the value of the transfer will be brought into your estate in calculating the IHT payable on death, if death occurs within seven years of making the transfer.

The amount of the transfer for IHT purposes is based on the value that has left your estate, rather than the market value of the shares. For these purposes, your shareholding is aggregated with that of your wife. Before the gift to Jo, you and Maggie had a combined 51% shareholding in Massive Bargains Ltd and were therefore able to control the company. After the gift to Jo, your combined shareholding has been reduced to 41%. As you can no longer control the company, there has been a significant decrease in the value of your shares.

The amount of the PET for IHT is:

	£
Value of shares before gift: 720 @ £3,000	2,160,000
Value of shares after gift: 620 @ £1,500	930,000
Value transferred out of estate	1,230,000

This amount could potentially be covered by business property relief (BPR) at 100%, as the shares gifted are unquoted shares in a trading company you had owned for at least two years. The availability of BPR to reduce the value of the estate on death will depend on whether Jo still holds the shares at that date and whether the company continues to qualify for the relief.

I suggest that we arrange a meeting with you and Maggie to discuss your succession plans for the company and means of mitigating potential IHT liabilities. There are advantages and disadvantages to making gifts during your lifetime, which I would like to discuss with you.

Stamp Duty

There should be no *ad valorem* stamp duty due on the transfer of shares, as there was no consideration. It will be necessary to have the stock transfer form stamped to effect the transfer. I suggest that you discuss these requirements with your solicitor, if you have not already done so.

To summarise, there are no immediate tax consequences for you as a result of the gift to Jo, but there is a potential income tax liability for Jo. I would be happy to discuss this with her in more detail.

Please call or e-mail me with any further queries.

Yours sincerely,
Tax Advisor

Chapter 7

Question 7.1

Your answer should include the following points for each of the potential courses of action.

(a) Harper Ltd acquires the property

  (i)   SDLT will be payable on the acquisition value of the property, i.e.:

£150,000 @ 0%	0
£100,000 @ 2%	2,000
£350,000 @ 5%	17,500
	19,500

  (ii) Where VAT is charged by the vendor on the sale of the property, SDLT will be payable on the VAT-inclusive amount, i.e. £600,000 @ 1.2 = £720,000:

£150,000 @ 0%	0
£100,000 @ 2%	2,000
£470,000 @ 5%	23,500
	25,500

(iii) Harper Ltd can borrow funds to acquire the property and obtain a tax deduction for the interest.

(iv) Industrial buildings allowance is no longer available, but the company will be able to claim capital allowances at 8% on integral features in the building.

(v) On a sale of the property, any chargeable gain will be subject to corporation tax.

(vi) Indexation allowance will be available to the company to reduce the amount of the gain.

(vii) If Jack wishes to receive the proceeds from any disposal of the property, additional tax will be payable on extracting the funds from the company.

(viii) Holding the property in the company may allow it to obtain bank financing for its operations on better terms, as debt can be secured on the property.

(ix) The downside of holding the property in the company is that it will be available to the company's creditors if the company gets into difficulties.

(x) The value of the property will be reflected in the value of the shares, which should qualify for 100% BPR for IHT on the death of Jack.

(b) Jack acquires the property and rents it to Harper Ltd

(i) SDLT will be payable at 4% of the acquisition value of the property, i.e.:

£150,000 @ 0%	0
£100,000 @ 2%	2,000
£350,000 @ 5%	17,500
	19,500

(ii) Where VAT is charged by the vendor on the sale of the property, SDLT will be payable on the VAT-inclusive amount, i.e. £600,000 @ 1.2 = £720,000:

£150,000 @ 0%	0
£100,000 @ 2%	2,000
£470,000 @ 5%	23,500
	25,000

(iii) There will be SDLT payable by the company on a lease in respect of the property. It may be possible to avoid this by granting a non-exclusive licence to occupy rather than a lease.

(iv) If the option to tax is, or has been, made on the property, Jack must register for VAT and charge VAT on the rent. As Harper Ltd should be able to fully recover any input tax, this should be a cash flow issue rather than a real cost.

(v) Jack will pay income tax (assumed to be at the higher rate of 40%) on the net rental income received from the company. The company will obtain a corporation tax deduction for the rental payments. This can be a tax-efficient means for Jack to extract funds from the company, as there is no employers' or employees' NIC on the rent.

(vi) Jack can borrow funds to acquire the property and set the interest payable against his rental income.

(vii) The rental income will have to be sufficient for Jack to make capital repayments to the bank. As no tax deduction is available for capital repayments, he may have an income tax liability on the rental income without the funds to meet the tax from the rent received.

(viii) Where Jack incurs expenditure on integral features in the building, he can claim capital allowances at 8% on the expenditure in calculating his taxable rental profits. Where Harper Ltd incurs the expenditure as lessee of the building, it can claim the allowances.

(ix) On a sale of the property, Jack will be subject to CGT on the chargeable gain.

(x) If the property is sold by Jack at the same time as a disposal of the shares in Harper Ltd, this may be an "associated disposal" for the purposes of ER. However, the relief is restricted where a market rent has been charged to the company.

(xi) Jack will personally receive the proceeds on any disposal of the property, thereby avoiding the double tax charge that can arise where the property is held in the company.

(xii) 50% BPR for IHT will be available on the property on Jack's death, as long as the property continues to be used in the trade of Harper Ltd and Jack remains the controlling shareholder of Harper Ltd.

(xiii) The property will be protected from the company's creditors should trading difficulties occur. This is subject to any personal guarantees Jack may have given over the company's debts.

(c) The SSAS acquires the property and rents it to Harper Ltd

(i) SDLT will be payable on the acquisition value of the property, i.e.:

£150,000 @ 0%	0
£100,000 @ 2%	2,000
£350,000 @ 5%	17,500
	19,500

(ii) Where VAT is charged by the vendor on the sale of the property, SDLT will be payable on the VAT-inclusive amount, i.e. £600,000 @ 120% = £720,000:

£150,000 @ 0%	0
£100,000 @ 2%	2,000
£470,000 @ 5%	23,500
	25,500

(iii) There will be SDLT payable by the company on a lease in respect of the property.

(iv) If the option to tax is, or has been, made on the property, the SSAS must register for VAT and charge VAT on the rent. As Harper Ltd should be able to fully recover any input tax, this should be a cash flow issue rather than a real cost.

(v) A market value rent must be charged to the company by the SSAS.

(vi) There are strict borrowing limits imposed on pension schemes. The SSAS may only borrow up to 50% of the value of the assets in the scheme. As the SSAS has assets of £1.5 million, it will be able to borrow a sufficient amount to acquire a property for £600,000.

(vii) No income tax is payable by the SSAS on the net rental income. The company will obtain a corporation tax deduction for the rental payments. Thus, from an income tax perspective, it is tax efficient for the property to be acquired by the SSAS.

(viii) As no income tax is payable by the SSAS, it may be able to apply a greater percentage of the rental income to make capital repayments to the bank and reduce the bank debt more quickly.

(ix) In addition, tax-deductible pension contributions on behalf of Jack can be made by the company to the SSAS. This will reduce the company's tax liability in the period in which the contributions are paid and the funds can be applied by the pension scheme to further repay the bank debt.

(x) As it is not subject to income tax, the pension scheme cannot benefit from capital allowances. To the greatest extent possible, capital expenditure on integral features in the building should be incurred by the company to enable it to benefit from the capital allowances.

(xi) The SSAS will be exempt from CGT on the disposal of the property.

(xii) The exemptions from income tax and CGT make holding the property in the pension scheme very attractive from a tax perspective.

(xiii) One downside of holding the property in the pension scheme is that its value will remain in the pension scheme and Jack can only have access to the value of the property under the pension scheme rules.

(xiv) Under certain circumstances, the value of the pension scheme may not be included in Jack's estate for IHT purposes.

(xv) The property will be protected from the company's creditors should trading difficulties occur.

Question 7.2

Your answer should include the following points for each of the scenarios.

(a) Richard acquires the shopping centre for market value of £6.8 million from Dolly Investments Ltd

(i)   Richard will be required to finance the acquisition, including incidental costs such as SDLT. Bank financing is unlikely to be available for the full amount, so Richard will require access to personal funds.

(ii) On the basis that Richard will continue the business of letting the shopping centre, previously carried on by the company, the transfer of going concern (TOGC) treatment should be available for VAT so that no VAT will be charged on the acquisition by Richard.

(iii) SDLT would be payable by Richard as follows:

£150,000 @ 0%	0
£100,000 @ 2%	2,000
£6,550,000 @ 5%	327,500
	329,500

(iv) Corporation tax will be payable by Dolly Investments Ltd on the gain realised on the disposal of the shopping centre:

	£
Proceeds	6,800,000
Less: cost	(5,000,000)
Gain before indexation	1,800,000
Indexation allowance:	
Say 0.290 × £5 million	(1,450,000)
Chargeable gain	350,000
Corporation tax @ 20%	70,000

(v) Following the sale of the building, there will be cash remaining in the company:

	£
Proceeds on disposal	6,800,000
Cash held by company	2,550,000
Total cash	9,350,000
Less:	
Discharge of bank borrowings	(2,000,000)
Pay other creditors	(150,000)
Corporation tax on disposal	(70,000)
Net cash remaining	7,130,000

(vi) The full amount of the distributable reserves could be distributed to Richard to enable him to finance the acquisition of the property. Temporary financing would be required until the dividend was received.

(vii) Income tax would be payable by Richard on the distribution. If a dividend of £5 million was paid to him, income tax of £1.9 million would be payable, leaving him with a net amount of £3.1 million.

(viii) The company could be placed in liquidation before a distribution was paid. Under section 1030 CTA 2010 and section 122 TCGA 1992, this would be taxable on Richard as a capital distribution at 20%.

(ix) However, it would be likely in these circumstances that HMRC would seek to apply the anti-avoidance legislation on transactions in securities, at sections 682–709 ITA 2007, to counteract the tax advantage and to subject the distribution on a winding up to income tax rather than to CGT. The transactions in securities legislation is particularly likely to be invoked, following the introduction of the targeted anti-avoidance rule (TAAR) by Finance Act 2016, for situations where a company is placed into liquidation but the shareholder continues to carry on a similar business within two years of the distribution.

(b) The shopping centre is distributed *in specie* to Richard, and then Dolly Investments Ltd is placed in liquidation

(i) Richard will receive the property as a dividend *in specie*, so will not be required to finance the acquisition of the shopping centre itself.

(ii) On the basis that Richard will continue the business of letting the shopping centre, previously carried on by the company, the TOGC treatment should be available for VAT so that no VAT will be charged on the acquisition by Richard.

(iii) As Richard acquires the property as a dividend *in specie*, there should be no SDLT payable by him on the acquisition. This is subject to the treatment of the debt of £2 million attaching to the property.

(iv) The company will require sufficient distributable reserves to make the distribution. As a revaluation surplus has been booked in the accounts in respect of the property, the revaluation reserve will be treated as distributable and the company will have sufficient distributable reserves.

(v) Dolly Investments Ltd will be deemed to have disposed of the property at its open market value.

(vi) Corporation tax will be payable by Dolly Investments Ltd on the gain realised on the disposal of the shopping centre:

	£
Proceeds	6,800,000
Less: cost	(5,000,000)
Gain before indexation	1,800,000
Indexation allowance:	
Say 0.290 × £5 million	(1,450,000)
Chargeable gain	350,000
Corporation tax @ 20%	70,000

(vii) Following the distribution of the building, the company will have sufficient cash funds to repay its creditors and pay the corporation tax.

(viii) It may be possible for Richard to take over the debt of £2 million due on the shopping centre. However, this would be regarded as consideration for SDLT purposes, meaning that the SDLT exemption for distributions *in specie* would not be available.

(ix) Income tax would be payable by Richard on the distribution. The net dividend received will be equal to the market value of the shopping centre, i.e. £6.8 million. This will be taxed at 38.1%.

(x) Therefore, Richard will have an income tax liability of £2.59 million, but he has not actually received any cash from the company that he can use to pay the income tax.

(xi) After the distribution of the property, the company's cash position would be:

	£
Proceeds on disposal	0
Cash held by company	2,550,000
Total cash	2,550,000
Less:	
Discharge of bank borrowings	(2,000,000)
Pay other creditors	(150,000)
Corporation tax on disposal	(70,000)
Net cash remaining	330,000

(xii) Therefore, the company will not be able to pay a significant pre- or post-liquidation distribution to enable Richard to settle his income tax liability.

(xiii) If Richard does not have funds available to settle the liability, it is likely that he will have to raise finance and secure it on the shopping centre.

(xiv) This would be preferable to Richard taking on the £2 million debt of the company relating to the shopping centre, as it saves SDLT.

(c) **Dolly Investments Ltd is placed in members' voluntary liquidation and the shopping centre is subsequently distributed *in specie* to Richard**

(i) Richard will receive the property as a dividend *in specie*, so he will not be required to finance the acquisition of the shopping centre itself.

(ii) On the basis that Richard will continue the business of letting the shopping centre, previously carried on by the company, the TOGC treatment should be available for VAT so that no VAT will be charged on the acquisition by Richard.

(iii) As Richard acquires the property as a dividend *in specie*, there should be no SDLT payable by him on the acquisition.

(iv) As the company is being placed in liquidation but has sufficient cash to repay its bank borrowings, this should be done before the company is put into members' voluntary liquidation to avoid any complications arising with the bank.

(v) The company will require sufficient distributable reserves to make the distribution. As a revaluation surplus has been booked in the accounts in respect of the property, the revaluation reserve will be treated as distributable and the company will have sufficient distributable reserves.

(vi) Dolly Investments Ltd will be deemed to have disposed of the property at its open-market value.

(vii) Corporation tax will be payable by Dolly Investments Ltd on the gain realised on the disposal of the shopping centre:

	£
Proceeds	6,800,000
Less: cost	(5,000,000)
Gain before indexation	1,800,000
Indexation allowance:	

Say 0.290 × £5 million	(1,450,000)
Chargeable gain	350,000
Corporation tax @ 20%	70,000

(viii) Following the distribution of the building, the company will have sufficient cash funds to repay its creditors and pay the corporation tax.

(ix) CGT would be payable by Richard on the capital distribution, based on the open-market value of the property:

	£
Proceeds	6,800,000
Less: cost of shares	(1,000)
Chargeable gain	6,799,000
CGT @ 20%	1,359,800

(x) Therefore, Richard will have a tax liability of £1.36 million, but he has not actually received any cash from the company that he can use to pay the income tax.

(xi) After repaying the bank debt and distributing the property, the company's cash position would be:

	£
Proceeds on disposal	0
Cash held by company	550,000
Total cash	550,000
Less:	
Pay other creditors	(150,000)
Corporation tax on disposal	(70,000)
Net cash remaining	330,000

(xii) Therefore, the company will not be able to pay a significant post-liquidation cash distribution to enable Richard to settle his CGT liability.

(xiii) If Richard does not have funds available to settle the liability, it is likely that he will have to raise finance and secure it on the shopping centre.

(xiv) The tax payable under this option is lower than under option (b), but there is a risk that HMRC would seek to counteract the income tax advantage using the transactions in securities anti-avoidance legislation. The transactions in securities risk is increased by the introduction of the TAAR in Finance Act 2016. It should therefore be recommended that an advance clearance application under section 701 ITA 2007 be made.

Chapter 8

Question 8.1

Tangle Ltd

(a) The disposal of the 10% shareholding in March 2016 would be exempt as the substantial shareholding exemption (SSE) applies.

(b) The SSE will continue to apply until 1 March 2017 (a 10% holding is required in 12 months of the 24 months prior to sale).

If the sale of the remaining 8% shareholding will give rise to a gain, a disposal prior to this date will mean that the gain is exempt.

If the share sale would crystallise a loss, then the disposal should be after 1 March 2017, as the loss will then be allowable. A disposal prior to 1 March 2017 would mean the loss would not be allowable.

Question 8.2

Bon Ltd
Disposal 1 on 31 March 2016:
% shareholding is 3,000/20,000 = 15%
Shares held for the previous two years, therefore SSE applies.

Disposal 2 on 28 February 2017:
800 shares sold, which is a 4% holding.

The shareholding before the sale was only 9%. However, between 1 April 2015 and 31 March 2016, 15% was held. As this is within two years of the date of disposal, SSE applies.

Chapter 9

Question 9.1

MEMORANDUM

From:	Tax Assistant
To:	Tax Partner
Date:	25 April 2016
Subject:	Succession Planning for Polly North

Option 1: Sale of Shares in Circus Ltd to Polly's Son
Capital Gains Tax (CGT)
Polly's son is a connected party (section 286 TCGA 1992) for CGT purposes. Accordingly, the disposal is deemed not to be at arm's length for CGT purposes and, therefore, to take place at market value. Polly will be required to estimate the market value for the purpose of completing her tax return. The valuation should be undertaken by an independent qualified expert, as the valuation may be enquired into by HMRC.

If the consideration is paid by instalments, then the entire gain is still chargeable in the fiscal year in which the disposal takes place. The tax will be due for payment on 31 January following the end of the tax year in which the sale takes place. Polly may, however, take advantage of the provisions of section 280 TCGA 1992. If any of the consideration is payable more than 18 months after the date of the disposal, the tax due may be paid in instalments. The period over which the instalments are paid would be agreed with HMRC, but cannot exceed the lesser of eight years and the point when all of the consideration is paid.

Polly will pay CGT at 20% on the market value of the shares in Circus Ltd.

However, Polly may be eligible to claim entrepreneurs' relief (ER) on up to £10 million of the chargeable gain arising on the sale of the shares. Polly has owned the shares for at least one year and is a director; therefore it appears that the company is her "personal company".

However, the company has an investment portfolio and its "trading" status may therefore be in doubt. If the shares are to qualify for ER, then the company must not, to a "substantial" extent, carry on activities other than trading activities. Substantial is not defined in the legislation, but HMRC has indicated that it interprets this to be more than 20% of turnover or expenditure, assets or management time.

Inheritance Tax (IHT)

If the market value of the shares is paid in full by Polly's son, no immediate IHT consequences should arise, since there will be no diminution in value of Polly's estate. However, it should be recommended that Polly consider IHT planning after the sale, as she will be exchanging shares potentially fully qualifying for BPR for less IHT-efficient assets.

Option 2: Transfer of Shares in Circus Ltd to Polly's Son for a Nominal Amount

Capital Gains Tax (CGT)

If the shares are transferred for a nominal sum, then a charge to CGT based on the market value will still arise. The charge will be computed using the open-market value of the shares less their base cost. ER could be claimed on the same basis as set out above.

Alternatively, a claim for holdover relief under section 165 TCGA 1992 may be made. The effect of this claim is that the chargeable gain would be reduced by the size of the gain held over, which effectively reduced the gain to nil. The effect of the claim would be that the son inherits the base cost of the shares from his mother.

The key condition that needs to be met for holdover relief is that the shares transferred are shares in a trading company. The definition of a trading company is the same as that for ER, i.e. one that does not, to a "substantial" extent, carry on activities other than trading activities. It is worth emphasising that, if the claim fails, then Polly will be left with a tax liability and no means of paying it. It is therefore important to review this area carefully to see if holdover relief is available.

Inheritance Tax (IHT)

If the shares are transferred to Polly's son for a nominal amount, a potentially exempt transfer (PET) will have occurred, computed at the market value of the shares. No IHT is payable at the time of the transfer. However, should Polly die within seven years of making the transfer, the value of the transfer will be included in her death estate for IHT purposes, within the section relating to gifts and other transfers of value.

Business property relief (BPR) may reduce the value of the lifetime transfer. The key conditions for obtaining the relief are as follows:

1. The assets are relevant business property. This category includes any unquoted shares, such as those transferred by Polly, and a reduction of up to 100% can apply to the chargeable value of property falling into this category.
2. The business must be a qualifying business, which is defined as a company whose business does not consist wholly or mainly in making or holding investments.

"Wholly or mainly" is interpreted as meaning more than 50% and can be measured by different indicators, including the profits generated by the investments. Given that the company has an investment portfolio, there may be a difficulty here. Further information must be obtained from Polly about the value of the portfolio, and the income generated from it, before any conclusion on the availability of BPR can be reached.

The shares must also have been held for at least two years by Polly. This condition appears to have been met. Also, since this is a lifetime transfer, her son, as transferee, must still hold the shares at the time of Polly's death for BPR to apply.

BPR will also be reduced to the extent that the value of the transfer can be attributed to "excepted assets". These are assets not used wholly or mainly for the purpose of the business in the previous two years or required for future use in the business. The investment portfolio may fall into this category, unless it is a short-term repository for working capital. In this case, the BPR available will be reduced in proportion to the value of the investment portfolio as opposed to the value of the entire company.

Question 9.2

If Glenn were to gift the property to Freya, this would be deemed to be a CGT disposal at market value under sections 17 and 18 TCGA 1992.

Capital Gain

	£
Current market value	345,000
Less: cost	(35,000)
Gain	310,000
CGT @ 20%	62,000

The CGT payable by Freya would therefore be £62,000. The payment of this liability by Freya would be consideration for SDLT purposes. However, this is within the nil rate band for SDLT on commercial properties, so no SDLT would be payable by Freya.

As there is an option to tax in place, and the transfer of the property is a gift, VAT will be charged on market value. It is suggested that Freya also elects to waive exemption and registers for VAT, in order to reclaim this input VAT. It is assumed that VAT being charged on the rent will not be a concern for the new tenant, on the basis that the business previously carried on by Glenn is fully taxable.

Note that the TOGC treatment will not be available on the transfer of the freehold property to Freya, as she is not carrying on a similar business to her father.

Given that Glenn has used the property for business purposes, an election can be made to hold over the gain under section 165 TCGA 1992. This will be restricted by virtue of the periods of non-business use, so some gain would remain chargeable.

This will reduce Freya's base cost. She should weigh up the benefit of deferring the tax liability against any potential tax liability on a future disposal of the property.

The CGT payable and Freya's base cost if holdover relief under section 165 is claimed would be:

	£	£
Current market value		345,000
Less: cost		(35,000)
Gain		310,000
Gain available for holdover	310,000	
Less: restricted		
£310,000 × 66/192	(106,563)	
Gain held-over	203,437	(203,437)
Gain remaining chargeable		106,563
CGT @ 20%		21,313
Freya's base cost:		
Market value	345,000	
Less: gain held-over	(203,437)	
Base cost	141,563	

Note that the holdover relief is restricted as the property was not used for business purposes throughout the period of ownership. The total period of ownership is from March 2001 to March 2017, i.e. 192 months. The period of non-business use was from March 2001 to September 2006, i.e. 66 months.

From an IHT perspective, the gift is a PET and there will be no charge to IHT unless Glenn dies within seven years. The property would have qualified for BPR whilst used by Glenn for his business, but once separated from the business will no longer do so.

Chapter 10

Question 10.1

Corresponding UK tax:

		£
Chargeable profits:	£750,000	
UK tax @ 20%		150,000
Less: double tax relief – lower of:		
(1) £750,000 @ 20%	£150,000	
(2) Foreign tax paid	£25,000	(25,000)
Less: UK corporation tax paid:		
£45,000 @ 20%		(9,000)
Corresponding UK tax		116,000
75% of corresponding UK tax		87,000

Broccoli BV does not meet the tax exemption criteria in the year ended 31 March 2017, as the tax paid of £35,000 is less than 75% of the corresponding UK tax. The other exemptions should be considered and, if they are not applicable, the CFC charge gateway should be applied to determine the chargeable profits.

Chapter 11

Question 11.1

Olivia:

No tax liability on the gift to the discretionary trust in June 2009, as it was made more than seven years before death; however, it does affect the nil rate band avilable.

IHT liability on PET in March 2014:

	£	£
Gift of apartment		236,000
Less: annual exemption 2013/14		(3,000)
Annual exemption 2012/13		(3,000)
Original chargeable amount		230,000
Fall in value:		
Original value	(236,000)	
Value at death	185,000	
		(51,000)
Revised chargeable amount		179,000

Nil rate band:

Nil rate band at date of death	325,000	
Less: utilised in seven years before PET	(160,000)	
		(165,000)
		14,000
IHT @ 40%		5,600

Question 11.2

Seamus:

	£	£
Tax on settlement:		
Seamus's transfers in previous seven years		180,000
Initial transfer of value		350,000
		530,000
Tax:		
Total transfers	530,000	
Less: nil rate band	(325,000)	
	205,000	
Tax @ 20%	41,000	
Effective rate of tax @ 30%:		
(41,000/350,000) × 30%	3.51%	

No. of complete quarters 10/06/11 – 10/06/15 = 16
Exit charge:

£40,000 × 3.51% × 16/40		561.60

Chapter 12

Question 12.1

Since Parsley Ltd is already a taxable person, there cannot be a TOGC unless Thyme Ltd is also a taxable person or becomes a taxable person as a result of the transfer.

Section 49(1) VATA 1994 states that where a business is transferred as a going concern, the transferee (Thyme Ltd) will be treated as having carried on the business before, as well as after, the transfer for the purposes of determining whether the transferee is liable to be registered for VAT.

Paragraph 1(2) of Schedule 1 VATA 1994 confirms that where a business is transferred as a going concern and the purchaser is not already VAT registered, the purchaser (Thyme Ltd) becomes liable to register if the turnover of the acquired business exceeds the registration limit.

Prior to the transfer to Thyme Ltd, the cake business had turnover of £180,000 per annum. Thyme Ltd therefore becomes a taxable person at the time it acquires the business from Parsley Ltd.

The requirement of Article 5(1)(b)(iii) of S.I. 1995/1268 is therefore met, and Parsley Ltd can treat the sale as a TOGC, regardless of whether Thyme Ltd fulfils its legal obligations and becomes registered as soon as it acquires the business.

Question 12.2

Dear Johnny,

Thank you for your e-mail. The eligibility criteria for VAT grouping in the UK are:

- members of VAT groups must be bodies corporate;
- members must meet the control test in section 43A VATA 1994, which is that one body corporate, one person, or two or more persons in partnership controls all the bodies in the VAT group; and
- members must meet the residency test in section 43A VATA 1994, which is that all members must be established or have a fixed establishment in the UK.

Coriander Ltd and Spice Ltd would meet the criteria for group registration for VAT, even though they are not actually in a 'group'. It is sufficient that they are both controlled by Mr Spice.

Regards,
Tax Advisor

Question 12.3

At the transfer date, any liability belonging to Julian (the transferor) to pay VAT or to submit a VAT return becomes the liability of Gary (the transferee).

Gary would become entitled to any right to credit or repayment of input tax at the date of the transfer.

Any right to bad debt relief on pre-transfer supplies belongs to Gary, as does the obligation to repay input tax where Julian was the debtor.

From the transfer date, payments or credits are treated as having been made by Gary, even if actually made by Julian.

Once the number has been reallocated, HMRC cannot take enforcement action against Julian.

Chapter 13

Question 13.1

While it might be tempting to suggest to the client that they should propose recovery of 25/27ths of the VAT incurred on the refurbishment (on the basis that the current lease will expire 27 years after the refurbishment took place and there will be 25 years of taxable rent), HMRC policy is not to accept such proposals.

It is HMRC policy that, even if the refurbishment is not a capital item, the VAT recovery must be calculated as if it were, i.e. on the basis of a 10-year period.

Therefore it is unlikely that HMRC would accept any recovery greater than 8/10th of the VAT, on the basis that there has already been two years of exempt income.

Question 13.2

The grant of a rent-free period by a landlord does not normally trigger any VAT liability unless the rent-free period is given in exchange for something that the tenant provides for/to the landlord (e.g. the tenant carries out works for the benefit of the landlord).

This could be a barter transaction, where the rent-free period is a non-monetary payment for the works, and the works carried out are non-monetary consideration for the rent-free period.

If so, the landlord will be making a supply of land for six months to Grape in return for works being carried out to its satisfaction. The value of this supply will be equal to the six months of rent that it forgoes, which is the value implicitly agreed between the parties.

Grape will be making a supply of renovation works of equal value to the landlord and will need to account for VAT on this supply.

Both parties should therefore raise VAT-only invoices to the other. The landlord should be able to recover the VAT charged by Grape given that they have opted to tax, and Grape should be able to recover the VAT charged by the landlord on the same basis as they would recover VAT on rent paid, i.e. as an overhead of the business. As they are fully taxable, they will be able to recover the VAT in full.

Question 13.3

Mr G. Ingles
55 Fruit Drive
Belfast

Dear Gilbert,

VAT Implications of Recent Acquisition

I refer to our recent telephone conversation, during which you requested advice on the VAT implications of your proposed acquisition of the trade and assets of Berry Ltd, and set out my observations below.

Transfer of Going Concern

As the business being acquired from Berry Ltd is a going concern, the transaction is likely to be outside the scope of VAT. This means that no VAT would be charged by the vendor on the sale of the various assets. This is due to the transfer of going concern (TOGC) provisions, the conditions for which are:

1. the assets are to be used by the transferee in the same kind of business;
2. the transferee is VAT registered, or becomes taxable as a result of the transfer;
3. where part of a trade is transferred, it is capable of separate operation; and
4. there is no significant gap in trading.

Provided that all these conditions are met, there would be no VAT charged on the stock, plant and machinery and other assets acquired, and your business would therefore not have any input VAT to reclaim.

The only exception to this rule would be where the vendor transfers an "opted" property as part of the deal. An "opted" property is where the vendor has waived the normal VAT exemption in respect of the property. If the property is subsequently sold, standard-rate VAT must be applied to the consideration for the sale of the property, unless the purchaser also opts to tax the property. Under those circumstances, the transfer of the property would also be treated as a TOGC.

Partial Exemption

Where a business makes a mixture of taxable and exempt supplies, the input VAT recovery by that business is restricted. Where input VAT is incurred on costs that are directly attributable to making exempt supplies, none of that VAT may be recovered.

Where input VAT is incurred on costs that are directly attributable to making taxable supplies, all of that VAT may be recovered. Note that taxable supplies include both standard-rated and zero-rated supplies.

Where input VAT is incurred on costs that cannot be directly attributable to making either taxable or exempt supplies, the VAT that may be recovered in respect of these costs is reclaimed by using a method acceptable to HMRC. The standard method for apportioning this residual input VAT is to reclaim on the basis of the proportion of taxable supplies to exempt supplies.

In your circumstances, based on the projected turnover for the next 12 months, this would be 88.21% taxable supplies to 11.79% exempt supplies, meaning that 88.21% of this residual VAT could be reclaimed.

Where the input tax relating to exempt supplies is no more than the *de minimis* limits of £625 per month on average and no more than 50% of the total input tax, the full amount of input VAT may be recovered.

Capital Goods Scheme

As the premises to be acquired will cost more than £250,000, the Capital Goods Scheme (CGS) rules will apply to the £500,000 property. These VAT rules seek to restrict the input VAT recovery in respect of the costs of acquiring that building to the proportion of the building used for making taxable supplies. This would not necessarily be the same proportion as the partial exemption formula outlined above, i.e. 11.79%.

If, for example, 25% of the floor space in the building was used for making exempt supplies and the remaining 75% for making taxable supplies, the CGS restriction would be 25%. Thus, on the basis that £500,000 is the VAT-exclusive price of the building and that VAT at 20% is to be charged on all costs, the total input VAT would be £100,000. The CGS would restrict the recovery of this VAT to the percentage relating to taxable supplies – 75% in this example – so that only £75,000 of the £100,000 input VAT would be recoverable.

The usage of the property would then need to be monitored over a 10-year adjustment period, and an annual adjustment may be necessary. For example, should the exempt usage fall from 25% to 10% in the second year, then additional input VAT of £1,500 (calculated as 90% less 75% × £100,000 × 1/10) could be recovered for that year. If the exempt usage were to increase during the 10-year adjustment period, then additional VAT would be payable to HMRC.

Please contact me should you have any further queries.

Yours sincerely,
VAT Advisor